Travels With Our Kitchen

A Travelers Guiding Light

Travels With Our Kitchen

Where We Lived & What we Ate

Peter & Sheila Jenkins

Travels With Our Kitchen

Prologue

The idea to write this cook book, which was started during our first retirement to Cyprus in 2000, was based upon an article Sheila had written when we were in Sarawak, called **"Ex-pat in the Kitchen"**. This was included in a Shell publication called **"Life On The Move"**. In honour of this a scan of the original is included in the Syria section. When we began the initial idea was that it would just include recipes. Sheila had, on and off, kept a log of what we were cooking and eating in the different locations we have lived in over the years. With me going back to work in Oman in 2004 the project was forced to a halt. After our retirement to Edinburgh in 2011 its completion was given high priority. The trouble was its "intent" evolved with the passage of time. It now provided the opportunity for us to record not only what we ate, but why we were in the various places we were. And what we did whilst there. This significantly expanded the scope. It also forced many unexpected, and therefore surprising, discoveries to the surface. Mostly these, one way or another, are linked to the vagaries of memory. One such being the trouble we had remembering exactly what we did eat when and where? Also what were the most surprising changes forced on our diet in the different countries we lived in? When did we move from here to there? And the biggest mystery of all, considering Sheila's collection of over 400 hundred cookery books (we have downsized since Oman) which did we use, and when.

From the early days, Edinburgh (60's) until London (80's) there is little hard evidence of which books were a major influence. One thing we know, because it's written inside, the Good Housekeeping **"Picture Cookery"** was presented to Sheila when she completed her pre-nursing course at Fod House, Dunfermline, in mid-1964. We had that in Edinburgh even though we can't find several of the recipes that kept us alive during our student days. We also have a book with the necessary provenance **"Good Food on a Budget"**, by Georgina Horley, to have been with us in London. Another candidate from those early years was a double edition of Elizabeth David's **"A Book of Mediterranean Food"** and **"French Country Cooking"**. Sheila also had two very well used paperback cook books. **"Farmhouse Fare"** which had been sent by Grandma Coghil to Sheila's mother when she lived in Pakistan in 1947 so she could tell the cook what to cook. The other was **"Mrs Beeton's Cookery Book"**. Sheila had them rebound, and therefore they still survive, by the Borneo Bulletin press in Brunei. The Mrs Beeton was bought from an Oxfam shop in Aberdeen. Inside was a receipt from when Mrs Jones, the first owner, had bought some provisions. It is possible to get a fix on when, and where, we might have used other books by reference to publication date. This does have limitations though. On inspection books we thought we had been referring to since the ark were in fact 'first published' relatively recently in the context of this story. Things get better in the '90's as I tended to write 'where and when' the book had been bought on the inside cover. The trouble is many of these newer books, following the law of diminishing returns, have been less influential and less referred to.

Other more personal, and long lasting, food influences were the inspiration and practical help we received care of a long list of talented friends. Folks we got to know during our Edinburgh student days. My flat mates, their girlfriends, and there relations. Thank you Astrid, her sister Ing and husband Jim, Marlyne, and others now forgotten. This source of support, and help, from friends continued during our travels. The Richards, Geraldine and John Rose, Jamalat, the Thermistocleus's, neighbours from our overseas postings, and Fiasal Riyami (the Fisherman) and his family who provided us with a monthly "catch of the day" fish supply, and precious time with them at their house for the Eid celebrations. Finally, now with two Thai daughter-in-laws (Angkana and Wanvisa) and their families, we have been privileged to experience real "home" style Thai food. The delicious combined result of shopping every day; grinding with pestel and mortar fresh spices each time you cook; impeccable pre-preparation; and exquisite presentation.

As mentioned 'move' dates were a problem. Toward the end of this story's preparation I discovered that we were a year out on when we believed we had left Holland. This date distortion continued through to London. We did get our arrival in Syria, and our subsequent move dates, correct. I found the error when trying to fix when we had bought the Mini (6th June 1987). This did not fit well with the dates I remembered. Our old passports had the "stamp" that recorded we had arrived in Brunei on the 13th December 1980 – a year later than I'd assumed. Knowing we had stayed in Brunei for 4 years now meant we returned to London at the end of 1984 not '83.

On reflection having completed the final draft I realise the long term, almost undercover, influence of Thai cuisine on our eating choices. Obviously two Thai daughter-in-laws (Angkana and Wanvisa) helps cement this process. From our first visit to Bangkok in 1979, through to visits for Buddhist wedding blessings, Thai cooking and taste has slowly insinuated itself into our everyday food habits. Here demonstrated in that several Thai dishes are included in the Oman and Edinburgh chapters. The other reflection is that on our last visit to Hua Hin I tried to photo, list, and learn the Thai names of the ingredients, new to us, that Angkana prepared. This includes, 4 spices, 4 herbs, 13 vegetables, and 3 fruit we had never eaten before on our previous 6 visits to Thailand, nor in the numerous European Thai restaurants we have eaten in. An extraordinary realization.

Finally what are the top cooking secrets gleaned from the years of cooking in the nine differing countries we have cooked in, and during the lengthy time this story was in gestation?

Tip Number 1 - "Learn to butcher a chicken". A good quality, free range, chicken carefully butchered equals:- 2 breasts (enough for the recipe you had in mind); 2 thighs (stir fried chicken); 2 drum sticks (barbequed or sticky sauced); wings (lots of ways); and a carcase (chicken stock – essential for Thai Chicken Soup for the Soul). That is 5 meals for 2 people, 10 generous helpings.

Tip Number 2 - Get to know your butcher and fishmonger. The best way to do this is to "give feedback". For example an honest "our New Zealand guest thought your lamb was the tastiest she had ever eaten" has earned us support, advice, and if you are lucky the pick of the days offerings from Craigies Farm butcher. We also get advice and help following this tip from Mrs Noey Clark (who is Thai), of Clark Brothers fish shop, in Musselburgh. I also suspect that a cheery "Swadi Kap", the traditional Thai greeting, might help as well.

Tip Number 3 - Grow as many of your herbs as possible. Mint and Parsley are easy, as is Thyme, and Rosemary. Chives and basil are good. Tarragon is more difficult but worth the effort. Fresh herbs, added immediately to the pot, will make a world of difference to the taste and your satisfaction.

Tip Number 4 – Make your own stock. It is not a huge effort and the results can be frozen so there is no waste. We normally have as a minimum chicken, and fish, stock available in the freezer. Be it soup, or risotto, chosen for that evenings meal we are always ready to go.

Contents

		Page
1.	Introduction	6
2.	Edinburgh - Student Days	14
3.	London - First Job With Shell	28
4.	Aberdeen - Our Most Foreign Posting	40
5.	Assen - North Holland	52
6.	Brunei - First Overseas Assignment	64
7.	London - Back to Reality	78
8.	Syria, Damascus - Best Assignment	90
9.	Sarawak - Back to the Jungle	106
10.	Den Haag - Dutch City Life	118
11.	Cyprus - Life in the Holiday Home	128
12.	Oman - 3 Months Become 7 Years	142
13.	Thailand - Many Visits & Now Family	166
14.	Edinburgh - Final Retirement	184

1.0 Introduction.

Sheila and I were "travellers" long before the start of the period covered by this story. Both our fathers were in the Royal Air Force. Skipping past the fact that we had both lived in all corners of the UK we had also lived abroad. Sheila had lived in Pakistan, & Singapore. I had lived in Egypt, & Cyprus. Perhaps this had, unknown to us, given us a taste for travel, and the exotic. We had silently absorbed the idea there were a multitude of different aromas and spices that excited the taste buds. Part of it was undoubtedly the smell of 'heat'. Especially in arid areas such as the deserts of Pakistan for Sheila, and Egypt for me. The combination of high temperature, and low humidity, was a baptism into a completely different living experience.

The Summary "Route" map to the Travels.

Where did the route take us? We had first met in Leuchars in Fife where our fathers were both stationed. In the summer of 1962 I had just come back from visiting my parents in Singapore. Success in my 'O' levels meant that I could continue at Madras College and my mother had arranged that I stayed with a family, the Gordon's, who lived around the corner from the school. Sheila having left boarding school was about to start her 2 year pre-nursing course at Fod House in Dunfermline. Hearing I was back she tracked me down and we met for our first date on 23rd August '62. Over the next 2 years having almost immediately fallen in love we lived for the weekends when we could be together. In between Sheila managed to complete her training and I managed to gain enough "Higher" exam passes to attain University entrance.

Edinburgh

Wanting to stay together we then sought to go either to Edinburgh or to Glasgow. Sheila was accepted by the Edinburgh Southern group of hospitals. I had applied to Strathclyde (Glasgow) and Heriot Watt (Edinburgh). When the offer came for Heriot Watt I immediately accepted. The outcome was we were to live in Edinburgh for 6 years. We would marry; have our first son Darron; and eventually I would graduate BSc Mechanical Engineering. We would also begin the travels (evolution) of our kitchen there. Firstly necessity, and the arrival of Darron, meant we had to cook every day. Secondly the people we met at university, mostly through connections to Edinburgh Dentist School rather than the Heriot Watt, introduced us to a range of new tastes. John Lloyd / Mark Hill in the flat in Claremont Crescent always seemed to be brewing real French Coffee & Chicory. Through Astrid's brother in law, Jim Kempston, we witnessed new cooking techniques. And when we occasionally had money we could eat out. There were trips to an 'Italian' on Leith Road (mussel stew) and a Chinese in Stockbridge. Sheila, with a very restricted budget, turned for support to the Good Housekeeping cook book won as a prize at pre nursing college. Her food repertoire was also bolstered by reflecting on cooking that she had experienced during visits to the homes of friends from boarding school. The success of her efforts would successfully support me, and Darron, until final exams and then graduation. Next I needed a job.

London

My successful application, and interview, for the job of Economics Engineer led to me joining Shell Exploration and Production Ltd in September 1970. At that time this was a very small unit housed in Shell Centre, Waterloo. I travelled to London on my own first and stayed with John Lloyd. I managed to find a flat to rent in Canterbury Mansions, Lymington Road. It would not be free for a little while so I called for Sheila and Darron to come south and we stayed with Aunty Ann & her husband Donald for 2 months. Following the financial constraints of surviving on a student grant we were eagerly looking forward to the "good life". Reality, and the burden of renting at London rates, were soon to curtail our expectations. However whilst not being able to go out to the theatre, with dinner, very frequently we did expand our horizons. The shear range of ingredients available, and the impact this had upon our cuisine, was a lasting legacy of our move south. Here we would also encounter a new diverse range of food influences. Greek tastes via Chris Thermistocleous, and his Norwegian wife Nana. Our neighbours Vi and Andrew would make their own contribution by sharing recipes. We also remained in contact with Jim and Ingrid Kempston who lived in central London but had started to do set meals in their Norfolk 'barn' at the weekend. It was in London that Darron started school, Kevin arrived, and we set-to living a normal working life. After 3 years, and finally understanding what the financial benefits were likely to be, I accepted the offer to become 'International' staff. After 3 months of training in Holland we excitedly awaited the news as to where our first international assignment would be. The answer, greeted without over whelming enthusiasm by Sheila, was Aberdeen. This, in due course, became known as 'the most foreign posting we ever had'.

Aberdeen

In 1973 Aberdeen, as yet not effected by the soon to be oil boom, was a rustic, primitive back water. Pubs still had saw dust on the floors and ladies, if not banned, were certainly heavily discouraged from entry. There was, just a single restaurant. The cultural norm being that eating out was a waste of money, and the once every 10 years you did go out it was to a hotel. The final scene setter was when eventually exotic vegetables started to made an appearance Sheila had to explain to a supermarket manager just exactly what you did with green peppers so he could help his customers. The important, and long lasting, food influences were barbeques on Balmeady beach; baking all our bread as the available stuff tasted like polystyrene; and inspired by visiting our 'hippy' friends exploring the wonders of the hedgerows. I was already an expert 'black berrier' to which was added collecting rose hip berries and rowan berries. Aberdeen was a big turning point for us in many ways. Kevin started primary school there. We had a car for the first time. An MG 'B' rented from Callum Durran our dentist friend. And as Shell was paying the house rental we had at last a few spare pounds to spend. We visited auctions and started a 'woodcut' picture collection. We upgraded the MG for a Fiat 124 Sport. We even went on "proper" holidays where we didn't stay with relations. My final job in Aberdeen was being Project (though I wasn't so entitled) Engineer for the construction of a semi-submersible rig being built by SEDCO in Halifax, Nova Scotia. With this project, after many a scare such as breaking its moorings and hitting a bridge, completed and the rig ready to sail across the Atlantic my job, and time in Aberdeen, were up. Now it was off to pastures new in Holland.

Assen, North Holland

Aberdeen was to be followed by 4 years in Assen, northern Holland, working for NAM the Shell / Esso gas company. This was a food revelation. Firstly because you could buy custard at your doorstep. OK so the Dutch don't call it custard it's called vla. And you could also buy far more things than a British, now deceased, milkman would normally deliver. Beer, and potatoes, for example. And our 'milkman' spoke 5 languages. A marvellous service. We lived in a semi-detached house, with a garage, in Hertshoistraat. A sort of small Shell compound. It was here, inspired by the lack of English meat cuts, that we started buying ½ carcasses (lamb, pork, and beef). This is where the garage came in as it housed the buckets of brine in which we cured the pork belly.

The house had a garden to the back in which the previous inhabitants has planted some herbs. We not only kept up this good habit but branched out and one year grew courgettes. It was here that we met John Rose, who at the time was working for Schlumberger the French oil field service company, and his wife Geraldine. They were not only to become dear friends but as they had lived in Libya, Italy, Nigeria, and France were rather more practiced at eating local specialities, and adapting recipes to what was available. Several of the recipes herein were inspired by them. Assen was also where Kevin and I learnt to ice skate. Assen had a rink where we both went on to play recreational ice hockey. The biggest treat however was skating outside on natural ice. Normally on a frozen Dutch meer. I did once however travel to Germany (OK only just over the border) to play an international, Assen team v German football team, ice hockey match. What a fantastic experience. I can still remember how cold it was. When I came to drive home the gear box oil was so viscous with the low temperature the gears were hard to engage. All good things come to an end and our time in Assen was due to end. One of the central ideas of how Shell operated was to facilitate the spread of technical expertise by transferring staff between operating companies. In NAM we were the leading exponents of "well bore surveying". Measuring and calculating the path of our deviated wells from surface to reservoir some 3.5 km underground. I was to take this expertise to Brunei Shell.

Kuala Belait, Brunei

We set off to Brunei, on the north coast of the island of Borneo, arriving on the 13th December 1980. In the local, river mouth, town of Kuala Belait (Mouth of the Belait) was a covered market of the old variety. There were sellers of chicken, pork, fish, and vegetables. If you needed pork it was an early morning, killed and eaten that day, job. Fish was what was caught that night / day. Vegetables had dirt on them from growing in the ground. Our house was pretty well 'on the beach' with large terraces front and back. These encouraged us to get out the barbeque on a pretty regular basis. Also prawns are easy 'novice cook' fodder. They are colour coded. Bluish equals' raw – pink equals cooked. Job done. This was our first 'real' overseas taste of life and we enjoyed it to the full. There were Jungle Bungles (trips up jungle with the Army) that we both, separately, attended. Another new experience was the pretty hectic social life on the Shell camp. There were farewell parties where houses were converted into longhouses or caves. There were "on going" suppers – each guest cooked a course at their house before going to a new venue for the next course. There was even a 'shipwreck' party where the surrounding garden had been flooded and you had to wade through the water to enter. It wasn't all parties. There was sport. After my first day at work I was taken off on a "Hash". This I was to discover was a run in the jungle modelled after 'hare and hounds'. The 'hares' laid a +/- 1 hour duration run/walk marking the trail with toilette paper. The 'runners' then had to complete the run resolving the problems posed by "checks" - deliberate breaks in the paper markings. I eventually did 132 hashes. I also learned to windsurf becoming rather too fanatical in "wind watching" through the office window. Finally Darron, during his summer vacations, learned to play golf.

London – Second Time

When I accepted the transfer back to Shell Expro, London, Sheila thought I was mad. She was probably correct. My reasoning, if there was any, was that I had been to a 'fare-well' party soon after our arrival in Brunei Shell. It was in honour of a man leaving to return home after 23 years in Brunei! Now that's frightening. I felt we needed to reconnect to the mother country. Silly idea. We arrived back in the UK in December having visited New Zealand and Hawaii. What we didn't expect was 6 months in a hotel whilst we struggled to find a place we could afford to buy.

The only positive spin off was that a friend of Sheila's sister ran a restaurant close to our hotel in the middle of London. This allowed us to experience a working kitchen first hand. Both inspiring, and frightening, at the same time. During this time we still had our flat in Eastbourne, and having bought a Porsche 924, we commuted at the weekends. In mid-1985 we moved into the flat we had bought in Kenilworth Court, Putney. It was here we re-discovered the joy of window boxes and growing fresh herbs. Though working again for Shell Expro I did not work in Shell Centre. I was first assigned to Mathew Halls offices to work on the design of the north sea Eider platform, then to Shell Mex house to do the conceptual design of Kittiwake platform. In total we were to stay in London for 5 years. Important memories / events were visiting my Grandparents at Middle Shelspit farm; re-visiting our friends, the Roses, for holidays in their Gruisson apartment in the South of France; and going for runs along the Thames embankment. Sheila, home alone, decided that she needed to re-train and gain "portable" skills. To this end she successfully completed a "Steiner" Beauty Therapy course in 1986 and went on to work in a salon in Hammersmith. Once equipped with her own specialist "bed" this skill was to become an important export in our travels.

Damascus, Syria

Broke, and slightly desperate, I approached my boss in The Hague and asked for a 'hot and well paid' posting. As he promised, within a matter of almost hours, I had been offered and accepted a hardship posting. Working for Al Furat Petroleum, based in Damascus, Syria. What was to become the best posting we ever had. After our arrival our first shopping trip was whilst we were still staying in the Sheraton hotel. We needed lemons for the gin & tonics. In these days the company provided a car + driver. There was however no guarantee that he spoke any English. We made it to the souk and found a lemon seller. When asked how much we needed we showed 2 fingers remembering how expensive lemons were back in the UK. To our horror, and distress, we were handed 2 kilo's. For several minutes chaos reigned. Finally to our embarrassment the seller gave us 2 lemons, would not take money, whilst making it plain to all around that we were clearly mad. This was the shopping low point. We were soon to get much better, and more adventurous. In this we were greatly aided by driver Aymon, who having worked very hard at his English, could now help us learnt the ropes. Also our experiences of other markets enabled us to overcome the qualms of going to the "smelly" souk. Here you could buy all manner of meat. However it was all alive. It was to be a little while before we knew a butcher well enough to get him to 'hang' rabbits, not part of the Muslim culture for any meat, in his cold room. Later on Nabile, who's butchers shop was directly opposite our house, knew us well enough to invite us to inspect his sheep prior to their slaughter for the annual festivals. One other unique feature of the Al Furat assignment was you knew in advance exactly when you were leaving. The contract between Shell & the Syrian government for the supply of engineers stated that if a person stayed longer than 4 years Shell had to offer a discount on the going day rate. Naturally Shell arranged that our assignment ran for 3 years and +/- 360 days. Our time was up.

Miri, Sarawak

The theory was, like many other ideas more hope than reality, that if you survived Damascus you would be rewarded by a good posting. We in a way came up trumps. We were assigned to Sarawak. We arrived in Miri, about 25 miles down the coast from Brunei, in 3rd November 1993. We had, naturally, already some idea of what we were going to. The local pork and fish markets; excellent Chinese restaurants; and food stalls. We were quickly assigned a temporary house, immediately and for obvious reasons christened the "Purple Palace". Malay's do like bright neon lights, and garish colours. The glory of the house was it had 21 coconut palms in the garden. I must have bought the rum at duty free. With this to hand, and with fresh coconuts, it was time to experiment in getting the proportions just right for the Pina Colada's. I won't elaborate but just say whatever it was I intended to cook on the barbeque was left for sons to complete. Whilst there we rediscovered the joys of 'street' food something that was a little limited due to health worries in Damascus. There was a great place were all the food stall holders had different coloured plates. You walked around seeing what looked the best and placed your order. When it was time to pay you paid on the basis of how many plates of a particular colour you had. All good things have to come to an end. In 1995/6 Sarawak Shell was technically bankrupt. Drastic measures were called for. The workforce was cut from in excess of 4,500 to 1,750. I worked on the team charged with redesigning the company and it was within part of my remit that I made myself redundant. Luckily there was another job for me back in Holland.

Den Haag, Holland

Our departure from Sarawak, and arrival in Holland, was very rushed. I started work on the 1st October 10 days before the start of a training programme that I was to 'manage'. I imagine we first stayed in a hotel whist we house hunted but to be frank I cannot remember anything other than the trauma of my new job. Den Haag, the capital of the Netherlands, is however a very easy place to enjoy life. It's easy to get out of the city. Ten, or max fifteen, minutes are all that's needed. And you can get every delicacy you desire within walking distance. We lived right in the centre, near the Peace Palace, in Willems Park, on Zeestraat. Though in the city there was a very village feel to the place. There was a square close by that provided, in relative seclusion, a baker (OK so every place in Holland has it's baker); a fantastic multi-lingual grocer; a deli; a very well provided butchers; and an excellent wine shop. We were also surrounded by good restaurants. Excellent pizzas, Indonesian ricetaffle, and Singapore noodles, were available within easy walking distance. For fresh fish we used to go the short distance to Scheveningen harbour where the days catch was on sale. Scheveningen is also a great place for fish restaurants. My favourite dish became "kinder" fish and chips. The fish was a selection of off cuts from whatever was in supply, deep fried. Only available off the children's menu. For the first year of our stay I worked just outside Den Haag at the Shell Training Centre. During the last 2 years I joined the LEAP (Leadership) Team and spent most of my time travelling. I helped run training workshops for Shell employees in Oman, Nigeria, Norway, UK, and Syria as well as in the Holiday Inn in Soesterdiun in the middle of Holland. I'm not sure this travel broadened my taste pallet except to say there are some disgusting things on offer in other parts of the world. One thing that did expand our horizons was linking up with Geraldine and John Rose who were again based in Dusseldorf. They would visit us and we would go through to them. This set up was augmented by a variation – we would meet half way, at what we called the outback, for windsurfing and barbeques. In mid-1999 the oil price dropped below US$ 10/bbl making most of Shells North Sea production uneconomic. Shell senior management, in spite of previous commitments to stick to the long term vision, panicked. Some 5,000 of the +/- 12,000 "international" staff were made redundant. I was lucky in that I had a choice. I could stay with LEAP and run a 12 – 18 month transformation programme in Nigeria or accept voluntary redundancy. We chose the latter. This meant we were on the move again.

Cyprus

We didn't really plan to retire early to Cyprus. But leaving Shell in September 1999, after working for them for 30 years, the good news was I was eligible for a full pension.

Travels With Our Kitchen

Unfortunately redundancy made us homeless as well as jobless. We had recently sold up in the UK and our Cyprus holiday home was all that was left. This, combined with loosing UK tax free status if we went back home, compared to paying 5% in Cyprus as a retiree, sealed the deal. We moved to Limassol. Memories reminded us of delicious, seasonal, fruit, and veg. Of loading the cool box to take delicacies back to Syria. We were also encouraged by the thought that as a condition of EU membership the island, Greek and Turkish, would be reunited. Both ideas unfortunately evaporated in the heat of everyday reality. The growers had discovered Dutch "hydroponic" growing techniques. And the Greeks voted NO!!! Still we did have access to local markets and supportive gardeners. This ensured among other things a supply of virgin olive oil. Especially pleasing if you had helped harvest the olives. We also were lucky in that our local family included us in their food traditions. Family cooking and special traditional feast day recipes. As time passed, and I failed completely in getting any offers of employment, I started to do some consulting work. First in Cyprus for a Limassol company Audah who distributed cigarettes to "difficult" airports in the Middle East. This was followed by preparing, and delivering, 2 or 3 day workshops to various Middle East clients through a local company. Through this same company we were asked to bid for 3 months consultancy work in Oman Refinery. Success saw the start of the next chapter of our lives. I flew out to Oman via Abu Dhabi in June 2004.

Muscat, Oman

Unknown to us on arrival this 3 month job was to be extend to 6 months duration. We stayed in a serviced apartment in the Safir Hotel. Sheila and I, having visited Oman when I was in the LEAP Team, roughly knew our way around. Where the supermarkets were, and we could remember the restaurants and hotels we had enjoyed previously. We enjoyed ourselves knowing it was only a temporary assignment. Come Christmas and we would be back in Cyprus. Immediately upon our return Oman Gas requested that I come out and undertake a similar consultancy for them. Again toward the end of this job, and with suitcases packed, I got a 3 month job through SPIE with Petroleum Development Oman. No sooner had I started work than I was signed up to be Operations Manager for Shaleem Petroleum. Sheikh Abdul Aziz Al Mahri's oil well work-over (repair) company. I did this for nearly 18 months before taking a position directly in SPIE as Contracts Manager. This ultimately led to me becoming the Country Manager and our time in Oman stretching out to 7 years. Not bad for a 3 month job. Looking back the Oman period was in many ways defined by two supreme, divergent, threads. The PDO club fishing competition, where through the patronage of Faisla Al Riyami, we enjoyed many a "Fish of the Day". A 5kg Hamour is a sight for sore eyes, and empty stomachs, especially if needing scaled and gutted. The other key influence was "press and stir". This was the instruction given by the chef at the Oriental Hotel, Bangkok, cookery class we took. A far away influence but we could get lots of fresh, air flown, Thai produce in Oman. Our love of oriental food, combined with sons who both had Thai partners, easily squeezed us in this direction. That said it was also very easy to feel how "far away" you were. We could get all the cookery magazines, Good Food, Olive, etc, and easily relate to their pleadings – only use fresh, organic, market produce, in season. The problem was that in Oman the only seasonal ingredients were dates, and dried fish!!! To be fair the supermarkets were at times a treasure trove of regional, and worldwide fare. The issue was to gauge the ever changing availability you had to visit 3 or 4 different supermarkets. On the plus side compared with Cyprus the top hotels, the Al Bustan, the Chedi, and to some extent the Sheraton all had excellent restaurants. The Chedi was always first class be it breakfast, Thursday (1st day of the weekend) lunch, or Darron and Angkana's wedding. In addition there was the excellent, stand alone, Mumtaz Indian restaurant. We never had a bad dish there in the whole time we lived in Oman. Finally, worthy of all the fine dining superlatives, there was Shannon Bennet's Vue restaurant were we enjoyed some of the best food we've ever eaten. We were also lucky enough to take part in a full day cookery demonstration in his kitchen. Sadly the restaurant is no longer in the Al Bustan hotel.

Bangkok & Hua Hin, Thailand

We had first visited Thailand in 1979 en route to our first overseas Shell assignment in Brunei. We stayed at the Oriental Hotel. We did the usual touristy things. Visited the floating market; went to temples; and visited the "Rose Garden" to watch their cultural show. Subsequently we visited Thailand once again during our time in the Far East. Then after a gap of many years we visited again in 2008 to see Darron who was teaching English in Ayutthaya, the old Thai capital, upriver from Bangkok. We again stayed at the Oriental. This time taking advantage of their in-house Thai cookery course. We didn't visit Ayutthaya but Darron came down and stayed at the Oriental for a couple of nights. On our next trip in 2009 we went up to Ayutthaya to visit Darron, and Angkana, his new partner. This was where, in many ways, our real introduction to Thai food started. Angkana is an excellent cook. She bravely cooked for us, for the first time, then. The dishes, wonderfully fresh and fragrant, are now regular additions to our diet. After their marriage in Oman in November 2010, we visited Thailand again in March 2011 for the Buddhist blessing of their union. This took place up from Trat, in Eastern Thailand, near the Cambodian border. We gained another perspective on Thai life and cuisine. Coming up to date our last visit, November 2011, saw us stay with Darron, Angkana, Kain, Gerry, and Noey in their new home in Hau Hin. They have a small annex to the house which we set up as our 'granny flat'. This is where we stay when we visit them. This trip involved a drive over to Pattaya, Noch Noosh Gardens, for the Buddhist wedding, and blessing, of Kevin and Wanvisa. We left Thailand following a stay in Bangkok with Piyapon (Wan's mother). Another wonderful exposure to the joys of real Thai home cooking. We have stayed twice since then. Two months in early 2013, and 3 months in 2014. Angkana during these visits enjoyed, and rose to the challenge, of cooking with us watching on. She must have made over 60 different dishes which featured among the many other delights +/-18 herbs and vegetables we had never seen, never mind eaten, before.

Edinburgh - Retirement

When we prematurely retired to Cyprus in 1999 we didn't own a house in the UK. With Darron working in Edinburgh it turned our minds to buying there. After a false start we bought 17A Union Street, a garden flat. Proper retirement started in November 2011 after attending Kevin and Wanvisa's wedding in Thailand. The first challenge was combining, and downsizing, three kitchen equipment hordes into one. Which sauce pans to keep, and what to do with the 2 extra whizzers? We also needed to get used to, and understand, all the changes that had taken place in the 22 years we had lived outside the UK. A food revolution, in terms of both restaurant fare and general availability of ingredients, had taken place. In Edinburgh, and it's surrounds, we are blessed with marvellous 'farmers' markets; really world class specialist fishmongers; award winning butchers; and self-styled "...probably the best vegetable shop in the world", Tatty Shaws. Over our time we have come to consistently visit two particular favourites. One is Craigies farm shop for their excellent butchers and root vegetables. The other is Clarks Fishmongers of Musselburgh. We learnt of them from reading the autobiography of Clarissa Dickson Wright (she of the BBC television series Two Fat Ladies) where she praises them highly. As it happens Mrs Clark is Thai. Not only that but she comes from a village close to that of Piyapon, Wanvisa's mother. Ever since these two met at the shop I think we have been spoilt when it comes to our frequent purchases. All these different sources of food are in addition to the supermarkets with a range that covers Waitrose to Lidl. As for "eating" we immediately sought produce that was not available in Oman. We had time and fresh ingredients. Simon & Sarah Richards, with whom we shared our first retirement Hogmanay, gave me a large one day, one page, diary. This became our food log book. In this all manner of things were recorded including the entire extra special, and successful, meals we cooked. There are over 80 references to recipes which we had cooked for the first time. Not only new but the majority being memorably tasteful. Some of these are included below.

2.0 Edinburgh - Student Days, Sept '64 to Sept '70

Sheila and I had met at Leuchers, in Fife, Scotland, where both our Royal Air Force fathers were stationed in the early 1960's. I had just been given the opportunity to transfer from the Borough Secondary School to the local, I guess you would now have to say, grammar school. This was Madras College, St Andrews, an institution set up in 1832 by Rev Dr Alexander Bell on his return to Scotland having made his fortune in India. Sheila had just left her boarding school, Upton Hall, and had started her pre nursing training at Fod House, in Dunfermline. We had met earlier, all be it briefly, but took until 23rd August 1962, to fix the first date. I, having enjoyed success in passing my "O" levels, had just returned from visiting my parents in Singapore and taken up residence in digs in St Andrews. Sheila was spending the week days at Fod House and coming home to Leuchars for the weekends.

In mid-1964 Sheila completed her pre nursing studies. To commemorate this she was presented with a copy of Good Housekeeping's *"PICTURE COOKERY"* book. Perhaps they knew how soon she would need to live using these skills. I had managed to get good enough passes in my "Higher" exams to have attained University entrance. The question we faced was where were we to go to nursing / studies - "Glasgow or Edinburgh?" As Sheila was accepted by the Edinburgh Southern Group of hospitals, and the Heriot Watt College (just prior to being granted University status) accepted me to study a 4 year course in Mechanical Engineering, we moved to Edinburgh. She took up residence in the Edinburgh Southern Group Training school on Carlton Terrace where there was a boarding house for the trainee nurses. I moved into digs in Bread Street.

At the end of my first year I was devastated by failing "maths". I managed to get a summer vacation job in a naval munitions factory in Fife dismantling old cordite shells. I needed the money to survive. This however posed a problem re studying for my resit. How to balance the need for money with the need for unpaid time off work to study. I took a week off and managed to fail the re-sit. The option then became to take a year out, re sit the exam, and re-join in the 2nd year in the event of success. By this time I was sharing a flat and the need to pay rent meant I urgently needed a job. I joined Bruce Peebles, an Edinburgh electrical engineering company, and worked in their R & D Lab. My job was stress testing aluminium welds. It didn't completely fill my time so I used to make things, such as key rings, to take home. Sheila continued her nurses training working at the Deaconess, Bangower, and Bruntsfield hospitals.

To help with the revision I attended 'night school'. Come the June '66 exam I managed to pass. There was however another problem. Sheila had fallen pregnant and we had been married in April. We started life together moving into a rented room in Annandale Street. The baby was due in late October. I went back to Heriot Watt to continue my Mechanical engineering studies. The first problem was we couldn't afford the rent we were paying for our room. I had assumed that on my return to Heriot Watt I would be eligible for a "full" grant of GBP 350 per year. The reality was a reduced grant with a parental contribution. My parents were not overly impressed with me and probably thought I should get a proper job. Luckily we had Edinburgh University friends who were living in very cheap, University subsidised, flats around the University buildings in the Old Town. After a period of "squatting" we moved in with them. The imminent arrival of Darron meant again we needed a proper home. We found a small flat to rent in Muriston Road. As we were young, I can think of no other reason, we successfully coped with what were quiet extraordinary problems. Darron was born with a cleft pallet. Fortunately he didn't have a 'hare' lip. He just lacked the soft pallet that separates nose and throat. Swallowing was a problem. We needed special teats so that he could suck and take food. He needed an operation to correct the problem. However there was a complication. Sheila's Grandfather had suffered from the gene deficiency that causes haemophilia. He lived to a reasonable age, and the chances of a daughter in the line being a carrier is 50/50, so it was not definite that he would have haemophilia. However we had to wait until he was over 6 months before he was considered strong enough to undergo the 'tests'. In the early days I used to sleep so shallowly that when he couldn't swallow properly, and would start to choke, I would wake up and push my fingers down his throat to clear his airway. He on his part, once he was off his special bottle, had to survive for much longer than normal on minced food.

Once we settled in to parenthood it became obvious that the need to feed three on the grant required subsidising with paid work. A dental college student friend, Colin Watson, & I hired an ice-cream van. From early afternoon until the pubs closed we did a "round" covering the housing estates on the outskirts of Edinburgh. The money earner was the ice cream. The attractor was we also sold cigarettes.

Around the end of the '67 academic year our financial situation was helped by a move into Edinburgh University, subsidised, slum accommodation. I think we must have been helped by our university friends and undoubtedly a kind (unknown soul) somewhere in the administration. We were allocated 5 Ingleston Street. This was a two room, one toilet, tenement flat on the 2nd floor. Once we had redecorated, ripped up the lino, sanded the pine floors, painted the ceiling and one wall bright red / blue, and I had finished making a table, bench, and shelves, we moved in. The rent was 13s 6p (67p) a month plus yearly "fue" duties of a further 5 shillings a year. Within our modest budget.

Travels With Our Kitchen

Back to the ice cream round. The need to skip lectures to start the round, plus the sheer effort of doing it, perhaps not surprisingly, didn't help the 'academic' studies. That year I failed a couple of exams and repeated the failure of Electrical Engineering at the resits. This meant another year out. My summer vacation job was working in Edinburgh Parks department, in the "Meadows". It was during this time that Darron could have his test for haemophilia. Luckily he was not a sufferer and so the surgery to correct the cleft, soft pallet, could go ahead. He had the operation at the Western General. Our only solid, and harrowing, memory was visiting him soon after the operation when he was in a cot, hands tied to the side, to prevent him sucking his figures and possibly rupturing the stiches.

In my job in the 'parks' once the leaves began to fall I realised things had to change. If I was to achieve academic success I needed to earn enough money to finance uninterrupted studies. A higher paid job was essential. I took a job as a labourer for Nuttal & Son who had the contract for redeveloping Leith docks. Primitive conditions were combined with high levels of danger. Firstly there was always the risk of getting into a fight with one of the numerous "hard" men with whom, on and off, I worked. The job was digging clay, using pneumatic power drills fitted with a spade shaped head, on the landward side of the old harbour walls. These "holes" were about 40ft deep, though only 12/14ft wide. On one side there were steel piles, and on the other the existing, leaky, old harbour wall separating us from the North Sea. We spent most of our time below sea level. How I escaped serious injury / drowning I'll never know. One week I would work 5 by 10 hour days and Saturday morning. The next week I worked the Sunday as well. Some 65 hours a week which equalled 77 ½ paid hours. Take home pay at +/- 7 shillings (35p/hr) per hour was GBP 20 for the short week and GBP 27 for the long week. The combination of cheap rent, and my labourer's salary, meant for the first time we enjoyed a few of life's luxuries and saved money. Of the luxuries I remember a few Chinese, and Italian, meals out.

Further hiccups were to follow. On coming home from work I was greeted by a note pinned to the door saying Sheila had been admitted to the Western General hospital as an emergency. On attempting to open a drawer the disc between vertebrae S4 and S5 had ruptured. The released viscous fluid was pressing so forcefully on her sciatic nerve that she couldn't walk or pass water. The later problem meant she needed immediate surgery. By the time I made the hospital I had taken up smoking! Caring for Darron was of necessity passed to Sheila's parents & I guess they drove up to Edinburgh from Devon to collect him. He stayed with them for some 6 weeks before Sheila, now well on the way to recovery, travelled down to Devon to retrieve him.

Somehow in the midst of all this I was able to look after Sheila once she came home, continue to work in the docks, and do a bit of studying. Then helped by taking 2 weeks off work, and really pushing myself, I was able to pass the Electrical Engineering resit. Come the October of '68 I was to again return to Heriot Watt which by now had gained university status. Third and fourth years were navigated successfully. The summer of '69, accompanied by man 'walking' on the moon, we stayed with Sheila's parents during our 3rd year summer vacation and I worked in Barnstable, Wonderloaf, factory. I worked days one week, nights the next, making some 40,000 loafs a week. Sheila, and Darron, enjoyed their time with her Mum and Dad. This was to prove the only time we were together as a whole family. After yet another resit we returned to Edinburgh where I worked for, and passed, my final exams in May/June 1970. All 3 of us proudly attended the graduation ceremony in the following August. Throughout all these "interesting" times we always managed to have 3 meals a day, and often entertain our university friends when they needed some sustenance. This miracle was the result of Sheila's efforts. From her nursing days, when she looked after his dying wife, she knew a friendly butcher. He throughout our student days was a source of protein we could otherwise never have afforded. He would give us cheap, unpopular cuts like pork ribs, or liver. It's easy to forget from a 2014 perspective what a completely different world 1960's Edinburgh was. My guess is, compared to today, it was a time when everyone had known at some time the rigours of poverty. As such the people around us were much more supportive of young families like us. The Ingleston Street flat was above a Fish & Chip shop. Whenever we wanted to buy we would be sent back upstairs until the freshly made fish was ready. Round the corner in East Adam Street the local general shop would extend credit if you had no money. Most surprising was that even the nearest supermarket, Low's on the Bridges, would give us cut off's of bacon scraps. Along with the home made table & bench we had invested in a cooker – 4 gas rings, a grill, and an oven. Luxury. This combination of Good Housekeeping's **"Picture Cookery Book"**; Sheila's ever expanding cookery knowledge and skills; a steady supply of good basic ingredients; and our cooker, kept stomachs full and body and soul together.

One last, and how lucky we are they still going strong, key influence and inspiration on the food side of life was Jim Kempston. Jim is married to Ingrid, sister to Astrid Silins, who later on became God mother to Kevin. They used to come up from London to visit Astrid. We met Jim & Ingrid mid-way through Sheila's pregnancy during the time we stayed with Astrid & Marlyn, in Charles Street. Their visit promised the treat of good food, excellently prepared. I can only ever remember him cooking pork loin with onion and apples but I'm sure Sheila remembers other, even more exquisite, offerings. We would keep in touch when we moved to London. Later they moved up to Edinburgh where we were to eventually retire to. In the middle of this migration, in the mid '80's Jim would go on to be owner/chef at Stone Green Hall, Ashford, Kent, a Cromwelian farmhouse where before the name was invented they ran a boutique (romantic) hotel. He would also write a cook book, well ahead of it's time we now realise, entitled **"The Creative Cook"** published in 1993.

Returning to the main theme our travels and the different kitchens we have come to use one of the last acts in Edinburgh was to take the photo below.

This is the view from the kitchen/living room window into the common back yard. It was taken to act as a reminder of how we had succeeded through not giving up and not complaining. Also were we to ever feel hard done by in some future life it's a reminder of harsh reality that many did not, could not, escape from.

For us it was off to adventures new. Before we leave Edinburgh below are some of the recipes we can now recall from these student days.

Fried Egg Sandwiches

Edinburgh, with its soft morning rolls, is famous for its 'bacon sarnies'. I must say I think we always bought these. What I do remember is the first thing I ever cooked for Sheila. This was before we got married and I was living in digs with family Gordon in St Andrews. It was "fried egg" sandwiches. These can be a bit messy to eat so a steady, non-drunken, approach is best. Preparation of this treat was repeated many more times after our arrival in Edinburgh.

Ingredients - serves 2

2 eggs
4 slices of factory white sliced bread
Heinz Tomato Ketchup

1) Crack eggs into hot flying pan and fry until the white starts to crisp. Flip over and continue for a few moments to fry.

2) Place 1 slice of bread on each of 2 plates and flip the eggs out onto each slice. Cover in tomato sauces before covering with the second slice of bread.

3) Slice the sandwich in half to assess how much runny yoke will ooze out. Eat mopping up the yoke with the crusts of your sandwich.

Potato and Leek Soup

After getting married, and having Darron, we soon discovered that living on a single student grant was quiet a financial challenge. Even after we secured a cheap rental flat our food budget was rather limited. One answer was to cook cheap, but filling, dishes. Sheila soon developed two staple, repeated weekly, lunch time soups recipes. These were Lentil Soup, mentioned below, and this one Potato & Leek. Our fellow students soon learned the days on which Sheila made soup and soon came to realize there would always be more than enough to go around.

Ingredients - serves 4

2 lbs potatoes peeled and sliced
1 large onion finely chopped
2 leeks white parts sliced
1 oz knob of lard (butter was an expensive treat)
2 pints water
1 Oxo chicken stock cube
1 dried Bay leaf
¼ pint milk
Salt and pepper

1) Peel and slice the potatoes, slice the leek and chop the onion. In a sauce pan on medium heat melt the fat and sauté the potatoes, onion, and leek for +/- 10 minutes.

2) Add the water to the sauce pan, crumble in the Oxo cube, and add the bay leaf. Bring to the boil and simmer until the vegetables are tender and the potatoes begin to break up.

3) Mash with a potato masher, add the milk, and return to the heat. Taste and adjust the seasoning. When hot serve to warm bowls.

Spaghetti Bolognaise

At the end of my 1st year at Heriot Watt I took a summer vacation job at Rosyth in a munitions factory on the other side of the Firth of Forth. There they dismantled old Navy ammunition and shells. This meant I needed a place to stay. John Lloyd and Mark Hill having rented a flat in Claremont Crescent and wanting to keep it on for their next academic year needed a summer rental. That was me. In the end I was to stay 9 months. It was here we got to know Astrid Silins, and Marlyn Robson, friends to this day. At a certain point Mark & John decided they must entertain their Edinburgh University English Professors, Lecturers, and other undergraduates. The only issue was "What to cook?" Spaghetti Bolognaise was the eventual choice.

Ingredients - serves 30

Lots of minced beef
Many onions sliced thinly
Large quantity of tinned tomatoes
Tube of concentrated tomato paste
Garlic if you can get it (remember this was 1966)
Some oil
Some cheese (parmesan ??? - I sure we didn't know about this never mind being able to afford it)
Salt & Pepper
Tons of Spaghetti

1) Heat some oil in a frying pan then add the onions (& the garlic) and sweat down. Add the mince and cook, stirring to break down any lumps of mince, until golden brown.

2) Add the tinned tomatoes and a good squeeze of the paste. Bring to the bubble and simmer, occasionally stirring and checking the liquid content, for a couple of hours. If dry add a little water or wine if available.

3) Bring a large sauce pan of water to the boil and then salt. Add the spaghetti and cook as per the instructions. When cooked but still 'al dente' (an expression we didn't know then) drain and transfer to a large bowl.

4) Pour the cooked bolognaise over the spaghetti and gently stir through. Grate some cheese over the top. Serve in soup bowls and impress the academics by discussing "Piers Ploughman" texts 1 or 2, and or Chaucer.

Bacon & Potato Pie

Another diet 'staple' that filled our bellies and kept us warm. I imagine that the bacon bits came from the same source as quoted before – the bacon counter at Lows supermarket. One interesting point whilst searching our minds to try and remember what we ate, and going through the cookery book collection to see if we could find a book published early enough to have been the recipe source, we drew a blank. We definitely cooked this but the recipe below is how we would make it now and how we did indeed cook it in many subsequent cold locations.

Ingredients - serves 2 1/2

Bacon scraps
2 large onions finely sliced
4 large potatoes finely sliced
1 ½ oz knob of butter
2 * tblsp Flour
½ pint milk
Salt and pepper

1) Scatter 1/3 rd of the uncooked bacon scraps in the bottom of a pie dish. Next cover the bacon with a layer of sliced onion. Now do the same building a layer of sliced potato. Salt this first layer. Repeat twice more finishing with a good layer of potatoes on top.

2) Melt the knob of butter in a sauce pan. Slowly add the flour stirring as you go with a wooden spoon. Continue adding flour and stirring until all the butter is absorbed. Now start to slowly add the milk stirring continuously to make a lump free sauce. Once ready season with salt and pepper to taste. Gently pour the white sauce over the pie layers.

3) Place the pie on a rack toward the top end of the pre-heated (160C) oven and cook for 1 hour checking after 30 to 40 minutes to make sure the pie is not overflowing.

Grannie's Lentil Soup

This was another 'student days' life saver. It was always called "Grannies Lentil Soup" but Sheila is not completely sure she ever stood and watched her Granny make it. However her mother did. Given we could get bacon ribs for free, and the other ingredients were cheap, this was a regular wholesome treat. The photo below is a modern day recreation – I took it yesterday.

Ingredients – serves 4/6

- *Bacon ribs or slices from half a packet chopped*
- *1 large onion finely chopped*
- *2 carrots coarsely chopped*
- *1 large leek chopped*
- *2 sticks of celery coarsely chopped.*
- *1 cup red lentils*
- *Bunch of parsley chopped to garnish*
- *Salt & Pepper*

1) Put a good sized saucepan on a medium heat. If using packet bacon add the chopped slices to the dry pan as they will release fat as they cook.

2) With the bacon cooking underway add the chopped onions and begin to sweat down. With the onions softening now add the chopped carrots. Continue to sweat giving the occasional stir. Now add the leek and celery. Give the contents a good stir. Continue to soften.

3) Add the washed lentils and generously cover the vegetables with water. Bring to the boil and then simmer for 30 minutes. You are aiming to have all the vegetables cooked through and soft. Add salt and pepper to taste.

4) Remove the saucepan from the heat. Ladle +/- 1/3 of the soup into a separate bowl and liquidise with a hand held stick blender. Return the blended soup to the saucepan and mix in. If needed reheat.

Serve in generously sized soup bowls, garnished with the chopped parsley, and accompanied with slices of good country bread.

Smoked Haddock Kedgeree

Sheila had learned how to make 'kedgeree', a classic Anglo Indian dish, when she attended Fod House, Pre-nursing College, in Dunfermline. Later on, after we had Darron, and where living in Ingleston Street, this dish became a stalwart. The fish was cheap, it was easy to cook, it was (and is) very flavoursome. Now we always make a version (below) that more closely follows Rick Stein's kedgeree recipe from one of his earlier, 1995, TV series "Taste of the Sea".

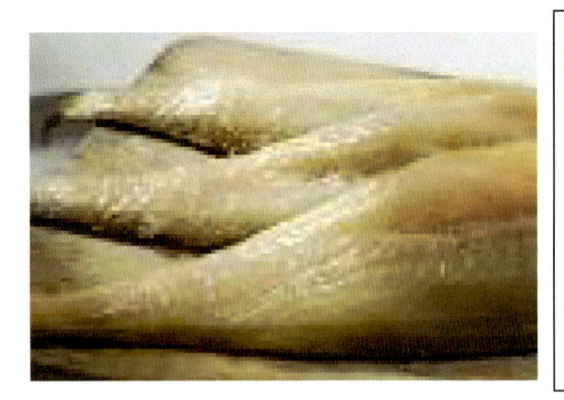

> On the other side of the "Bridges" from our flat was a wet fish shop. This is another example (dish) where we were supported by local shopkeepers. Sheila would put Darron in his push chair and set off to the shops. Invariably in the fish shop if she asked for "two pieces of fish" they would hand over two pieces and "an extra piece "for the bairn". I must also mention that in those far-off days the rice would have been cooked "plain" without any spices.

Ingredients - serves 4

400g smoked Haddock (avoid very yellow - artificially coloured - you want pale golden)
2 large eggs
1/3 rd cup of rice per person
4 Cardamom seeds, 3 cloves, a 27.5 cm piece of cinnamon bark, and 1/2 tsp turmeric
Knob of butter
8 - 12 small tomatoes
Large bunch of parsley
Salt and freshly crushed black pepper to taste

1) Place the haddock in a shallow sauce pan or frying pan. Just cover with cold water and slowly bring to the boil. Switch off the heat and leave for 10 - 15 minutes depending upon the thickness of the fish. Remove fish and set aside to cool. Reserve the cooking liquid.

2) Put the eggs into a small pan and cover with cold water and bring to the boil. Boil as per your preferred process. Whites hard; yokes soft, or hard. Remove cool and shell.

3) Wash the rice. Drain and add to a sauce pan. Cover the rice to a depth of +/- 1cm with the liquid the fish was cooked in. Add in the cardamom, cloves, bark, and turmeric. Place on the heat and bring to the boil. Place a tightly fitting lid on the pan, turn the heat down low and allow to cook for 12 minutes. Do not remove the lid whilst cooking. When the 12 minutes is up remove from the heat and fluff up the rice with a rice paddle and remove the spices.

4) Whilst the rice is cooking finely chop up the hard boiled eggs and set aside in a dish. Slice the tomatoes in half (if small) quarters (if larger) and set aside in a bowl.

5) Turn the rice out into a shallow dish and flake the smoked haddock over. Finely chop the parsley and scatter over the rice and fish. Carefully amalgamate. Season to taste.

Serve in bowls with the chopped eggs, and tomatoes, added to the side.

Cottage Pie

In thinking about the recipes for this journal has forced a deeper reflection about what were we actually doing back then. I've realised that I keep talking about 'freshly ground black pepper' which for penniless students sounds very grand. Well it was then that we first introduced a golden rule which we have successfully followed since those early days.

This is if we were lucky enough to be given some money we bought something long lasting and didn't blow it down the pub for example. The first such gift of money from Grandma Capel was spent on a wooden pepper mill. We still have it some 45 years later and it is in daily use when we cook.

Ingredients - serves 4

1 large onion finely chopped
1 large carrot chopped into fine cubes
1lb beef mince
¼ lb frozen peas (optional)
¼ pint beef stock or good gravy
Butter
Splash Worcester sauce
Salt and freshly ground black pepper to taste
1lb mashed potatoes

1) Put a knob of butter into a frying pan over a low heat. Add the chopped onions and the carrot and sweat down until soft. Add the minced beef, and if using, the peas. Now add the stock. Gently cook the mixture stirring occasionally for 5 minutes. Season to taste and add a few drops of Worcester sauce.

2) Grease a oven proof dish and transfer the meat mixture to it. Cover with the mashed potato a serving spoonful at a time working around the dish until all the potato is added. Using a fork flatten off the potato leaving ridges from the forks prongs.

3) Place the cottage pie into a medium hot oven, 180 C, and bake for 40 minutes. Check that the potato topping is nicely coloured on the 'ridges' and the meat mixture is bubbling at the dishes side.

Serve on hot plates with the vegetable of your choice.

Leg of Lamb

This photo of Darron gnawing on the leg bone was taken in the Ingleston Street flat. As I only had a camera after working with Nuttals & Son redeveloping Leith docks it has to be between late 1968, when I restarted my studies, and when we left Edinburgh in mid-1970.

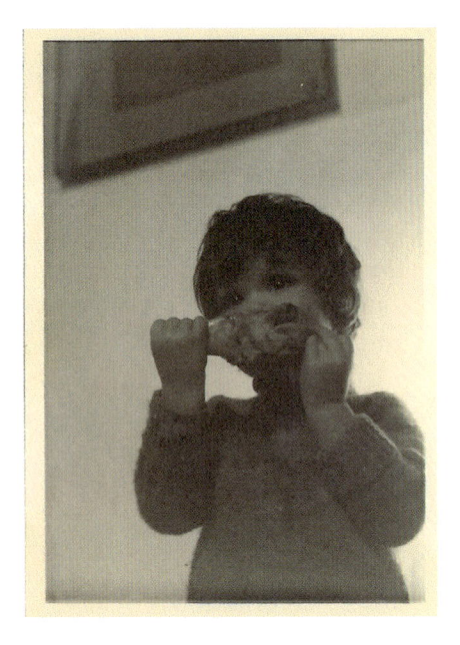

The puzzle is - how could we afford to buy a whole leg of lamb??? Another clue that it was toward the end of our time in Edinburgh is the picture on the wall. This was given to us by Mike Wilkin when he quit Medical studies at Edinburgh University to do Accountancy in Glasgow. Perhaps there was a bit of cash left over from my labouring days. I'm not even sure how we would have prepared it for cooking. The one luxury we did have was a gas cooker so it will have been roasted. Here is how we would do it now.

Ingredients   - serves 2 ½ at least

1 leg of lamb (+/- 2.5 kg)
1 large onion sliced
3 or 4 cloves of garlic sliced
3 sprigs of Rosemary
White wine or Vermouth to de glaze the pan (we never had wine in our student days)
Small new potatoes & spring veg.

1) With a sharp and pointed knife (a boning knife would be ideal) make incisions in the fleshy side of the leg. In each incision push a slice of garlic and a small sprig of rosemary detached from the main stem. Repeat in an organised, equally spaced pattern until all the garlic/rosemary is used up.

2) Place the slices of onion in the bottom of a roasting dish then add a sprig of rosemary. Now balance the leg of lamb on top of them with the 3rd sprig of rosemary on top of the leg.

3) Gently slide the roasting dish into a pre heated, hot, oven trying to keep the leg balanced on the onions. Roast for 20 minutes per 500g plus 20 minutes. Once cooked remove.

4) Take the leg out of the roasting dish and set aside, covered with aluminium foil, to rest. Place the roasting tin on a medium heat and add the Martini to the dish and deglaze. You can also add some of the vegetable cooking water for flavour. Bubble down. When ready strain through a sieve into a heated jug. Finally as the gravy will be pretty fatty pour into a fat separator.

Carve the leg and serve with the potatoes, spring veg, and the gravy poured over the meat.

Queen of Puddings

Along with soups another staple was 'pudding'. This seems quiet strange remembered as it is from our perspective of our retirement to Edinburgh. Once your children leave home the incentive to make puddings declines. That, and the combination of weight controlled diet and Sheila's gluten intolerance, means such treats are a long forgotten memory. In the spirit of revival we offer another recipe from the Good Housekeeping's *"Picture Cookery"* the Queen of Puddings.

Ingredients - serves 4

½ pint milk
¼ pint bread crumbs
½ oz butter
½ oz sugar
2 egg yolks
2 tblsp raspberry jam

For the Meringue

2 egg whites
4 oz sugar

1) Bring the milk to heat without boiling in a pan. Add the breadcrumbs, butter and sugar and set aside for ½ hour for the bread to swell.

2) Beat in the egg yolks and pour the mixture into a greased pie dish. Bake in a moderate oven 170 C for about ½ hour until set.

3) Spread a thick layer of jam on top of the pudding heating the jam if necessary so that it spreads easily.

4) Whisk the egg whites until stiff and then fold in nearly all the sugar. Pile this on top of the pudding and then dredge with the remaining sugar. Return to a slightly cooler (160 C) oven and bake for 20 to 30 minutes until the meringue is lightly coloured and crisp to the touch.

3.0 London - First Job With Shell, Sept '70 to Aug '73

I had been in the students union and chanced to ask if I could borrow the paper someone had just finished reading. In it was an advertisement in the jobs section placed by Shell Exploration and Production Ltd in which they were looking for an Economist with mechanical understanding or a Mechanical Engineer with some economics. Having done a 2 year course in Economics as part of the varied subjects I had included in my Mechanical Engineering degree I applied. Somewhat to my surprise, as at the "milk round" interview with Shell I was told "no way" would I get a job with them, I was invited down to London for an interview. The excitement was tinged with a slight degree of panic as we didn't have the money for the fare. I was therefore forced to approach the bank. Once I mentioned "interview with Shell" the skin flint attitude of yore was replaced by:- "Come into my office, would you like a cup of coffee?". At the end of my interview with Guy Fussilier, who would be my boss for the first 2 years, I was left with a real sense that I would be offered a job. With my expenses to hand I prematurely celebrated by buying Darren a car transporter Dinky toy. On my return to Edinburgh our hopes were confirmed when the telegram arrived offering me a job as an Economics Engineer on a salary that seemed a fortune.

I headed off down to London. Sheila and Darron initially stayed behind as I house / flat hunted. I stayed with university friend John Lloyd. Dreams of immediate wealth and luxury were soon dashed. I found out how much it cost to rent in London. After 10 days or so I was able to find a flat but a "fee" needed to be paid for the "fixtures and fittings". One way or another we found the money and moved into Canterbury Mansions, Leamington Road, West Hampstead. This was our home for the next 3 years. After the Edinburgh flat this was rather luxurious. We had a kitchen, a bathroom, two bedrooms and a 'day' room. Quite a step up from the 2 small rooms, a tiny box room which was were Darron slept, and a toilet, that made up Ingelston Street.

We soon settled in. I got used to the daily "tube" (Bakerloo Line) ride to and from Waterloo which had an entrance straight into Shell Centre. Sheila soon met other 'mothers' on the traditional school run which in those days was done on foot. We also became friends with our neighbours across the road, Andrew and Vi, who had a son about the same age as Darron. Vi was a good cook and Andrew who sold early 20th century pictures were soon making a big impact.

Darron's school was up the road, just the other side of Finchley Road. In another sign of the times, quite extraordinary given today's perspective, was that he quite quickly (within a year) wanted to walk home by himself. I know at the beginning Sheila, out of his sight, was monitoring his progress but soon he had earned a high level of freedom.

Travels With Our Kitchen

As a result of knowing Andrew and Vi two distinctly new elements were introduced to our lives. They were knowledgeable about the good places to eat out in London. One excellent place we 'found' through them was The Ark in Nottinghill Gate. And it was through Andrew that Sheila did 2 weeks work for him at the Chelsea Antiques Fair. Following this, again through contacts of Andrew's, Sheila did another two months, earning more than I did, selling oil paintings from a gallery in Masons Yard.

Other memories are not as joyous though perhaps with hind sight we were extremely lucky. Sheila, heavily pregnant, was knocked down when a parked police car was rammed and jumped across the pavement. Sheila was badly shaken and Darron had his jaw broken. With his teeth wired together it was back to 'baby' food for him that he could eat through a straw.

Kevin arrived in November 1971. The medic's at Westminster Hospital, having given up on his natural arrival, sent me home. This did the trick he popped out early the next morning. With Sheila's back problem, and low blood pressure, they were to stay in hospital for some 2 weeks. Once we did get him home our lives shifted down a gear as we adjusted to a new wee person. One associated twist was that Shell where desperate for me to get back to work (see the bid below). As such they insisted we were assigned a Norlands nanny for a few weeks. We joke now that she was also on a salary higher than mine but it did help Sheila get into the swing of having two boys to look after.

At work the size of the Shell Expro unit I was in grew from being 12/14 staff, when I first started, to in excess of 50 employees. Initially focused on the discovery of gas in the Southern North Sea the emphasis shifted to the North and the waters off Aberdeen. Drilling rigs initially capable of drilling only in the good weather summer months were replaced by much larger rigs that could operate all year round. The other big deal was that the 5th North Sea Licensing Round included the option of 'bidding' on specific oil exploration prospects. I worked with Guy on the Shell bid for block 211/21. After much secret effort we calculated that a bid of GBP 21.0 million should be offered. At the time, with the 2nd bid some GBP 11 million lower, the press thought Shell Expro must be mad. As now so was it then. The media tend to be extremely poorly informed about the realities of the oil and gas world. What we knew and nobody else did was that the 1st exploration well in block 211/29 had found oil in what was to be known as the Brent sandstone. In fact some 2 billion barrels of oil. Today there are now some 12 to 14 oil fields in this 211 block. What we were not so good at guessing was the long term price of oil. We assumed US$ 3.40 per barrel. Todays, 5th Sept '12, price for Brent crude is US$115/bbl. We were no better at guessing how much it would cost to build a production platform, and drill oil wells from it. My 'wee' black book records that we estimated it could cost +/- GBP 35 million. I think the actual costs for the 4 Brent platforms installed, and wells drilled, exceeded GBP 1,000 million.

We didn't have a car in London. My salary just about covered our running costs. I had however, on my first work holiday, passed my driving test. My parents lived outside Salisbury, in Wiltshire, and my brother who still lived at home was working as a driving instructor. This was my 2nd attempt. The first attempt, in Edinburgh in my 1st year at Heriot Watt and I guess financed by my parents, ended in failure as I didn't "halt", and pull on the hand brake, at a stop sign. I do however remember the car was a 1.5 litre Wolsely. Now with Allan's help I managed to pass my Salisbury driving test. We were later on able to benefit from this success as friends were to lend us their cars. Chris and Nana Themistoclaus who were doing up a house in a neighbouring street, and in fact stayed with us when the roof was off their house, occasionally lent us their Audi. Another friend Jim, who worked for Clive Jenkins ASTMS union, had a company Ford Escort, which he lent to us during an extensive period of hospitalisation. It was in this car that we drove to Norfolk and stayed with Jim and Ingrid Kempston in their barn / occasional restaurant. My cousin Paul and his wife Jenny had fostered a West Indian / Irish boy called Byron. I remember he came with us on this trip and that he suffered travel sickness. I also recall the car never smelt the same again.

With Shell Expro expanding fast, and me being rather well positioned enjoying working in my Economics Engineer job, I was offered the chance to join Shell International staff. To initiate this transfer I had to go to Holland and do the Graduate Training Scheme, which when I first joined Shell Expro as a local staff employee, I had not been eligible for. This would be followed by me being assigned to one of the +/- 162 worldwide Shell International exploration and production operating companies. We hoped, and looked forward to being sent on our first, exotic, overseas posting. Before revealing the outcome here are some of the food highlights from our radically changed, London, diet regime.

Vi's Pate

Our across the road neighbours in London where Vi & Andrew. He was an 'art' dealer. He told us the story that when he first started he bought items at the cheap end of Portobello Road and sold them at the expensive end. By the time we met he had his own gallery, shared with several partners. Continued success would see him strike out alone. Vi, though a source of interesting recipes, couldn't bring herself to put her hand in a chicken to pull out the giblets. Sheila used to get the call tom help out. This recipe, among others, was the quid pro quo.

Makes 8 servings as a starter, 4 as a main.

Ingredients

6 rashers of streaky bacon (to line the loaf tin)
2 oz lard
4 oz streaky bacon (chopped)
1 sliced onion
½ lb lambs liver
3 oz crust less bread crumbs
1 tsp salt
1/3 tsp freshly ground black pepper
1 tsp anchovy essence
½ tsp ground mace
2 tbsp sherry

1) Stretch each rasher of bacon with the back of a knife then line a 1 lb loaf tin.

2) Melt the lard in a frying pan then add the chopped bacon & onion. Fry off until soft.

3) Put the fried bacon & onion in a blender. Blitz to a coarse mix combined with the liver, garlic, seasoning, anchovy essence, mace, and herbs. Pour into a bowl.

4) Blend the bread crumbs into the pate mix and then add it to the bacon lined loaf tin. Cover with a double thickness of foil.

5) Place in a ban Marie with water to half loaf tin height. Place in a pre-heated oven, gas mark 3 / 140 C, for 2 hours. Remove, allow to cool, and turn out.

Slice into good sized servings and serve with toast, baby leaf salad, and chutney or gherkins.

Potato & Watercress Soup

We know we did this soup recipe in our early days in London. Sheila had been inspired by, and bought, a double Elizabeth David publication. The first half was **"A Book of Mediterranean Food"**. The second half was **"French Country Cooking"**. Sheila and I both love watercress (Sheila remembers watercress at Ewelm primary school, me from the stream at Middle Shelspit) so we thoroughly enjoyed it. Darron however started to suffer unexplained nausea attacks. Somehow we correlated the occurrence of his sickness with the consumption of the potato & watercress. I don't think we have made this soup since.

Ingredients - serves 6

900 g of floury potatoes (King Edwards, Maris Pipers, Desiree)
2 onions or shallot chopped
Salt and freshly ground pepper
A good pinch of nutmeg
250 mls milk
2 bunches of watercress (reserving some fine leaves)
2 tomatoes skinned and chopped (optional)
1 glass white wine

1) Peel and dice the potatoes and finely chop the onions. Add to 1 litre of water and bring to the boil. Salt the water and cook for +/- 20 minutes until soft.

2) Remove from the heat and puree using a stick blender, a food processor, or as we probably did back then a fine sieve.

3) Return to the heat and stir in the 250 mls milk. Add plenty of freshly ground pepper, a good pinch of nutmeg. Bring back to the boil.

4) Add the finely chopped watercress and stir in. If using add the chopped tomato. Finally carefully add the white wine so as not to curdle the milk.

Serve in bowls garnishing each with the reserved watercress leaves.

Fish Cakes

Darren started primary school just after we moved to London. Holy Trinity primary school was up the road from our flat, on the other side of Finchley Road. As in primary schools across the country the teacher asked the class of 46 children to write about their favourite food. The overwhelming consensus, from this multi ethnic sample of children, was "fish fingers".

> We heard the following story from Darron's teacher, who thought it was magical. When seeing what the other children liked he explained that his parents were so poor they couldn't afford to buy "Fish Fingers". They had to make do with fish cakes made from real fish. In honour of this we offer the recipe set out below.

The origins of this recipe go back to Sheila's time at pre-nursing college, Fod House. They were taught how to cook food suitable for patients. Over time it has also been influenced by Jane Grigson's version which includes Anchovy paste. As Sheila has now become 'gluten' intolerant we don't do the bread crumb bit any more.

Ingredients - makes 4 cakes

250 g of floury potatoes (King Edwards, Maris Pipers, Desiree)
250 g cooked white fish (cod, or hake, for example)
1 egg
A bunch of parsley finely chopped
1 tblsp Thai fish sauce (or Anchovy paste)
Salt and Pepper

1) Peel and dice the potatoes. Boil until cooked. Mash and salt and pepper. Add the Thai fish sauce to taste.

2) To the cooled mashed potato add the egg and chopped parsley. Stir in and amalgamate.

3) Break the fish into bite sized pieces ensuring all bones, and skin, are removed. Incorporate the fish in the potato mixture. Once thoroughly mixed fashion into balls – we use a ladle to make sure the cakes are equal size. Place on a tray and refrigerate for +/- 30 minutes.

4) In a hot frying pan shallow or deep fry as you prefer.

Serve in hot with a poached egg on top, with a salad, or on their own.

Taramasalata

When Sheila and Darron were knocked down in London Darron suffered a broken jaw. To ensure it re-set properly, correctly aligned, he had to have his upper and lower jaws wired together. As he could now only eat liquefied food we bought with the help of Carol, Sheila's sister, who worked for Sunbeam, an electric liquidiser. Looking back I'm sure we would never have owned one of these but for the accident. Once we had the machine you then start to think about all the other things you can use it for. Making taramaslata, which while available in restaurants was not widely available in the shops or supermarkets, was one such use. There was one further small difficulty. It was also nigh on impossible to buy smoked cods roe. Sheila had to go to down to Mayfair Village, with its upmarket purveyors of fine produce to the rich and wealthy, to source some.

Ingredients   -   Serves 4

3 slices of white bread crusts removed and soaked in cold water
½ small onion finely chopped
Juice of one lemon
100g smoked cods roe
225 ml extra virgin olive oil

1) Place the soaked bread, onion, and lemon juice in a food processor and process to a smooth paste.

2) Now add the smoked roe and process for another minute or so. With the motor still running very slowly add the extra virgin olive oil as if making mayonnaise until it is all amalgamated.

Remove from the processor and chill until needed.

Jamalat's Mousaka

Jamalat, who was Nigerian, and her husband Patrick, lived on the end house in Sumatra Road. Down the road in fact from our friends Chris and Nana Themisocleaus. Next door to the house was a small play park with swings, and a sand pit. If the weather was good the mum's would gather there whilst the children played. This is Jamalat's take on this Middle Eastern classic.

Ingredients - serves 6

4 aubergines (you used to have to salt them before use but now its not necessary)
Olive oil
2 onions finely chopped
750 g lamb (traditional) or beef minced
Black pepper
½ tsp ground allspice or 1 tsp ground cinnamon (optional)
1 tomato skinned and chopped
2 - 3 tblsp tomato puree
4 tblsp butter
4 tblsp flour
600 ml hot milk
Good pinch ground nutmeg
2 eggs
Grated cheese - parmesan or annari

1) Modern day aubergines hardly need salting and rinsing. Wash the outside and dry. Slice into nice equally thick slices. Place in a greased baking tray in a single layer basting with olive oil. Brown on both sides. Place on paper to cool and dry.

2) Heat a good glug of olive oil in a heavy saucepan over a medium heat. Add the onions and sweat down until they start to take on colour. Add the lambs (or beef) mince to the pan and season. Continue to cook until the mince has 'browned'. Now stir in the tomato, tomato puree, the allspice or cinnamon,

3) For the white sauce add the milk and the butter to a saucepan and heat. Slowly whisk in the flour until the sauce thickens. Add the nutmeg and season to taste. Crack the eggs into a bowl and whisk. Now remove the sauce from the heat and carefully stir in the egg mixture.

4) Layer the base of an oven proof dish with some of the sliced aubergine. Add a layer of the cooked mince and a sprinkle of sauce. Now add a layer of aubergine. On top of this add the second layer of mince and sauce. Finally add the remainder of the aubergines neatly arranged and the remains of the sauce. Add a sprinkling of cheese, and a little nutmeg. Place in a pre-heated oven, 160C, for 45 minutes.

Serve in warmed pastor bowls

Hare (Reserved for the Cat)

Grandpa Capel was a great hunter. He had been given a "hammer" action, 16 Bore, shotgun when he was young. This is a fairly small guage gun so you have to be a good shot to bring down game. He told the story that as a teen ager he was earning more than his father by shooting vermin and claiming the bounty. Foxes in particular earned a good return.

By the time I can remember, 1954 / 5 when we lived in Thornborough waiting to join my father who had been posted to Egypt, rabbits and pheasants were the choice, with maybe a pigeon or two. During a visit, up from London, we saw a hare, something of a rarity hanging in the outside shed. On asking we were told they didn't eat hare so were thinking of giving it to the cats. Following Sheila's protest at this outcome we were sent off back home with the hare. We think we used Elizabeth David's book **"Mediterranean Food"** as guidance and inspiration when faced with this challenge. Here's how we cooked it.

Ingredients

4oz fat bacon cut into squares
2 onions finely chopped
2 or 3 shallots finely chopped
1 large clove garlic finely chopped
1 hare carefully butchered into nice pieces
2oz plain flour
½ pint red wine
½ pint good chicken stock
½ lb Mushrooms (wild if possible)
A sprig or two of Thyme

1) Into a medium heated heavy oven proof pan add the bacon squares, the onions, and the shallots. Slowly sweat them down in the released bacon fat until they just start to colour.

2) Add the pieces of hare to the pot and brown them on all sides.

3) Carefully stir in the flour taking care it does not burn.

4) Now pour in the wine and the stock. Cover the pan and bring to the boil. Simmer for 1 hour.

5) Clean and slice the mushrooms. Gently fry then in some butter with the Thyme sprigs. Add to the pan after an hours cooking and continue to simmer for 30 minutes.

Remove the hare to a serving dish. Boil down the remaining juices. Serve the hare with the juices pored over with potatoes and veg of choice or croutons.

Stifatho

As already mentioned one of the joys of our first stay in London was the eclectic range of people we got to know. This recipe must have come from Nana & Chris who stayed with us for a while when their home was being renovated. That said there were several other sources that could quite readily have passed this recipe on.

Ingredients   -   Serves 4

1 1/2lb stewing beef
Splash olive oil
2 tblsp flour
2 onions chopped
2 cloves of garlic finely chopped
1 large tin tomatoes
2 oz tomato paste
1 tsp oregano
1 tsp cumin (optional)
2" piece of cinnamon bark (optional)
2 bay leaves
1 glass red wine or water
Salt and pepper to taste

1) Cut the beef up into evenly sized 1 inch cubes. Put a glug of olive oil into a hot frying pan. Add the beef cubes and brown evenly. Add the flour, chopped onions, and garlic and continue to fry and stir for a further 4 - 5 minutes.

2) Transfer the beef to a large casserole. Add the tinned tomatoes and the tomato paste. Transfer to the stove bring to the boil. Add the herbs, as selected, the bay leaves, and the seasoning. Finally add the wine or water to cover the meat. Put the lid on the casserole and bring back to the boil.

3) Place the casserole in a pre-heated oven 170C / Mk 3 for at least 2 hours.

Serve with rice and a nice green salad.

Date Cake (Sheila's Mummies)

When Sheila lived in Pakistan as a child her Mother would turn this cake out on a regular basis. There she used real fresh dried dates from the souk. For the recipe below Sheila used packaged (cooking) dates that come in ½ pound, cellophane wrapped blocks. With the boys getting bigger now was the time to revert to Mothers best.

Ingredients

½ Lb dates
¾ cup boiling water
¾ cup sugar
1 ¾ cups plain flour
1 tspn bicarbonate of soda
1 tblspn butter
1 egg
1 tspn baking powder

1) Grease a loaf tin well and line with grease proof paper.

2) Put dates in a bowl with bicarbonate of soda. Pour over the boiling water. Press and stir.

3) In a separate bowl cream the butter and sugar. Gently stir in the egg and mix. Then add 1 tablespoon flour, and 1 tablespoon of dates, alternatively mixing in as you go. Finally add the baking powder.

4) Pour the mixture into the loaf tin. Bake in a slow oven for 1 hour. Test with a knitting needle. It should come out 'clean' when cooked through.

Turn out and allow to cool on a cake rack.

4.0 Aberdeen - Our Most Foreign Posting, Sept '73 to Nov '76

Early 1973 I had been offered the opportunity to transfer to work for Shell International. I was to appreciate, much later, that this opportunity was a very rare, and privileged, one. I had attended the 3 months "basic training" with the newly recruited graduates. At that time this training was run in Wassenar a small village just outside Den Haag. Once the training was completed we were to be assigned to our first 'international' posting. People were sent to the Far East, Middle East, and South America. We got Aberdeen. Not exactly what we had hoped for or expected. I was to work there as a "Drilling Engineer" whatever that was.

Never the less my salary increased by +/- 30% and we would get a housing allowance so it was not all bad news. On arrival I was taken by the HR department and shown houses that were available. The most suitable was a relatively new build in Carlton Road reasonably close to a school. I then headed south to Edinburgh to meet up with Sheila and Callum our dentist friend. They had driven his mother's MG which I was to 'hire' up from London. They had brought Harry the hamster in the car and now it was my turn to continue the drive up north to his new home. Sheila and the boys would arrive soon thereafter to start our new lives 'up north'. I must mention here that as you can see the MG is a convertible. We were a family of two adults and two growing children. They used to travel squashed in the space behind the front seats. I can't remember that they complained. They do however to this day hang onto the back of the front seats whenever traveling in the back of a car. Thus began a very different life for us.

For a start we were suddenly living in a detached house with a garden in suburbia. For the first time in our lives we had a car and enjoyed the mobility it offered. Following Sheila's London introduction to early 20th century art, and a bit of extra cash, meant we started to go to antique shops and buy woodcuts. In these same shops we saw and bought a few nice pieces of Clarice Cliff pottery. All of which we still have. Both boys had bikes. Life was really not too bad.

The other contrasts were not necessarily immediately evident, or positive. House prices were rising in Aberdeen as increasing number of oil workers moved to the city. This was not seen positively by the locals. Darron with his English accent, and an oil field worker as a father, was the butt of much prejudice at school. This was not just from the other children. The Headmaster once commented that he was lucky in that he was 'intelligent' and did not have to end up working on a drilling rig as a labourer like his father. In addition some of our neighbours also thought we were over paid brat's and anyway it was "oor oil".

On balance however it was to be a good time. We used to go for weekends up to Knockaddo and stay with our hippy friends who were running the oldest woollen mill still operating in the UK. Steve's parents had two cottages up there. The one by the road was reasonably civilised but the one across the wooden suspension bridge over the river was pretty basic. I can still remember being in bed with all our cloths on trying to dry the bedding with our body heat. Another great delight was to go to Balmede beach, North of Aberdeen, for barbeque lunches. The technique and the recipes are given below.

It is difficult to say much good about the local Aberdonian food supply. The bread was processed sliced white. Vegetables were 'neeps' (turnip) and not much else. You couldn't buy decent fish in Aberdeen in spite of its history as a fishing port. Also our local "Fine Fare" supermarket didn't sell garlic. This was the same shop that didn't know what you did with a green pepper. Meat availability and quality was good as we were well served by a local butcher. To compensate for these local deficiencies we were forced to frequented an upmarket vegetable shop in Rosemount that sold a small range of imported goods. We also became early foragers. We used to go mushrooming. And as you will see from the recipes below rose hips, and rowan berries, harvested from the hedge rows were added to our diet.

In addition to the limited ingredient availability 'eating out' possibilities were non-existent. At that time some pubs still banned women from entering them. Going to a dinner dance, at a local hotel, once a year was the gastronomic tops for the minority of Aberdonians who did go out to eat. In general eating was only to maintain life and the cheaper you could get by the better. However soon after we arrived an Italian restaurant, the first in the city, did open. Their target guests clearly where the growing number of oil related expat's who were moving to the town. There was some food progress over the 3 years of our stay but it was glacially slow.

At work I was trying to find out what a Drilling Engineer did. This (unknown to me at the time) was a newly created position and nobody really knew what we were supposed to do. As such there wasn't a clear career development path. All that was known was that the title included 'drilling' so we better do some time off shore.

"It's just like the one daddy works on," says seven-year-old Darren Jenkins, 50 Craigton Road, to his mum, Sheila, after he won a prize in the Lego competition. His dad is a drilling engineer on an oil rig.

I was sent out to Shell's floating, mobile, semi-submersible drilling rig, named ship fashion Staflo, and told to report to the 'Tool Pusher'. He was a guy called Greg McGregor. Tool pushers in general thought they were the 'real' drillers and hated us upstart drilling engineers. Greg however took me under his wing, gave me an oily rag, and said go and polish that 'mud' pump. Because I was happy to do this I think it helped overcome the prejudice that existed towards new, young, graduates. Also my experience labouring in Leith docks helped. In a way I knew the ropes and couldn't be pushed around. After this I volunteered to work 12 hour shifts on the 'drilling floor' (the bit you always see on the TV when they talk about the oil business). My first 2 weeks passed off quickly thereafter. My time on the rig was recorded in LEGO by Darron seen here after winning a prize.

Travels With Our Kitchen

After a few more trips off shore, sometimes at the mercy of fog which meant the helicopters couldn't bring the relief crews out from the Shetlands, my initiation was over and I was assigned to an office job.

Another memorable event was me looking after the boys for 2 weeks whilst Sheila holidayed in Barbados. Carol, Sheila's sister, worked for Freddy Lakers airline. She could get cheap concession tickets. After Sheila's father died, at the unnatural age of 54, Carol thought it would be good to take their mother on an exotic holiday. She didn't want to go. With the tickets bought Sheila enquired if she could go. I happily volunteered to take 2 weeks off work and look after the boys. I quiet fancied long peaceful days with the boys at school. The reality, of course, soon became obvious. I was run off my feet. Getting them ready for school, doing the shopping, washing, cleaning and cooking, soon filled my days and frankly exhausted me.

The "Prawn in Vermouth" recipe below is a monument to this time. Sheila returned wonderfully tanned and relaxed. I slunk off back to work for a rest.

It was in Aberdeen, in spite of the paucity of exotic ingredients, that we started to expand our culinary horizons. The extra disposable cash naturally encouraged us to become more adventurous. Having the MG / Fiat meant we could extend our reach in terms of the shops, and suppliers, we could access. In Aberdeen itself, on Union Street was an excellent book shop. It was from their extensive stock that Sheila started her, even after recent downsizing, impressive collection of cookery books. To supplement the newly acquired knowledge what we needed now were the ingredients. Around Aberdeen if you were prepared to travel you could find good seasonal supplies of meat and vegetables of superior quality to that available in town. Farm shops had not really been invented but "pick your own" options existed. At the weekends we used to combine the joys of antique hunting, possible in many of the towns surrounding Aberdeen, with sourcing from local suppliers. This not only led to an antique collection, many pieces of which we still have today, but also provided an expanded source of cooking ingredients. The results of some of our culinary efforts are set out below.

The ZEN of Bread

Moving from the extensive range of fruit, vegetables, and breads, available in London to the wastes (at that time) of Aberdeen was a shock. It was 1973 and the luxuries that would be bestowed by 40 years of oil production were far in the future. The Auk oil field, discovered in 1971 would not begin production until December 1975.

As a student summer vacation job I had worked in the "Wonderloaf" bakery in Barnstaple, N Devon. It was therefore natural for me to start to make up for one of the omissions from the Aberdeen diet, good bread. I should also say that making your own bread is a deeply therapeutic exercise, particularly if you go for a good strong "knead". In addition the aromas emulating during the baking build both the anticipation and the appetite.

Ingredients

2 ½ pints lukewarm water
1 ½ - 2oz dried baking yeast or 4oz ordinary yeast
2 lb wholemeal flour
2 tblsp sugar
2 tblsp olive oil
2 tblsp salt
¼ lb Strong white flour

1) Pour the 2 ½ pints lukewarm water into a large bowl. Add the yeast & sugar. Mix well to dissolve. Add wholemeal flour a cupful at a time. Continue to add flour mixing it in until the 'sponge' is the consistency of paste

2) Cover the bowl with a damp cloth and set in a warm place (airing cupboard) to rise to +/- 2 ½ times its initial size. Knock back and add the olive oil and salt. Fold in the strong white flour a little at a time until the dough no longer sticks to the side of the bowl.

3) Flour a board and turn out the dough. Now vigorously knead with the heal of your hand until the dough "bounces back". Oil the bowl and return the dough into it. Set the dough aside to rise until approximately double in size.

4) Turn out and again knock back and gently knead. Now cut to size depending on whether making a couple of loafs or some rolls. For loafs place the dough in oiled baking tins and allow to rise. If it is rolls place the roll on an oiled tray and set aside to rise.

5) Set the oven to 450 F (120 C). When to temperature place the risen rolls in the oven and bake for +/- 25 minutes. For the loaves cut shallow slits in the top of the risen dough and bake for 1 hour. Turn out and cool on a rack so the bottom of the loaf does not sweat.

Rose Hip Syrup

A friend, Jenny, who we had met in London introduced us to friends of hers who were living in central Scotland. They lived in Altnahar and worked in a wool mill in Knockandhu. In fact this was and joy of joys still is the oldest working wool mill in Scotland. There was no electricity, running water, or anything else at the house and they lived and worked a semi hippy, self-sufficient, life style. Also around that time *'Food for Free"* by Richard Maybe, and *"Self Sufficiency"* by John Seymour, were reminding us of the pleasures of getting some of our daily intake from the hedgerows.

Hence it was that we got into making our own Rose Hip syrup. There were tons of berries to be harvested and having 20 times more vitamin C than oranges must be good for you. I have to confess that the photo is not from that time but taken on a beautiful day, on the road up Carlton Hill (Edinburgh) behind the old High School building, Autumn 2012.

Ingredients

1 kg of freshly harvested rose hip berries
2.75 l water
750 g of sugar per litre of syrup

1) Wash the rose hips and blend in batches until you achieve a course texture. As the quality of the rose hips will deteriorate with time crack on here to the next step.

2) Bring 1.75 litre of water to the boil in a large saucepan. Once to the boil add the rose hips and bring the mixture back to the boil. Turn off the heat and allow to stand for 15 minutes.

3) Using a colander over a large bowl, and a freshly washed muslin cloth / tea towel strain the rose hip mixture retaining the solid rose hip residue.

4) Return the residue to the pan and add 1 litre of water. Bring the mixture to the boil remove from the heat and allow to cool. Repeat the straining process.

5) Return the strained rose hip liquid to the large saucepan and add 750 g of sugar per litre of liquid. Place on a medium heat and stirring in the sugar to dissolve bring to the boil.

6) Take off the heat and using a ladle and using a funnel fill sterilised jars.

Macaroni & Cheese

Kevin, after the age of 4 or so, became a very selective eater. A guaranteed winner with children, and something that had always been in Darron's diet was "macaroni and cheese". Now was the time to introduce this treat to Kevin. It was to continue as a "staple" being both wholesome and filling. The recipe is based on that in the much used and trusted Good Housekeeping's *"Picture Cookery"* book that Sheila was presented on completion of her nurses training at Fod House.

Ingredients   - serves 4

2 oz macaroni
1 oz butter
1 oz flour
¾ pint of milk
Salt & pepper to taste
2 - 3 oz grated cheese
Brown breadcrumbs

1) Cook the macaroni as per the packet instructions. When cooked drain well and set aside.

2) In a suitable saucepan melt the butter, add the flour, and cook for a minute. Now gradually add the milk and stir until it boils. Add the macaroni, season to taste, then stir in the cheese - reserving a little for later.

3) Pour the mixture into a greased 'au gratin' dish. Sprinkle the top with the breadcrumbs and the reserved cheese. Cook under a hot grill until the top takes on a nice brown colour.

Serve in pasta bowls with optionally Heinz Tomato Ketchup.

Cullen Skink

Sheila, with family roots in the fishing town of Kiess in North Eastern Scotland, probably had absorbed this recipe unconsciously just from contact with the women folk of the village. The picture is Kiess harbor with typical Scottish weather. Not the place, or the climate, for a swim.

Cullen, which is a small town further south than Kiess on the Murray Firth, is the home of one of Scotland's most famous dishes Cullen Skink. This is a hearty soup and traditionally made with Finnan haddock (smoked haddock), potatoes and onions. As mentioned avoid heavy yellow, artificially, coloured fish. You want the "un-dyed" version

Sheila's recipe always adds potatoes chunks. Some recipes however will add mashed potato.

Ingredients   Serves 6

1 ½ lb (700 g) Smoked haddock
2 pints (1L) milk & water mixed
1 rounded tablespoon finely chopped parsley
2 onions peeled
2 oz (50 g) butter
add some cream if you wish
3 medium potatoes - peeled & chopped
Freshly ground black pepper and a good grinding of nutmeg
A good handful of chopped parsley or chives to garnish

1) Put the fish in a sauce pan and cover with the milk & water. Add one onion quartered. Over a gentle heat bring slowly to the boil; simmer very gently for about 5 minutes. Remove from the heat and allow to stand for 10 minutes. Strain off the liquid and reserve.

2) Chop the 2nd onion. In another pan melt the butter then add the chopped potatoes and onion. Cook for about 10 minutes over a gentle heat, stirring from time to time, until the onion begins to soften. Pour on the strained fish liquid and simmer until the potatoes are cooked. Remove from the heat and allow to cool. Puree the potato/onion and fish liquid in a blender.

3) Pour the pureed ingredients back into the sauce pan. Flake the cooked fish removing all bones and skin. Stir the fish into the soup, add black pepper, and a good grind of nutmeg then gently re heat. Check for seasoning.

4) Add the finely chopped parsley just before serving. If you want to be flashy you could add a dessert spoon of cream to each soup bowl.

Prawns in Tomato & Vermouth

Sheila's sister, Carol, worked for Freddie Lakers airline, Lakers Airline. She had thought it a nice idea to take their mother on a holiday to Barbados one of Freddie's destinations. As an employee she could get cheap flights. Mum wasn't really interested so at the last moment Sheila took her place. I took time off work to look after Darron (9 years) & Kevin (4 years). During this time I cooked the prawn dish listed below. The most memorable thing about it was when in answer to a neighbour's question "What are you guys surviving on?" I mentioned this recipe. It elicited the comment "Well when you can afford prawns cooking is easy". I must have followed this recipe from Jane Grigson's **"Fish Cookery"**. But even with a recipe you still have to "do it".

Ingredients - serves 4

1 ½ lb Cooked Prawns
1 small onion chopped
2 cloves garlic chopped
2 oz butter
8 oz peeled and chopped tomatoes (can be a tin of small whole tomatoes)
1 sprig sweet Basel or Rosemary
1 tps suger
2 - 3 oz Vermouth
2 - 3 oz thick double cream
A good pinch of cinnamon
Salt & pepper

1) Shell the prawns if necessary. Melt the butter in a frying pan and sweat down the onions and garlic till soft.

2) Add tomatoes, rosemary or basil, and cinnamon. Season with salt and pepper tasting as you go. You may need to add a little sugar if using raw chopped tomatoes. Bring to the boil and simmer for 30 minutes. Sieve into a clean pan.

3) Into the tomato mixture add the vermouth, and the cream. Stir together. Now add the cooked prawns and reheat.

Serve in bowls with boiled rice or with chunks of rustic bread.

Rowan Berry Jelly

Another treat from our hippy-day weekends with our friends in Knockandu was gathering rowan berries to make jelly.

These bright orange berries are high in vitamins A and C and in combination with crab apples make a delicious jelly to accompany game or lamb. They should be ready to pick August to November but are at their best in October. Wild crab apples if you can find them are ready to harvest over this period.

The addition of apples is to provide the pectin such that the final result will set. If you can't get crab apples you can use cooking apples

Ingredients

1 ½ kg rowan berries - washed
1.0 kg chopped cooking apples or less wild crab apples if available
1lb sugar per 1 pint of resultant juice

1) Put the rowan berries and the chopped crab apples into a preserving pan. Just cover with water and bring to the boil. Simmer for 20 minutes until the fruit is cooked and soft.

2) Sieve the fruit and juice overnight through a jelly bag, muslin and a colander, or if neither are available a pillow cover hung over a bowl.

3) Measure the volume of juice as you return it to the preserving pan. Add 1lb sugar per 1 pint of juice. Bring to the boil and simmer for 10 minutes occasionally stirring to dissolve all the sugar.

4) Increase the heat to a good rolling boil for 5 minutes. Test the jelly sets by taking a tea spoon sample and dipping it onto a cold plate.

When setting point is reached divide between hot sterilised jam jars. Seal the jars.

Beach Barbeques

What we knew as Balmedie beach (actually called Sands of Forvie) north of Aberdeen is a long hike from the road but that's the joy. Number one is that other folks will be put off by the walk so we seldom shared the sands with others. The second advantage was it discouraged the transport of excessive equipment or supplies. This means "bare bones" beach barbeques. These beach barbeques were the predecessors of similar outdoor cooking repeated in every one of the overseas locations we lived in from Holland to Oman.

Equipment
Matches
Sharp knife & a couple of small spoons
Tin opener (in those far off days before easy open cans)
BBQ griddle

Ingredients - serves 4
1 lb good quality pork sausages
2 small cans of Heinz baked beans
4 - 8 Morning rolls

1) Now this sounds easy but can in fact be quiet tricky - find 4 or 6 reasonably sized stones to make the "walls" around the fire and to support the BBQ griddle.

2) Collect a good quantity of dry fire wood. Drift wood stranded at the high tide line is often the best source. Light the fire using the kindling placing the small fire wood around the kindling like a wigwam. Slowly add the larger pieces and allow the fire to burn down.

3) Place the griddle over the fire balanced on the surrounding stones. Now ¾ open the beans bending the lid back to form a handle. Place the beans on the outer edge of the griddle. Keep an eye on them and stir to stop sticking. If boiling remove to the edge of the stones.

4) Scatter the sausages on the griddle. Fashion a pointed stick to turn the sausages (that's where the sharp knife comes in). Cook until browned on the outside and cooked through.

Open the rolls and insert a sausage. Enjoy accompanied by the occasional spoonful of beans.

Travels With Our Kitchen

Fresh "Johnshaven" Scottish Lobster

Sheila, and the lad's, had been taken off to Perth by a neighbour for a days "strawberry picking". On the trip home they decided to detour to Johnshaven a wee fishing harbour south of Aberdeen. We now know that, Murry McBay, supplies live lobsters, and crabs, to many corners of the globe. Back then without the knowledge of our neighbour I'm sure we would otherwise never have found this 'treasure'. They bought fresh (live) lobsters. All was fine until they got home. Firstly we needed a pot large enough to cook in. Secondly by the time Sheila had located one the lad's had decided that the lobster was really the pet they had always wanted.

Ingredients - Serves 4

- *1 large lobster preferably with the claws bound*
- *Ample boiling water*
- *Enough salt to make "sea" water*

Method

1) The first issue is how to 'humanely' kill the lobster. I prefer to speedily immerse the lobster in a very large sauce pan of fiercely boiling, salty, water. Other techniques include 60 minutes in the freezer prior to cooking. Also I have read that lobsters can be humanely killed using a sharp skewer inserted first between the eyes

2) If you're using the 'boiling water' method get a large sauce pan (almost the bigger the better as you have to get the lobster in and ensure it cooks completely submerged) and bring the water to the boil. Add salt in sufficient quantity that it tastes as salty as sea water. .

3) With the water fiercely boiling take the lobster (firmly) and immerse. Put the lid on the pan & bring back to the boil. Turn down the heat and simmer for 15 minutes (weight +/- 750 g) or 20 minutes (weight +/- 1.25 kg). Using tongs remove the lobster and set aside to cool.

4) Once cool enough to handle place the lobster belly side down, head towards you, on a chopping board making sure none of the legs are underneath. With a heavy, sharp, knife pierce the shell at the back of the head on the light coloured line you can see in the photo above. Now cut down through the head. Turn the lobster around & cut the tail in half linking with the cut in the head.

5) Carefully lift the tail meat out and remove the intestinal tract. Now break off the claws from the body. Again use the heavy knife to open the claws. Hold the claws upright then use the sharp side and chop into the middle of the top. Once you've made an impression twist the blade to crack the claw shell. Remove the claw meat.

Divide among your guests and enjoy with spicy mayonnaise.

5.0 Assen – North Holland, Nov '76 until Dec '80

Our first stay in Holland started at the Brink Hotel in the rural northern town of Assen. We moved there at the end of November just in time to celebrate Sinta Claus, the Dutch Christmas on the 5th December. This tradition celebrates the arrival of the Saint from Spain accompanied by Zwarte Peits - Black Peter's. I had some previous experience of life in Holland with my 3 month basic training in Wassenar, just outside The Hague. Some aspects of our new life in the north were therefore a bit familiar. Some were very different.

We moved into a NAM (Nederland Ardolli Maachappij the Shell/Esso company I was to work for) house, Hertshooistraat, 24. It had a garden & a garage. Both played a part in our food adventures. Just like Aberdeen once we settled into our house the first challenge was to get to grips with food shopping. For example the cuts of meat were different. In fact the British expats were known as the "vlees" (meat) eaters. The Dutch tending to eat their meat ready cooked, and sliced, rather than in big chunks. We cured pork in the garage and grew courgettes in the garden. Some aspects of this new life were very strange to our eyes and ears. The milk man, who could speak 4 or 5 different languages, sold beer as well as milk. He also sold sliced meat, cheese, 'vla' - Dutch bottled custard - and potatoes. The town boasted a twice weekly market and a supermarket – the K Mart. Early on we met our dear friends the Rose's. Geraldine, who having lived in Libya, married and moved to Italy where she learned to cook, and then had lived in Nigeria, and France, had an inspiring list of recipes.

We soon settled into life in our new house once the fleas, a memory of the previous tenants, had been eradicated. We had initially thought that maybe Darron could go to the Assen based British school. However there were only a very small number of children at that time at the school and they were all several years younger than him. It was fine for Kevin (5 years) but Darron would have to go to boarding school. He went off to Michael Hall (Steiner) school in Forrest Row, E Sussex. I got down to my new job. Kevin started to learn Dutch at school as the small English class were guests at the local Dutch school. And Sheila learned to cope with the new unfamiliar range of ingredients. We needed a car. Somehow I wrangled a trip to the Hague and bought a bright red BMW 1602L. This was a very serious car all be it the little brother to the BMW 2002tii. Now we had to look for activities, other than bike riding, to get fit.

Assen had an "ijs baan" (ice rink) which had the normal indoor rink and also an outdoor circuit for 'speed' skaters. The default activity for the small expat community was to take ice skating lessons. These were run by Duncan a Canadian, married to a Dutch lady, who had played ice hockey for Holland. Both Kevin and I learned to play (recreational) ice hockey. Holland has a skating tradition. If cold enough and the canals completely freeze they hold the "Elfstedentoch". This is the eleven villages, 200 km long, race. Some 200 elite skaters' race, and 16,000 skaters complete, in this event. As you can see we didn't participate but the sheer pleasure of skating on natural ice, outside, has to be experienced to understand how marvellous it is. In Holland it is also traditional to drink jagerstee (tea with Rum) which also lifts the spirits.

Travels With Our Kitchen

Another treat was the annual Assen Grand Prix for motorbikes. During our time Barry Sheen, on his number 7 Suzuki, was the leading man in the 500 cc class. I don't think we ever went to the actual race but we took full advantage of the practice sessions in the week leading up to the race. Assen is a street circuit. You can drive around it for most of the year. In fact when Sheila was learning to drive, and it had snowed, her instructor took her there for skid control training. By the time Sheila had passed her test (first time) we had sold the 1602 and bought a BMW 3.0L CSA. A very beautiful coupe.

In Assen I joined a Drilling Engineering Team. Following on from my last, and very interesting, job in Aberdeen this was all rather mundane. There were some interesting projects but the problem of 'what to do with Drilling Engineers' persisted. The only project I recall was me designing a set up whereby the mud (water with a set density and viscosity achieved through adding chemicals) which carries the formation cuttings up from the bottom of the well was treated to recycle over 95% of the water that was previously lost. Unfortunately a member of the Dutch royal family was to visit the rig. The water used, and therefore wasted, cleaning everything exceeded my savings. After some 18 months to 2 years I became an Operations Engineer writing "Well Programmes" – the detailed instructions to be followed when drilling – for an offshore platform in the Dutch K block sector of the southern North Sea. I enjoyed this much more and I continued in this job until we left.

It was from Assen that we made our first visits to France. John and Geraldine had bought a holiday flat in Les Dromedaries' in Gruissan, near Narbonne, in the Languedoc. It was on the 2nd floor and had a terrace looking out over the swimming pool. We were invited to stay in the summer of 1978. John, who for a Liverpool lad, had developed a taste for things 'fine' during his time in Schlumberger, was to introduce us to more new eating experience. The harbour in Gruissan was surrounded by open air restaurants. We would always (we were to stay several times over the coming years) try a selection first but tended to end up focussing on a few favourites. These always included a provider of moules a la mariniere, and a source of cassoulet. The only down side in those early days at the end of the '70's was the local wines were pretty poor. However one cave made a wine named after the limestone hills, just inland from the flat Etang de Mateille, called Montagne De La Clape. The wine was named, obviously, La Clap, This became such an in joke that we always bought plenty just to give away. On our first trip Darron (the oldest of the brood), Kevin, Lucas, and Anna, aged between 12 years and 4 years, had a fabulous time. It was great for the parents as well. On the several trips we did the only friction I can recall was when (maybe in '79) we went to a Michelin 'starred' restaurant to eat and John insisted that Darron eat with the 'children' rather than the adults. At thirteen that hurts.

As our time in Assen drew to a close we learned the next posting would be Brunei and that my initial job would be to update the well bore surveying techniques they were presently using. Our departure was preceded by a garage sale. From memory we priced everything at the same fixed price and entertained our customers with 'gluhwein' (warm spiced red wine). I'm not sure we covered the costs with the sales. The packers came, cleared the house, and we departed for the Shell Exploration & Production research laboratory in Rijswijk just outside The Hague. We were put up in a hotel for two weeks whilst I did an immersion course in how to survey angle, and azimuth, of oil or gas wells such that you can calculate their path through the subsurface en-route to the reservoir. It was whilst here that we realised that we had forgotten to ask the removal people to clear the loft. Darron and Kevin had built a sort of den up there and it was full of treasures. Once sorted the race was on to get out to Brunei before the boys Christmas holidays started. It would have been embarrassing if they had arrived first. Before we go out East we recall some of the new ingredients, and recipes acquired, during these Assen days.

Apricot Chutney

Darron had started boarding at Michael Hall School, in Forrest Row, East Sussex, soon after we arrived in Holland. He would come home to Hertshoistraat in his holidays. One of the English things he missed when he was with us was "Branston Pickle".

Sheila remembered there was a recipe in a book she had bought in Aberdeen called **"The Penguin Book of Jams, Pickles and Chutneys"** by David and Rose Mabey which used either fresh, or dry, apricots. The use of dried apricots made this a much more year round, spur of the moment, option. This book, published in 1976 in paperback, is still with us having been rebound by Lellos Bookbinding, Limassol in January 2002. Quoted below are the pre metric measures.

Ingredients

8 oz dried apricots
1 lb apples chopped
4 oz sultanas
2 cloves garlic
1 lemon juice and rind
1 tsp salt
3 tsp picking spice
1 pint malt vinegar
1 lb dark brown sugar

1) Chop the dry apricots and let them soak overnight in water.

2) Put the drained apricots in a large pan and add the chopped apples, sultanas, and all the ingredients except the sugar and the pickling spice. Put the pickling spice in a muslin bag, tie it up and add to the pan. Place the pan on the heat and cook slowly until the apples are soft. Now add the sugar stirring well as you bring the chutney to the boil.

3) Continue to bubble the chutney stirring occasionally and checking its thickness by pulling your spoon through the mixture. If it is thick enough that the furrow stays up and you can see the bottom on your pan you are done.

4) Remove from the heat. Recover the pickling spice. Pour into sterilised jars filling them well. Cover with a circular grease proof paper 'jam' cover, and seal with the lid.

This chutney does not need a long term maturing. In fact it has a better flavour when young. Enjoy after a day or two.

Sardines & Spinach Pate

I've asked Sheila several times for the details of this recipe without getting a clear reply. The problem I think is that after all these years of making it, in many of the locations we have lived each with its unique availability problems, it isn't a recipe anymore it's a set of broad principles. It's origins are Sheila's sister Carol, when she lived in Barnes, London, taken from the local Conservative political party association cook book. What I do remember is that our stay in Assen, Holland, introduced us to the glories of frozen Spinazee al la Crème, frozen spinach. I had hated spinach as a child as my Mum, for whatever reason, decided I needed to be force fed it. This gentle reintroduction allowed Sheila to start using the real thing.

Ingredients - serves 4

2 * Tins of good sardines in olive oil
1 * Small can of Anchovy fillets
1 * 400 g pack of frozen spinach (you can if you have the time to clean use fresh)
2 * hard boiled eggs
Generous nob of butter
1 * large onion finely chopped
2 * garlic cloves finely chopped (optional)
Zest of ½ a lemon
Tarragon (dried or fresh dependent upon availability)
Generous grating of nutmeg (caution - taste as you add as it is powerful)
Salt and freshly crushed black pepper to taste

1) Melt the nob of butter in a heavy frying pan over a medium heat. Add the chopped onions and garlic and sweat down until they turn translucent. Turn out into a food processor. Now cook the spinach. You can do this in the frying pan, or in a micro wave, the most important aim is to ensure the spinach is not too wet. Too wet and the pate will be too runny. Empty into a colander and squeeze out any excess liquid then add to the food processor.

2) Add the Anchovies, tarragon, and lemon zest to the food processor and pulse until it develops a course texture. Turn out into a large bowl.

3) Drain and break up the sardines and add to the fixture in the bowl and carefully fold in. Coarsely chop the eggs (whites bigger than the yokes) and stir into the pate mixture. Now progressively season with salt and black pepper, tasting as you go. Remember you need a little more seasoning as the pate will be eaten cold. Finally add the grated nutmeg.

4) Transfer the pate to a serving dish. Cover with cling film and set aside in a cool place until needed. This pate is best eaten within a day of being made.

Bring to the table letting your guests help themselves. Serve with toast.

Carbonara

This is another example of how another friend's favourite dish became transposed into our diet and eaten on a regular basis over the years ahead.

Geraldine Rose, who had already lived in Libya, Italy, Nigeria, and France, before we met her and her family in Assen, had already acquired a food repertoire tailored to different influences and availabilities. We speedily became friends and learned to plunder this extensive, exotic, source of recipes. She had learned this basic, store cupboard, staple from her neighbour whilst living in Italy. You don't need to tart it up by adding any exotica it is delicious as is.

Ingredients - serves 4

8 rashers of streaky bacon - chopped into small squares
Dried spaghetti
3 large Eggs
Grated Parmesan
Freshly ground black pepper
Salt for the spaghetti
Olive oil

1) Cook the spaghetti as per the instructions on the packet. Enough for 4 people normally equals 4 medium handfuls.

2) Heat a dash of olive oil in a large frying pan and then gently fry off the bacon pieces.

3) When the spaghetti is cooked but still 'al dente' drain off most of the water. Add the spaghetti to the bacon in the frying pan.

4) Take the hot frying pan off the heat and gently stir in the eggs. You want the heat in the spaghetti to cook the eggs. It is done when it is nicely mixed together and all the egg is cooked. Finally fold in ½ the grated parmesan and a good helping of freshly ground black pepper.

To serve divide between 4 pasta bowls and add the remaining grated parmesan over each serving.

Cheese and Corn Soufflé

Kevin, as noted above, was a very picky eater with a very limited range of dishes he would accept. At one stage he seemed to survive on only cheese and then only "jong belagen" (young Gouder), and pork chops.

One of his particular hates was eggs. Therefore Sheila was forced to seek recipes which presented them in different guises to get him to eat eggs. This soufflé recipe was one of the few successful ways of disguising the eggs such that he would eat them.

Ingredients - serves 4

5 oz garlic and herb cheese
Half a 5 floz carton of sour cream
7 oz can sweet corn
4 eggs
Salt and pepper to taste

1) Grease a 2 pint soufflé dish.

2) In a separate bowl cream the cheese and the sour cream. Drain the sweet corn. Separate the egg yolks and whites. Add the sweet corn and the eggs yolks to the cream mixture. Fold them into the mixture. Season well.

3) Whisk the egg whites until stiff and fold into the mixture. Turn into the prepared soufflé dish.

4) Bake in a pre-heated oven 180 C for 40 minutes until golden and well risen.

5) Allow to cool.

Serve with a nice fresh salad (I don't expect that Kevin would eat this though).

Guinea Fowl with Juniper Berries

We were introduced to Guinea fowl, as with many other additions to our food repertoire, by Geraldine and John Rose. This would have been after they moved from Holland and moved to Germany. Whether it was because they were available in Germany, or whether we first ate them with the Roses in the South of France we can't now remember. What we do have however is the recipe which Sheila wrote out in her cooking log from that time.

Ingredients - serves 6

3 Guiney Foul
12 Juniper berries
1 carrot, 1 onion, 1 stick celery roughly chopped
6 oz softened butter
1 onion finely chopped
6 pepper corns
Zest of ½ a lemon
6 – 8 sprigs of Thyme – remove leaves
Small bunch parsley
1 pint water
¼ pint red wine
Salt & black pepper

Beurre Marie   -   1 level tblsp butter, 1 level tblsp flour.)

1) Mix into the softened butter the chopped onion, lemon zest, thyme leaves, and crushed juniper berries. Now thickly coat each of the guinea fowl breasts with the butter. Place in a shallow baking dish and set aside in a cool place for 2 hours.

2) Make a strong stock by adding the Guinea fowl innards, the chopped onion, carrot, and celery, pepper corns, parsley, and salt & pepper to 1 pint water in a pan. Bring to the boil and simmer for 1 ½ hours.

3) Place the Guinea fowl in a pre-heated oven 200C / gas Mark 7 and roast for 20 – 25 minutes. They are cooked when the juices run clear having pushed a narrow bladed knife into the thickest part of the leg.

4) Make the sauce with ¾ pint of stock and the ¼ pint wine thickened with the Beurre Marie.

Half the birds and serve on hot plates with the sauce poured over.

Pork Fillet with Prunes

This is another recipe that whilst staying a firm favourite has evolved over the years dependent upon local availability of good quality ingredients. The initial inspiration was from Jane Grigson's classic *"Charcuterie & French Pork Cookery"*. When we began buying ½ sides of pork early on in our time in Assen this book became indispensable.

> The original recipe emphasised the use of a ½ bottle of white "Vouvray"; a pork chop per person; and using Californian prunes. There is mention of Agen prunes, if obtainable, as being the preferred choice. The first version Sheila cooked was initiated by buying Agen prunes whilst en route Assen to Narbonne to stay with the Roses in their Dromedairres apartment. The moment we returned home this was on the menu. Further evolution substituted 'fillet' for 'chops' as detailed below.

Ingredients - serves 4

2 * 1lb pork tender loin
8 - 12 large "Agen" prunes soaked in good white wine
Flour to dust the fillets
Salt and freshly ground black pepper
½ pint Stock

2 glasses white wine
12 small onions - outer dry skins removed
1 tsp arrowroot

1) Soak the prunes overnight. Drain retaining the liquid. If necessary de-stone the prunes.

2) Cut a length wise split down each fillet and gently open out and flatten. Lay out the first fillet, cut side up, and evenly space down its length half the prunes. Position the second fillet, cut side down, on top and carefully tie them together with string.

3) In a heat a hot heavy bottomed casserole melt the butter and add the fillet dusted with seasoned flour, and brown on all sides. Cook for 3 minutes. Add the stock, and the prune liquid, put the lid on the casserole and cook for a further 40 minutes.

4) Meanwhile cook the remaining prunes, and onions, in the white wine with arrow root seasoning. If necessary add water to cover the onions. Simmer for 20 minutes. Remove to a serving dish and retain the cooking juices.

5) Take the fillet out of the casserole when cooked and set aside to rest for a few minutes.

6) Add the onion cooking juices to the casserole and bring to the boil. Reduce by half.

Carve the fillet into generous slices. Serve garnished with the cooked prunes and onions and some of the gravy juices.

Roast Goose with Stuffing

A year, or 18 months, into our stay in Assen our good friend John changed job and he and Geraldine moved to Dusseldorf. This added a whole new dimension to the ingredients we could discover and use. Though only 2 - 2 ½ hours apart the diets of the northern Dutch, and the Karls Ruhe Germans, was surprisingly different. Goose was one of the several staples we bought on visits to the Roses. This recipe could however have been inspired by our Hertsheostraat neighbours Sheila & John.

Ingredients - serves 4

10 lb goose – skin pricked, I usually use my carving fork.
Goose giblets & neck
1 onion sliced
1 cup giblet / chicken stock

Stuffing

1 ½ lb cooked, mashed, potatoes
1 chopped onion
Liver from the goose (If available)
1 tblsp parsley
1 tsp sage
Salt & Pepper to season

1) Mix the stuffing ingredients together and season. Fill the goose's cavity with the stuffing.

2) Place the giblets, neck, and sliced onion in a roasting tin and place the stuffed goose on top of them. Add 1 cup of stock.

3) Cover with foil. Roast in a hot oven Gas 5 for ½ hour. Then lower the heat to mark 4 and cook for 20 minutes per lb (some 3 hours). Frequently check on progress as the goose will yield up an impressive amount of fat. This should be drained off at intervals and reserved for doing roast or fried potatoes. It will keep refrigerated for up to a year.

4) Some 20 minutes before the end of the calculated cooking time remove the tin foil and return to the oven to brown up the skin.

Serve with the stuffing and the potatoes, vegetables, or salad of your choice

German Red Cabbage

Another example of how with a move to a different location our diet evolved. Here the cooking method had moved on from Sheila's mothers style – "Lunch should be ready in 45 minutes I've just put the cabbage on !!!!" – to a very much more Continental approach.

Ingredients - serves 4

1 medium red cabbage
2 oz butter
2 cloves garlic crushed / very finely chopped
1 large cooking apple diced
2 onions finely chopped
1 tsp caraway seeds
½ tsp cinnamon
½ tsp nutmeg
Grated zest of ½ lemon
Bouquet garni
2 tsp soft brown sugar
1 small glass wine

1) Shred the cabbage finely. Melt the butter in a flame proof casserole. Add cabbage and cook for 5 minutes over a medium heat.

2) Add all the rest of the ingredients except the brown sugar and the glass of wine. Stir well. Heat a dash oil in a large frying pan and then gently fry off the bacon pieces.

3) Finally add the sugar and wine. Give one last stir and place in a pre-heated oven 300 F (90C), gas mark 2, and cook for 2 to 2 ½ hours checking half way that the cabbage is not too dry. If dry add a little water as necessary.

Very good when served with pork or roast goose.

Geraldine's Chocolate Chiffon Cake

Sheila first enjoyed this cake in the garden of Geraldine's Assen house on her 33rd birthday. We had been for a walk in the Assen bos (wood). Returning home Geraldine provided tea and cake for us all. Since that time Sheila has relied on this cake to make any celebration a little bit special. For example she used to make it in Brunei for Darron and Kevin before they returned to boarding school as we knew we would miss their November birthdays.

Ingredients

1 * cup of flour
1 cup caster sugar
2 tblsp good cocoa powder
3 tsp baking powder
½ cup sun flower or corn oil
½ cup boiling water
4 eggs
1 tsp vanilla essence
200g good quality dark chocolate
250 mls double cream

1) Sift together the flour, cocoa, and 2 teaspoons of baking powder.

2) Separate the eggs. Beat the yokes with the vanilla and the sugar. Mix in the oil and the water. Add the sifted flour mix and carefully combine.

3) Beat the egg whites with the remaining 1 teaspoon of baking powder until stiff and holding its shape. Fold into the baking mixture.

4) Divide the mixture between two 7 inch (+/- 28cm) diameter baking tins. Bake in a pre-heated oven 170C (325F) for 20 to 25 minutes.

5) Remove the cakes from the tins and set aside to let them cool.

6) For the filling / topping carefully melt the chocolate. Once fully melted stir into the whipping cream. Whip the mixture to thoroughly combine.

7) Place the first cake slice on a plate and cover with approximately ½ the chocolate mixture. Place the other cake on top and cover its top with the remaining chocolate mixture.

6.0 Brunei - First Overseas Assignment, Dec '80 – Nov '84

Moving to Brunei was our first real "overseas" assignment with Shell. In the late '70's the Northern half of the island of Borneo still retained the remnants of its UK imposed imperial past. We enjoyed a relatively leisurely outward bound trip. Our first stop- over was in Bangkok, staying at the Oriental Hotel. This was followed by going to Singapore where we stayed at Raffles. The purpose of the Bangkok visit was to introduce us to the sights, sounds, and tastes of the Far East. Hot weather accompanied the spicy, coriander garnished, dishes from the "Veranda" overlooking the river Chao Phraya. Lord Jim's (still in the old building then) provided a more sophisticated alternative. An enormous sea food platter presented with a protective plastic bib I recall. We decided to commit to the full tourist offering given that we had a relatively short time available. We did a visit to the floating markets; from shops situated close to the hotel Thai cutlery was purchased; and the Rose Garden, with its traditional dancers and elephant demonstrations, was very much enjoyed.

The visit to Singapore was a step closer to work. Shell encouraged its staff to shop in Singapore en-route to Brunei as after your arrival it would be at least 12 months before we could leave on holiday. In the mean time you had to survive on the limited range of supplies available locally. We bought ourselves among other things our first proper dinner, and tea, set by the Japanese company Noritaki. Also loads of material to be made up into curtains for the new home we were going to.

Brunei, situated on the northern coast of the island of Borneo, shares many features dictated by geography, and climate, with the other Borneo nations. Kalimantan (Indonesia) in the south, and Sarawak and Sabah (Malaysia) to the west and east respectively. All the major towns are at river mouths on the coast. Roads follow the coastline hardly daring to enter the tropical rainforests that cover the entire island extending down to the edge of the beaches.

After a short stay in the Shell guest house we moved into our new home. The house was off the Shell camp, in a small compound with 5 other houses, backing onto the beach. We had arrived during the winter monsoon. This converts a tropical paradise into a windy, and very wet, all be it hot, non-stop downpour. I can't recall that it dampened our spirits. As the photo shows certainly not Darron's, nor that of the out of shot Kevin.

When Shell had first 'drilled' in 1910 for oil in Borneo (Well "Miri 1", in Sarawak) there was no infrastructure. Having successfully found oil it then had to build all the infrastructure facilities needed. Hence the port, roads, power station, water supply, houses, the 'Commissariat' supermarket, hospital, schools, and club where all built and run by Shell. The cost of air travel, and even sea freight, was still very expensive when we were there. You survived on what you brought with you, and what was available locally. As for food supplies there were two main sources. The first were the mostly Chinese shops on Kuala Belait high street. We were soon instructed by helpful neighbours to source our soft drinks, and beer, from the 'Fat Chinaman'. Other specialist shops sold household 'plastic' goods. I always admired the plastic sauce pans. These I was later to learn were for scooping water to wash yourself. You could buy Chinese style kitchen equipment. Steamers, meat cleavers, bamboo handled sieves. Tinned food was widely available. I remember tinned sardines and bully beef. There were also some pretty unusual to Western eyes food products available. Many of them dried, and highly pungent. These offerings were complemented by what was available at the local markets. Pork, if your anatomy was good, or if you could delegate this early morning task to the amah, was available as they slaughtered the pigs daily. Soon after we arrived we moved into our rental house and were blessed with an introduction to a neighbour's (the Woods) Chinese amah, Susan. She had three daughters but no apparent husband. She worked part time for us Mondays, Wednesdays, and Fridays. Her other talent's included shopping at the local fruit and vegetable market (much cheaper if I go Madam), and sowing. In time she became our source of early morning pork as she would buy for the Wood's, and ourselves. There was also a thriving local fish market situated at the mouth of the river Belait. Some of the fish on offer was easily recognised, prawns and squid for example. Some was completely alien. As we were to learn in other postings your diet had to be dictated by whatever was available.

The other alternative, the Shell run Commissariat store, did cater for Western palates. However for most of the time "tinned" offerings were in the ascendency. There were a few times a year when fresh, otherwise unavailable products, were specially flown in. For the Dutch these treats coincided with Sint-A-Clause (5th December) and their Orange Ball (celebrating the Dutch Queens birthday). For the Brit's it was Christmas, and Burns Night. For example fresh 'Haggis and Neeps' were always flown in by British Airways.

In these far off, expatriate days, those who were already settled into local life; wives of colleagues in the Department you were assigned to work in, or new acquaintances met through a shared sport or social interest, immediately helped out with practical tips on how to survive / cook with the available ingredients. Many recipes were shared in this knowledge pooling environment. It was also a time when if you wanted entertainment it meant "do it yourself".

With both D & K away at school Sheila had the time, and the desire, to get involved in several camp social activities. She joined Petroleum wives; was on the Penaga Club committee; did newcomer welcomes; and generally helped out. This was particularly true for the Shell kids, back in Brunei from UK boarding school, during the summer holidays. Sheila did "fashion" shows for the girls. For my part I ran windsurfing lessons. Outside the holidays, see below, Sheila was a prime mover in organising "jungle" bungles, guided weekend treks, for the more adventurous Shell folks; and she also did several up-jungle trips to Iban longhouses delivering charitable donations for example after a longhouse had been damaged by fire.

When I first started work my job had been to write a borehole surveying manual, and initiate the re surveying of Brunei Shells oil and gas wells. The wells, some up to some 3,500m or more deep, were deviated. That is they are drilled vertically to a depth of 1,000 to 1,500 m and then they are "kicked off" building angle along a chosen azimuth. Regular angle, and azimuth, measurements have to be taken to accurately plot the wells path. After about a year or 18 months with this project up and running as a routine I moved to a new job. I first worked on computer data recording systems collecting the 24 hour drilling activity reports. Later I was to work in Drilling Contracts. Both these jobs were enjoyable and challenging having to learn new ways of working.

Our time in Brunei introduced 2 new activities that have followed us throughout the following years. Hashing and windsurfing. Hashing is a run for runners with a drinking problem. Started by the British tea planters in Malaya it was based upon the public school activity "Hare and Hounds". The Hash was run once a week, on Mondays, to help work off the weekend over indulgence in alcohol. Two or more "hares" would lay a trail out through the jungle using toilet paper. Typically in Brunei where the rains could be torrential they would set off at 4 o-clock. The runners assembling at the prearranged start would follow on at 5pm. There are 'breaks' in the trail included from which several false, and only one good trail, would lead. The idea being to allow the slow runners to catch up with the fast guys. The hope was that the runners didn't catch up with the Hares and that all the runners would safely return to the start around 6 o-clock before it got dark. If they didn't the Hares had to go back into the jungle and find the stragglers. If they failed the Ghurkhas', whose job was also to bring the after run beers, would go in and find them. Luckily this was seldom required though we did once loose over 20 runners including BSP's deputy CEO. I did a total of 132 runs and Darron managed 17. Living on the beach, during the time that windsurfing was just going main stream encouraged a group of us to take up the sport. I soon became fanatical. Many, many, hours were spent out on the water.

The other passion, shared by both Sheila and I, was the jungle. We were able to do several "up river" trips. These normally involved a very early start with a drive to the mouth of the Barrum river. A water taxi, which looked like a WW2 torpedo boat, would be taken up river to Marudi. From there it was dugout canoe with an outboard motor that took you further upstream you hoped in the direction to get you to the Iban long house you were supposed to visit. Another jungle exploit pursued by Sheila was the annual Jungle safari organised for Shell wives. The routine was they were driven to the top of the Labi road where they disembarked from the bus. Then there was a walk of several kilometres into the jungle to a pre-existing, Ghurkha built and manned, camp. On arrival the Ghurkhas would serve PIMS with fresh mint. Now that is attention to detail.

Other lessons given by the Ghurkhas included cooking jungle food. Ingredients included snails, snake, boar if you were lucky, mouse deer, or monkey if you were desperate. Other ladylike activities included rifle shooting practice, trapping game & fish, sourcing drinking water, and finding edible plants. It was on one such adventure where following a tropical rain storm, which caused a river level rise of several meters, the ladies had to be helicoptered out.

Sheila also organised the Jungle Bungle. From its start as a two hour demonstration of jungle survival techniques for the Panaga ladies it graduated into a 3 day self-survival challenge. Unable to go on the first trip I was able to get onto the second. Your rations for 2 people were a live chicken, hard tack, and water purification tablets. As equipment we had to have a pocket knife, a water bottle, matches, and a candle. The Ghurkhas provided us each with a kukri (their traditional curved bladed knife). As we had to make our own bashers (bed) to sleep in from sticks and young saplings this was essential. I thoroughly enjoyed my 3 days even though a jungle dog ate our chicken. This, and other Brunei food treats, are set out below.

Tinned Seafood Pate

In Brunei there where basically two shopping options that bore some resemblance to what we had become used to in Europe, and one that certainly didn't. There was the relative familiarity, and convenience, of the Shell run 'Commissariat' store. A sort of mini supermarket. Then there were the side walk Chinese stores of Kuala Belait's main shopping street. These two were the food source for most of the expats. However if you were a little more adventurous you could buy local cuts of meat, south Eastern varieties of fish, and indigenous varieties of vegetables at the local markets.

In the commissariat, with its supermarket like layout, we drifted naturally to the makes and range of preserved food, mostly tinned or frozen, that we knew from the UK. Given that this was a time when transport from Europe was still very expensive and storage conditions were fairly primitive. This meant supply was always a bit iffy, and even at best the choice was relatively limited and unvarying year on year. The cooking challenge was how to be inventive and create a variety of delicious meals, from this tinned fare. This recipe reflects those times and we think came from our neighbour Millicent Gresham.

Ingredients - serves 6 to 8

6 ½ oz (150 g dried weight) can of Tuna
7 ½ oz can of Salmon
6 oz Cottage cheese
4 Anchovy fillets
4 oz smoked salmon (not very often available) coarsely chopped
4 – 6 stuffed olives
1 garlic clove
Juice of ½ a lemon
Salt & Pepper

1) Put all the ingredients, except for the smoked salmon, in a liquidizer and blend well.

2) Carefully stir in the chopped smoked salmon pieces.

3) Put into a dish, cling film, and chill in the refrigerator for at least a couple of hours.

Serve with 'fingers' of toast.

Colour Coded Barbequed Large Prawns

I think this was the first thing, and certainly the first barbeque, we cooked in our beach side house in Brunei. The previous tenants had left the oil drum barbeque & I guess we had discovered a source of local charcoal. Certainly we must have already found the river mouth fish market. Things could only get better now.

Two tips: one for buying & one for cooking. The prawns head MUST be firmly attached with all the feelers, legs, and claws intact. They are cooked, and ready to eat, when they have turned pink (remember this is an extremely old photo so the colour isn't ideal) on both sides. I personally believe when barbequing it is best to keep flipping the prawns over several times rather than "4 minutes on the first side and 2 minutes on the other.

Ingredients - serves 4

Large prawns - 3 or 4 per person - shells on
1 sweet corn per person
Butter
Dried chilli flakes
Lemon zest

1) Mash / combine the lemon zest, dried chilli flakes to taste, with the butter. Place each sweet corn in the middle of aluminium foil large enough to make a neat parcel. Spread the butter mix onto the sweet corn and close up the parcels.

2) The lit barbeque has by now burned down to red hot embers. Place the sweet corn parcels onto the griddle. Cook for 10 - 12 minutes steadily turning to evenly expose to the heat. Move to the outer area of the griddle.

3) Add the king prawns to the centre of the barbeque and cook as above.

Serve and eat with the sweet corn and if available some nice crusty bread.

Banana, Bacon, & Prawn Kebabs

It's easy to forget that in late 1970's in the UK there was no idea of "fair trade" bananas. If anyone did think about it the banana choice was probably just Fyffe's, and whether to eat them in a bright yellow, or in their more black, speckled sweeter state. Once we settled in our house by the sea in Brunei it soon became clear the local banana choice was somewhat more extensive.

Entire 'stalls' were devoted to only selling numerous different types of banana. None of them looked like the large yellow Fyffe's UK norm. They tended to be small, and were sold either green or yellowy green. They were very sweet but were more grainy (seedy) on the palette. The large ones, plantain, which were also green needed to be cooked. Doing things with bananas, other than peel and eat raw, became a necessity.

Ingredients - serves 4

12 small, green, sweet bananas
24 rashers of streaky bacon
16 raw, shelled, and de veined, prawns
8 wooden skewers pre-soaked in water

1) Peel the small bananas cutting each in half. Wrap a piece on banana in a rasher of streaky bacon. Once the parcel is bound up take a skewer and skewer cross ways to hold the bacon on. Then add a prawn to the skewer. Wrap up and skewer a second banana parcel. Add a second prawn. Finally add a third banana, bacon wrapped, parcel to the skewer. Check that the parcels are positioned roughly central on the skewer.

2) Repeat for the other 7 skewers - note the skewers need to have been soaked in water in water prior to use to prevent them burning.

3) The lit barbeque has by now burned down to red hot embers. Carefully place the skewers onto the griddle. Cook for 4 - 6 minutes (actual time will depend upon the bbq heat) steadily turning to evenly expose to the heat. The signal they are cooked is the 'colour' change on the prawns and the bacon wrapping beginning to crisp up.

Serve.

Rock Cornish Hen – Coronation Chicken

My boss's wife, Millicent Gresham, introduced Sheila to Rock Cornish hens. There were only two other sources of chicken in Kuala Belait at this time. Either alive from the local market, or hormone stuffed frozen Danish. Neither that attractive. Rock Cornish hens are the result of crossing Cornish Game and White Rock chicken breeds. Being just the right size for 2 people, and having ample breast, and minimum leg meat, made them a favourite. Also the left over bones make an excellent base for stock. We could buy them from the "Commissariat" frozen in a double wrapped pack of two. We tended to cook them together eating one hot, and one cold.

Ingredients   - serves 2

2 by 500g double pack Rock Cornish hen
Sea salt and freshly cracked pepper
Olive oil
1 medium onion – thinly sliced

Quick Curried Sauce

1/3 homemade mayonnaise (or good quality bought in)
2/3 thick Greek, or goats, yogurt
Fresh lemon juice – to taste
Patak's Tikka curry paste – add to taste
2 or 3 tsp mango chutney (or apricot if mango not available)
Season to taste
A good handful of chopped coriander

Optional – great if you are having it for a party

1 by 500g pasta shells cooked as per the packet instructions

1) Roast your pair of Rock Cornish hens as you would poussins. Rub with salt and pepper and a drizzle of olive oil. Put the onion rings into a roasting dish sitting the birds on top of them. Place in a preheated oven 190 C and roast for 20 minutes. Check on progress. Return to the oven and roast for a further 20 minutes or until the juices run clear if pierced with the point of a knife. If you have a meat thermometer core temperature of +/- 70 C. Set aside to rest.

2) Carve the cold rock hen as thinly as possible and arrange the slices in the bottom of a shallow dish.

3) Mix the mayonnaise and the yogurt together until smoothly combined. Now stir in lemon juice, the curry paste, and the mango chutney a little at the time tasting as you go. When you have a good balance season as necessary. If using pasta you will need +/- double the quantity of sauce.

4) Spread the sauce evenly over the meat (and pasta if using) and gently mix to coat all sides. Finally sprinkle with the chopped coriander.

Beef in Guinness with Orange

After a while, and certainly once we established a good working relationship with Susan our part time Chinese Amah (maid), we became more aware of, and comfortable with, buying from the local markets and stalls.

> There was a covered market in KB that sold meat, fish, fruit and vegetables. There were also a variety of street side stalls. Part of the acclimatisation process was not just finding the locations of the various providers but recognising the far Eastern varieties and knowing how to prepare and cook them. Two things easily identified, Guinness beer and oranges, were in good supply. Guinness because the Malays liked the promotion - "A baby in every bottle". Oranges because they are indigenous. This recipe played to both these strengths. The beef no doubt came from the Commissariat and I expect originated in Australia.

Ingredients - serves 4 to 6

2lb of rump steak cut into 2" (5cm) cubes
1 onion chopped
1 carrot chopped
½ a small turnip chopped
1 stick of celery chopped
1 pint dark Guinness beer
2 oranges – juice and rind
A Good grate of Nutmeg and a Pinch of Allspice
Seasoned flour to coat the beef
Salt and Pepper

1) In a frying pan brown the onions. As the onions cook coat the steak with seasoned flour. When the onions are done transfer to a large casserole dish.

2) Add the chopped vegetables to the frying pan and quickly seal. Add to the casserole. Then in the same frying pan, possibly in batches, brown the steak cubes. Add to the casserole.

3) Deglaze the frying pan with the pint of Guinness. Pour into the casserole. Now add the spices, orange juice and rind. Give a quick stir. Put the lid on the casserole and place in a pre-heated oven at 120C, and cook for 6 hours occasionally checking all is OK.

4) Remove from the oven and cool overnight. Reheat the casserole prior to serving accompanied by mashed potatoes and a green veg.

Belly Pork, Apple, and Prune Casserole

As mentioned it was a wise tactic to use, if possible, the services of a Chinese amah to do the pork buying. Firstly, because they are much better qualified then ourselves to recognise both the type, and quality, of the pork joints on offer, and secondly you might also benefit from a price discount not available to Europeans.

This photo I must explain is not contemporary with our time in Brunei. It does however give a really good illustration of what a local pork market would have on offer. It is also easy to understand the need for pig anatomy knowledge in order to make sensible buying choices. You really can eat all of a pig but its squeal.

Ingredients - serves 4 to 6

1 ½ belly pork or spare ribs cut into cubes
6 juniper berries crushed
½ tsp chopped thyme
½ lb onions peeled and sliced
1 clove of garlic crushed
4 oz prunes halved and stoned
1 large cooking apple peeled and sliced
Dusting of caster sugar
1 ½ lb potatoes peeled and thickly sliced
¾ pint dry cider
Butter
Salt and freshly cracked black Pepper

1) Put a casserole on a medium heat, melt a knob of butter, and fry the pork to brown it nicely on all sides. Season with salt and pepper and add the juniper berries and the thyme.

2) Fry the onions and garlic. When softened work it around the pork and dot in the prune halves. On top now arrange a covering of apple slices. Dust with caster sugar. Now arrange the layered potato slices, over lapping one slice on another, on top. Lightly season and dot with small knobs of butter. Finally pour over the cider.

3) Put the lid on the casserole and place in a pre-heated oven at 150 C and bake for 1 ½ hours.

4) Remove from the oven, turn up the oven to 200 C, take the lid off and bake for +/- 20 minutes to brown the potatoes. Alternatively you could brown the potatoes under a hot grill.

Serve as a "one pot" supper or with a good, strong tasting, green vegetable.

Travels With Our Kitchen

Jungle Barbeque Chicken

Our stay in Brunei from '79 to '84 coincided with the existence of the British Armies Jungle Warfare School. To raise money they, at the prompting of Sheila, organised a yearly "Jungle Bungle". This was 4 days/3 nights in the jungle coping by yourself. Permitted equipment included matches; a candle; a knife on a bit of string; a live chicken; water purification tablets; a Kukri (Ghurkha knife); and a pack of 'hard tack' army rations. The programme was we were lorried up as far into the centre of the island as the Labi Road went. Then we dismounted and hiked through the jungle to a pre-selected area. It was to here that the chickens were flown by helicopter. The first night we slept in hammocks, made from parachute sections, under a ground sheet as cover. Now we had to make, and sleep the two remaining nights in, our own "bashers".

The first problem we encountered, night 1, was that the chickens had died on route to the jungle. It seemed also that no one in my group had any idea of how to pluck, and gut, a chicken. Forcing myself to stay awake I volunteered to do the job and also to cook the result. I must have absorbed some latent knowledge watching Grandpa Capel doing rabbits, or pheasants, at Middle Shelspit farm. As it turned out the real challenge was neither the plucking, nor the cooking, but what do you do with a hot cooked chicken at 23:30 in the middle of the jungle with temperature still in the upper 20's, and the humidity even worse. I decided to hang the chicken from a high'ish branch of a tree covering the string with anti-insect cream to prevent ants from descending the string and attacking the chicken.

Exhausted I fell into my hammock & quickly fell asleep. Waking the next morning I was surprised to see that we had been joined by a (jungle) dog. On closer inspection from my hammock I noticed it looked rather sleepy and well fed. Somehow it had managed, strangely undeterred by the anti-insect, to jump high enough to catch my chicken. The results of my cooking efforts were being digested as I watched. For the next couple of days we would have to survive on hard tack, and purified jungle water.

Chilled Pawpaw Mousse with Hot Chocolate Sauce

Again a story of "ingredients". Pawpaw – or Papaya as it is more commonly known in the UK – grew if not in our garden (I think the maid had a tree), certainly in the farming neighbour's garden. We were blessed with a continuous supply of excellent fruit. What we couldn't get was "fresh" cream. We had to make it. To this Sheila would sometimes add lemon juice. This thickened the resultant mixture and made it more suitable for recipes such as that below.

Ingredients   - serves 6

500 g Paw paw peeled and pureed (should yield +/- 400 mls)
Caster Sugar
50 mls lemon juice
125 mls sour or fresh cream (we couldn't get fresh cream in Brunei)
30 mls hot water
15g gelatine
2 egg whites

The Sauce
250g Chocolate
*4 * 15mls Brandy*
*2 * 15 mls honey*
30g butter

1) Sweeten the pureed pawpaw with caster sugar to taste (Sheila tended not to but let your palate be the judge as it depends upon the fruit). Now add the lemon juice.

2) With the hot water make up the gelatine and stir into the fruit. Leave until just setting.

3) In a separate bowl gently whisk the cream. You don't want to stiffen things too much. In another bowl gently whisk the egg whites. Fold both into the fruit mixture and taste for flavour. Once ready divide the fruit mixture into 6 ramekins or nice glass desert dishes. Place on a tray and put into the fridge to cool.

4) For the sauce either melt the butter in a metal bowl over heated water in a sauce pan, or use a micro wave. Now melt the chocolate into the butter. When fully melted and incorporated add the brandy and the honey and mix in.

Just before serving reheat the chocolate sauce if necessary. Serve the individual dishes to your guests allowing them to add a ladle full of hot chocolate sauce.

Sylvie's Black Cherry Clafouti

There tended to be two large, single interest, groups that didn't intermingle much. The sailors and the golfers. As a "windsurfer" we were grouped, but I think probably only tolerated by the proper dingy sailors as they needed the club membership numbers, as sailors. Through this grouping, at a regatta, we met Toni, and Sylvie, von Tiel. Toni who was Belgium was a proper sailor. Sylvie, who was French, was an excellent cook. We got to know them well enough that she gave Sheila this recipe. Much later, when we met them again in Oman, Sheila was to remind her of her generosity.

Ingredients - serves 6

2 lb black cherries
4 eggs
3 oz caster sugar
2 tblsp flour
1 tsp vanilla extract
2 tblsp rum
3 oz (1/2 cup) milk
2 tblsp double cream

1) Stone the cherries and put into a buttered china flan dish

2) Crack the eggs into a bowl and add the sugar and flour. Beat until foamy. Then gradually beat in the vanilla extract, rum, milk, and cream.

3) Pour the mixture over the cherries.

4) Bake in a pre-heated, moderate, oven 170 C for 40 minutes.

Serve warm.

7.0 London - Back to Reality, Dec '84 to Sept '89

There had been some hesitation about returning to London from the sunny shores of Brunei. We appreciated that there would be some compensations for leaving our unworldly, neo colonial life, behind. But I recalled an early Brunei Shell farewell party for a geologist who had worked there for 23 years. I thought it must be impossible to re-adjust to UK life after a spell like that. I though it wise therefore to leave after our 4 year stay.

We had bought a flat in Eastbourne in the early Brunei years so we had somewhere to stay on our return. In addition I had assumed as had been the case in Aberdeen that Shell would provide a London rent allowance. This was not to be the case as apparently the duration of our stay would be over 4 years. I had tried 'commuting' from Eastbourne but it was not sensible though others did it. We realised we would have to buy in London. Shell put us up in the Royal Trafalgar hotel in the middle of London whilst we house hunted. Unknown, and unimagined at the time, we would take over 6 months to find and buy a flat.

I was assigned to work as the resident Drilling Engineer working in Mathew Hall's office off Tottenham Court Road. They had won the contract to do the detailed design for Shell's Eider North Sea platform. As there was parking at work I used to drive my newly acquired, second hand, Porsche 924 the short distance to the office.

This was a completely new experience / challenge for me. I had worked for a few weeks on a North Sea platform but had never been involved in their design. Luckily the "conceptual" design which pretty well solves all the issues had been completed. Detailed design was more about deciding which of the various suppliers to buy a specific piece of equipment from. Other help was also to hand. As Mathew Hall didn't know much about drilling they had subcontracted KCA a specialist drilling company to do the hard graft. Also a sister platform, Tern, was being designed at that time and the 2 designs were supposed to specify identical rig equipment. Owen Jenkins, no relation, who was the contract Shell Drilling Engineer on Tern seemed to know what he was about & I was able to learn the ropes in large part from him & the KCA boys.

The 6 months spent living in the Royal Trafalgar Hotel might sound attractive in theory but in practice it soon became tiresome. A hotel bedroom seems to shrink the longer you stay. Even the novelty of eating out every night, all be it on a reasonable meal allowance, ceases to excite. That said in the early days we happily sampled the food on offer from a wide range of London's finest restaurants adding to our food knowledge, pallet, and taste experience. Of particular note was eating at *J. Sheekey* fish restaurant on St Martins Court. Sheila remembers that Simon Richards (also transferred back to London from Sarawak) had skate wings. We can't remember what we had but Sheila remembers wishing she had ordered the wings. At this time we also ate Thai food for the first time at restaurant, **Chang Mai**, one of the first of its kind in London. Vatcharin Bhumichitr (Vatch), who had come to the UK in 1976 and opened a shop selling genuine Thai products, had moved on to run this restaurant which specialised in Northern Thai cuisine. He is also the author of several books on Thai cooking which have become indispensable sources of reference when we yearn for food with a good chilli kick. In between these cuisine extremes we sampled traditional British, Italian, Greek, Indian and much more. Finally a friend of Sheila's sister, Gino, ran an Italian restaurant not far from the hotel. Toward the end of our time we used to eat there quite regularly. One attraction being we could more easily influence the size, and ingredients, of our evening meal. Also Sheila, given that it was reasonably quiet in the restaurant, enjoyed giving a helping hand in a proper "working" kitchen.

By mid-1984 we had managed to find, and successfully buy, 18 Kenilworth Court on Lower Richmond Road, Putney, overlooking the Thames. Now all we needed to do was sell Eastbourne. Selling is a Sheila job. For whatever reason we experienced difficulty in finding a buyer. At first this didn't matter because Shell helped out covering the cost of the bridging loan. We could also escape London for weekends in Eastbourne. As Darron and Kevin continued to 'board' at Michael Hall School, Forrest Row, West Sussex if they were free we could pick them up en route.

However as the clocks turned toward a year without a sale Shell mentioned that their help would soon come to an end. At about this time we had in fact found a buyer. They however were being stroppy and trying, no doubt thinking we must be desperate to sell, to renegotiate the price. I still remember the horror when I heard Sheila tell the agent to - "Please explain to the prospective buyer that we are in no hurry to sell". It worked we got the asking price.

With us settled in Kenilworth Court, and Eastbourne sold, Sheila could turn her mind to what she wanted to do. Various options where considered before opting to do a 'beauty therapy' course at the Steiner (beautician to the Royal family) school on Grosvenor Street. On graduation she started work part time at a Hammersmith salon. The skills gained here where to be a portable, work from home, option practised in several overseas assignment to come.

From our London base we were reunited with our friends the Roses, who by this time where living in Egypt. They visited us there and we holidayed with them in their apartment in Gruissan.

In June of 1987 I had sold the Porsche and bought UJA 557 S, our brown, Wood & Picket converted (1976) Mini Cooper. Also by this time both John and I were very keen windsurfers. Now there was no way we could drive to the south of France in the Mini so we used to put it, loaded here with my brothers windsurfer, on the train at Dover & get off in Narbonne.

The 'eating out rules' were changed on these subsequent holidays with the Roses. We would eat out one night and then Geraldine would cook. The third night would be eating out followed by night four being Sheila's turn to cook. This cycle was then repeated throughout the holiday. To support the holiday our chefs needed at least 4 recipes that they could execute, and feed to, 4 adults and 4 or 5 growing teenagers. That's when you learn.

A recurring food influence, during our Edinburgh student days, and our first time stay in London, was Jim and Ingrid Kempston. Their 'barn' in Norfolk had now gone but they had taken charge of a Cromwellian farmhouse in Kent, Stone Green Hall, and were running it as a restaurant with a few adjoining bed rooms. In mid-1985 Marlyn, dental undergraduate from Edinburgh days now established in New Zealand, came to visit. We all piled into the Porsche and set off for a weekend at Jim's place to celebrate Peter's 40th birthday. Jim and Ing were not there but it is a tribute to how they set the place up that our treatment was truly royal.

Other highlights of this period were visiting my maternal Grandparents. They lived outside Thornborough on the farm at Middle Shelspit they rented for over 60 years from the council. Grandpa Richard Capel had started his working life, after leaving school at 12 or 14 years, as a gardener for a Buckinghamshire estate. He therefore understood 'gardening' and the Shelspit farmhouse garden provided a very high percentage of their daily needs. This was supplemented by milk; making their own butter; eggs and the occasional chicken; and what you could hunt. Pheasants were the prised quarry followed by rabbits and pigeon. Hares we had already learnt were cat's food.

Lastly we continued to enjoy some of the fine dining experiences the capital city had to offer. Darron, who had by now left school, went to work for Maurice at his Putney High Street restaurant Cassis. Once he became established we started to get the inside line and what was happening in the London food scene. One interesting snippet was that it transpired that Maurice kept losing his most promising chefs who left to work with some new guy called Marco Pierre White. This was how we were able to sample his take on fine dining as the "White Heat" worked to earn his 2 Michelin stars at Harveys.

Liver & Sage

Living in London meant at weekends we could on a fairly frequent basis drive up to Thornborough, in Buckinghamshire, to visit my Grandparents at "Shelspit Farm". There are times when it needs someone from outside the family to give you an insight into the quirks you live with without noticing. On a one such trip Sheila saw liver in the pantry and asked if that was what we were having for supper. A shocked Grandma replied "Of course not. That's for the cat". Here is how Sheila cooked it. She still remembers how Grandma watched in amazement as we enjoyed eating the result of her efforts.

Ingredients - Serves 2

1 onion finely sliced
Olive oil
Knob of butter
Generous helping of fresh Sage
2 tblsp Flour for dusting
Salt and pepper
250g lambs liver
Juice of ½ a small lemon

1) Cut the liver into fine strips.

2) In a frying pan heat a glug of oil and fry the onion until soft and golden. Remove the onions and set aside

3) Add the flour to a plastic bag along with the finely chopped sage, pepper and salt. Thoroughly fix together.

4) It is important in this step to work quickly. You don't want the liver to become too gloopy with attached flour. Add the liver to the mix in the plastic bag and lightly coat each slice. Remove the liver from the mix shaking each slice to remove excess flour. Set aside on a clean plate.

5) Bring the frying pan to a high heat having added a little extra oil and a knob of butter. Now "flash" fry the liver until sealed. This should only take a minute or two as you want it to be pink inside. Quickly add the lemon juice and almost immediately remove the liver to a hot serving dish.

Serve on hot plates with spinach and mashed potatoes.

Horseradish Sauce

After we were truly settled in to our life in London, and living in Kenilworth Court, we got all our fresh vegetables from an excellent shop on Lower Richmond Road. They got to know us very well and appreciated that we were "up" for new suggestions.

When Josceline Dimbleby didn't collect the horseradish she had ordered they knew we would give it a try. My abiding memory of this effort was coming home from work and being offered a "sniff" of the ground horseradish. I can still recall the searing pain as my brain dissolved from the inside out. This is very powerful stuff.

Reference to *"The Perfect Pickle Book"* by David Maybe and David Collison helped us get some form of attack on these far from elegant looking roots.

To Make about 900 ml (1 ½ pints)

½ tblsp salt
1 tblsp sugar
½ tblsp dry mustard powder
1 heaped tblsp corn flour
1 egg beaten
1 pint milk
½ pint malt vinegar
1 large, or 2 medium, roots of horseradish

To Make the mayonnaise

1) Mix the salt, sugar, mustard, and corn flour together in a large, heatproof, bowl then blend in the egg. Stir in the milk and then very slowly add the vinegar stirring continuously.

2) Sit the bowl in a saucepan of water, put it on a low heat and gently cook stirring occasionally to break down any lumps until the mayonnaise thickens. Remove from the heat and allow to cool.

3) Meanwhile wash and peel your horseradish. Now grate the horseradish. This can be done using a food processor or and old fashioned hand mincer. The resulting vapours from this are extremely strong so caution is best exercised

Depending upon the quantity of horseradish either in batches, or all together, add the mayonnaise stirring as you go until you get a thick flavoursome mix. Store in airtight, sterilised, jars.

Stuffed Shoulder of Lamb

Soon after getting housing sorted in London Sheila did a beautician course at Steiner's Beauty School. Once qualified she started work at a beauticians located in Hammersmith. On Thursdays she had to work late. The arrangement was that I would do the cooking getting everything ready to eat when we returned home after me collecting her from work. On one memorable Thursday, inspired I think from a GQ boy's recipe, I decided to cook a stuffed shoulder of lamb. Having bought the shoulder, bone in, I discovered the only help from the recipe was the instruction "First bone your lamb shoulder". Setting to I managed to bone the shoulder then make the stuffing. The next instruction was to "tie up the shoulder". After much desperate searching I finally located some string. It was tied around the window box. Time being short I had no other option. I tied up the lamb, bunged it into the over and drove off to pick up Sheila from work duties. The lamb was extremely tasty. However that night the wind picked up and the next morning we sighted the window boxes 3 stories below.

Ingredients - serves 4 to 6

2 oz butter
1 large onion chopped
2 cubby garlic cloves finely chopped
3 rashers of back bacon chopped
4 oz small mushrooms - halved
2 tblsp chopped parsley
4 lamb kidneys - halved core removed and sliced
1 tsp chopped sage
4lb shoulder of lamb
Cooking oil for basting

1) "First bone your shoulder of lamb". I'd recommend getting the butcher to do this.

2) Heat half the butter in a frying pan. Fry the onion till soft. Add the garlic and bacon and continue to gently fry. Now add the mushrooms, and the parsley.

3) To a separate pan add the rest of the butter and bring to a high heat avoiding burning the butter. Add the kidney slices and cook until they colour.

4) When cooked add the kidneys to the first pan and add the sage and seasoning. Once amalgamated transfer to a mixing bowl and allow to cool.

5) The de boned shoulder will have flaps of skin and flesh around the central meat. Take a large needle and thread with black cotton. Stich up the flaps to form a pocket into which the cooled stuffing can be transferred. Continue packing lightly until all the stuffing is used. Stich up the opening. Now tie the lamb around with string to maintain a nice shape.

6) Place the joint in a roasting tin and brush with cooking oil. Cook in a pre-heated oven 190C for 1 hour 50 minutes. Check occasionally during the cooking to monitor progress. Once cooked remove from the oven and set aside covered with aluminium foil to rest for +/- 15 minutes

Carve the lamb. Serve on warm plates with roast potatoes, green vegetables, and juice poured over the lamb. Remember to re tie the window boxes.

Grown Up Chocolate Marquise

In July 1985, with our friend Marlyn Robson visiting from New Zealand, we went down to Kent to stay at Stone Green Hall, to coincide with my birthday. This is a Cromwellian farmhouse, run as a restaurant with a small number of bedrooms, by other friends Jim, and Ing, Kempston.

Jim had been a long term influence, and source of knowledge, on all things 'cooking'. From Edinburgh student days; via the Norfolk barn when we were first in London; and through visits to Stone Green Hall. The influences were formalised through the publication of his book *"the Creative Cook"* in 1993, and now continue with us both domiciled in Edinburgh. The recipe below was given to Sheila on a visit and a version is included in Jim's book.

To Make about 5 or 6 ramekins

12oz dark chocolate
¼ pint double cream
4 oz unsalted butter
4 egg yolks
2 oz caster sugar
¼ tblsp brandy, or ¼ tsp instant coffee melted in 1 tblsp boiling water

1) Cream the butter and sugar till pale. Then gradually beat in the Brandy or coffee solution.

2) Whisk the double cream until it "holds" its shape. Then combine with the butter and sugar mix.

3) Melt 8 oz of the chocolate. Once molten beat in the egg yolks. Then mix into the creamed mixture.

4) Fill the ramekins to just below the top and cover with cling film to prevent a crust forming. Refrigerate until set.

To serve remove the cling film and grate the remaining chocolate over each ramekin.

Casseroled Pheasant

Once upon a time in the UK you could send someone a pheasant (or a brace if you were lucky) through the Royal mail system by just attaching an addressed label to its leg. I seem to remember one unsuccessfully being sent to us by my Grandparents Capel when we were in Edinburgh during our student time. Grandpa who was an excellent shot would claim some of the local estates birds every year as they would innocently wander into his fields. In our London, Kenilworth Court, days a more secure route resulted in us being given a fine brace of pheasants.

Barkley, a friend of Darron's, who in the season would go shooting, was the source. Upon receipt of the pheasants we used to hang them outside (I have seen recommendations of from 1 ½ to 3 weeks). When we considered them ready (I'm sure well under the 3 weeks) we would take them to our local butcher who would pluck and dress them for us. Here's how we cooked them.

Ingredients – serves 4

1 large pheasant, hung, plucked, and drawn (as for chicken)
1 tblsp oil
¼ lb diced bacon
1 oz flour

For the Marinade

1 onion sliced
2 carrots sliced
2 garlic cloves crushed / finely sliced
2 bay leaves
Salt & black pepper
4 juniper berries
2 glasses red wine

1) Cut the pheasant in 4 pieces and marinate for two days. Drain retaining the marinade juices and pat dry with kitchen paper.

2) Sauté the diced bacon in a heavy bottomed casserole. Add the pheasant and brown all over. Sprinkle on the flour and pour the strained marinade. Bring to a simmer on top of the stove. Put the casserole, with a closely fitting lid, into a pre heated oven and cook for 1 ½ hours.

3) Take the casserole out of the oven and remove the pheasant pieces. Set aside on a nice dish to rest. Cover with foil to keep it hot. Put the casserole back on the stove and bring the sauce to the boil. Pour over the pheasant pieces.

Serve divided between 4 plates with a puree of potatoes.

Mrs Dimbleby's Greek Island Chicken

In retrospect it seems as if in our kitchen cook books go through phases of almost continuous use followed by periods when they are forgotten. This is then often reversed by a chance encounter. Suddenly a recipe remembered. Sometimes something seen on TV, or read.

Josceline Dimbleby's book *"A Taste of Dreams"* is a case in point. First published in 1976 and bought, can you believe it for £3.95, by Sheila just before we left Aberdeen. Like an old friend there are times when it's almost forgotten. But when remembered, and brought down off the shelf, it immediately reminds you of all the good times you've had together. This recipe was to become, when we were in Damascus, part of Sheila's cookery demonstrations.

Ingredients – serves 4

4 chicken breasts or thighs skin on, bone in
2 cloves of garlic crushed
Virgin olive oil
A Cinnamon stick, broken into pieces, and a good pinch of ground cinnamon
Freshly crushed black pepper
Sea salt
3 - 4 tomatoes sliced
1 orange sliced in rounds
1 lemon sliced in rounds
Handful of black olives pitted and halved
1 good glass white vermouth or white wine

1) Put the chicken pieces in an oven proof dish. Add the crushed garlic, the cinnamon stick and ground cinnamon, black pepper, and a glug of olive oil. Massage the marinade into the chicken pieces until both sides are coated. Cling film the dish and allow to rest for 1 to 2 hours.

2) Ensure each chicken piece is skin side up and season each piece with a good pinch of sea salt. Slice the tomato and halve the pitted olives. Arrange evenly around the chicken. Slice the orange and lemon and place a slice of orange, and a slice of lemon, on each chicken piece. Pore over the vermouth or white wine.

3) Place the dish in the centre of the pre heated (190 C) oven and bake for 40 minutes. Remove from the oven and check the cooking process. Return to the over for the final 20 minutes cooking to crisp up the top side skin.

This chicken dish goes particularly well with the potato dish described below.

Potatoes, Tomatoes, with Garlic and Herbs

As with the recipe above this one is also inspired by Josceline Dimbleby's *"A Taste of Dreams"*. We have cooked this particular recipe in just about every location we have lived. Helped I imagine by the almost universal availability of the ingredients. It goes extremely well with Josceline's Greek Island chicken recipe. Over the years with our growing love of camping, with its obligatory barbecuing, it became an almost indispensable side dish on these occasions as it can be prepared in advance and reheated as needed.

Ingredients

1 lb potatoes
1 - 1¼ lbs tomatoes
2 cloves of garlic crushed
1 tblsp dried oregano (imported returning from holidays in the UK)
Butter
Salt and pepper
Double cream diluted (Single cream was unavailable)
Handful Parsley - finely chopped

1) Peel and boil the potatoes in salted water until just cooked. Drain and set aside to cool. Once cool enough to handle slice into +/- 1 cm slices.

2) Using a sharp knife cut shallow crosses into the bottom of each tomato. Transfer to a bowl and pour boiling water over them to cover. Leave for a minute or so. Transfer to a bowl of cold water. Using a small knife skin the tomatoes. Slice up the tomatoes to a thickness slightly smaller than the potatoes,

3) In the bottom of a casserole dish lay out a single layer of potato slices. Spread a little of the crushed garlic; dot with a few small knobs of butter; carefully salt and pepper; then cover with a layer of tomato; finally sprinkle over some of the dried oregano. Repeat this process until all the potato and tomato are used.

4) Pour the cream over the top layer of tomatoes. Cover the dish and place in a pre-heated oven at 180C for 30 minutes.

5) Remove from the oven and sprinkle chopped parsley over the dish prior to serving.

Bread and Butter Pudding.

First off I should confess that the picture, unlike the majority of the others in the recipes, is not mine. As Sheila has now developed a "gluten" intolerance, and therefore this dish is definitely off the menu, I took the liberty of going to the web. The recipe is however 100% Sheila's. I am pretty sure that we ate versions of Bread & Butter Pudding in many of the places we lived. This is included in the London section as from Sheila's record of dishes cooked, and enjoyed, I can see it was written up then.

Ingredients

1 tblsp raisins
1 tblsp brandy
10 floz double cream
10 floz milk
4 oz caster sugar
3 eggs
Pinch of salt
1 vanilla pod
*14 * ¼ inch slices of dry French loaf buttered with unsalted butter*
Apricot jam
Icing sugar

1) Soak raisins in brandy

2) Heat the cream, and the milk, with the vanilla pod

3) Beat the eggs and sugar then add the hot cream mixture. Continue to beat.

4) Layer up the buttered bread, with the brandied raisins, in a suitable dish.

5) Strain the cream and milk mixture evenly over the buttered slices of bread.

6) Put in a bain marie and cook for 35 to 40 minutes in an oven at 150 C. Once cooked set aside and allow to cool for about ½ an hour. Dress with a good shake of icing sugar.

Serve with hot apricot jam.

Grandma's Chocolate Cornflake Cakes

When I was much younger, and Grandma and Grandpa Capel were still working full time at Middle Shelspit farm, I was always spoilt during our visits there. In particular having the choice of 3 puddings at lunch, and having a range of my favourite cakes at tea time.

Perhaps it was influenced by the fact I would always follow my Grandpa around and help out with any jobs I could manage. I think these began with collecting eggs; advanced through "farming out" - cleaning up after milking; included being sent off on the "Fordson" tractor to plough fields by myself; and culminated in me looking after the farm during my student days when Grandpa was taken ill.

This privilege of being spoilt continued for Darron and Kevin whenever we subsequently visited. Here's one of Grandma's recipes.

Ingredients

6 oz butter
6 oz Golden Syrup
6 oz good quality chocolate
6 oz Corn Flakes

1) Melt the butter, then add the syrup, and finally melt the chocolate

2) Carefully fold in the cornflakes and thoroughly coat in the mixture.

3) Spoon out to fill the greaseproof cake cases. Set in a cold place, or refrigerate, until set.

Serve with 4:00 o-clock tea after the cucumber sandwiches.

Travels With Our Kitchen

8.0 Syria, Damascus – Best Assignment, Sept '89 to Sept '93

Five years of living in high cost London had destroyed our finances. After a visit to our friends the Richards, outside Aberdeen, I had travelled to The Hague to visit the Well Engineering godfather Brian Ward. I explained I needed to be sent to a "hot and well paid" assignment. He said he would see what he could do. I was no sooner back in the UK when the phone rang and the question was "how did I fancy Syria?". I met Sheila, who had travelled back south by train, at the station in London and relayed the question. On her yes we signed up to go.

The trip to Damascus was memorable for 2 very different reasons. After leaving London the plane developed a problem & we had to overnight it in Holland. We were ferried to the Golden Tulip hotel just outside Schiphol airport. That evening we ate in their restaurant one of the tastiest meals we have ever had. Next day we completed the flight to Damascus. On arrival there was no "entry visa" at immigration. As we hadn't arrived the day before it had been disposed of. When I asked I was pointed to a mountain of discarded visas on the floor behind the desk. Luckily I was able to find ours and we could enter. We were initially to stay in the Sheraton hotel just off what we would christen crazy roundabout. The hotel was pretty crazy as well as the traffic at the roundabout. It was full of rich Lebanese fleeing the civil war raging at the time. As they didn't need to work they seemed to sleep all day and run around at night. The norm was that the doors of rooms opposite each other would be left open so that the residents could shout to each other across the corridor. It also hosted garish, and extremely loud, Syrian weddings. These seemed to start late in the evening and go on well into the early hours accompanied by over amplified Arabic music. This cacophony, and the inevitable "Damascus" diarrhoea caused by the salads, herbs, and I guess night soil contaminated vegetables, meant little sleep just when we most needed it. There were compensations. We had our duty free gin, we could get tonic, and we had been assigned a car & a driver. Now for the missing ingredient.

"No; No; NO!!!! Not 2 kilos of lemons, we just want 2 lemons."

This was how our first visit, with our driver who had very little English, to the "Friday" market ended. The stall holder, I recall, only very reluctantly gave in and let us have 2 lemons. We of course were still working with a UK mind set. Back home two kilos of lemons would cost the earth. In Damascus they were so cheap you had to buy by the kilo. This was to be the start of many a 'mind' changing experience during our 4 years we were there.

Unknown to us on first arrival we were to be introduced to a most wondrous Arab cuisine. Evenings sitting cross legged at our driver's aunt, or his father's, house manfully trying so as not to cause offence eat through a mountain of delicacies watched by the whole family. In the UK we have forgotten that a meal is a social occasion that should last late into the evening. Syrians have no idea of the quick meal, either in preparation, or in consumption. This was food lovingly prepared, using fresh seasonal ingredients, carefully chosen.

Travels With Our Kitchen

Damascus brought many new food experiences. There were trips to Tartus for fresh fish. We had to choose the leg of lamb we wanted whist the animal was still alive, tied up at Nabil the butchers, across the road. We came to terms with NOT being able to eat fresh salad greens like parsley. The amoeba could not be totally eliminated. Their digestion guaranteed an unpleasant experience which was heralded by your colour draining from head to feet just prior to the need for the "Damascus" dash. What could we get that was outstandingly good? We re-discovered the tasty delights of seasonal apricots, cherries, and pears. Field grown, sun ripened tomatoes, broad beans, cauliflower, and cabbages bigger "than 'yr head".

We tended to avoid the water melons that were piled high in the season and on sale from every other road side trader. They were sold by weight and we believed injected with water to 'up the price'. There was also the health issue. Where had the water come from? We did buy pretty well all our other vegetables from the souk, stalls, or if you saw a lorry loaded with excellent looking sun ripened tomatoes from the driver.

Unlike vegetables, and fruit, meat availability was very restricted. The local butchers didn't have beef but there was one source (smuggled?) in Malki. There was even pork reared by Philippine maids but it was not really tasty even if you could get it. What there was as standard fair were sheep, goats, and baby camel. In the 'smelly' souk however you could also buy live rabbits, chickens, Guiney fowl and other stuff you might not want to eat.

If anybody from the small expat community, faced the limited local availability of suitable entertainment, wanted to participate in some form of social, or sport, activity then they had to organise it themselves. Sheila having worked as a beautician in London decided to ship a specialist treatment bed to Syria. This meant she quickly found a niche doing beauty treatments, and facials, for the diplomat, and Shell, expat wives. Also Sheila being able to cook, and more importantly given the erratic supply of ingredients, being both knowledgeable and adaptable in the kitchen was to find another source of meeting people and enjoying herself. Soon after our arrival Sheila became a committee member of the British Women's Guild. This organisation ran various events to raise money for local good causes. One such was a "fashion" show. This was followed by the idea to organising a dinner to raise additional funds. A group of BWG members volunteered to cook an identical main course. The dish chosen was Greek Island chicken. Sheila demonstrated how to cook it, which was followed by a tasting, in our kitchen. On the night some 30 tables were arranged in Julia Armours garden and an army of paying guests were duly well fed.

Another expat organised activity was the weekly 'Hash' – the run for runners with a drinking problem. In total I was to do 151 runs. Sheila didn't run but would always attend and helped look after the kids and help with the after run food. We both ended up on the organising committee. Sheila as Hash Cash and in our last year I became Hash Grand Master. We had typically +/- 120 runners every week made up of Diplomatic community (Canadian & Australian being the most active) folks as well as people working someway connected to oil. I should also not forget the

Travels With Our Kitchen

Syrians who would run even if we quietly suspected that many were representatives of the 13 different 'muhabarats' (secret services) there to check on what we got up to.

A Hashing high light was the distinction of us helping organise DH3 500th Palmyra Hash. We organised the entire logistics of getting people to "lay" both the 499 "Night" run, and the mid-day, 15kl, 500th run. We also arranged for the "six" fingered restaurant man (check out the Lonely Planet Guide) to erect a huge Bedouin tent, and provide food and toilets for the over 200 hundred runners who participated. Sheila also organised Queen Zenobia bronze medals, hung with ribbons the colours of the Syrian flag, which were presented to each runner as they crossed the finishing line under the famous Palmyra Roman arch.

In the West Palmyra is known for its Roman era gate, and as the city of Queen Zenobia. The Syrians call it Tadmor (dates) as it is famous for their quality. The travel guides also talk about (or did in our time) the 6 fingered man. We, especially after he provided the food for the 500th Hash, always stopped at his café when en route to the oil fields the other side of Deir az-Zor, and again on our home ward trip.

Other serious physical activities included windsurfing at Qattinah Lake. The artificial lake lies between the anti-Lebanon hills and the high land to the north which include Homs and the Krak De Chevaliers. To the east you have the Mediterranean and to the west the desert. During much of the year this fairly extreme temperature differential develops in-land thermal winds. These in turn are accelerated as they head inland between the twin hills. I think I have sailed in winds in excess of 30 knots there. I also took up cycling. Our friend Hank Koelemij decided on his first leave to buy and import 4 bikes. Two for himself and his wife and two for my Sheila and I. We started pretty easily but things soon got serious. In the end there was a dedicated cycling group. For exercise I used to cycle from the house in West Meze up the highway that connected Damascus to Beirut. One of our farewell events was a handicapped speed trial in which I managed to accomplish my long held ambition of going under 30 minutes for the round trip. For Sheila a key activity was walking around the track at Tishreen sports stadium. Here, among many others, she met one of the few Syrian, female, Olympians a hep-athlete. And on one memorable occasion she panicked our driver Ayman by saying "Good morning" to Rifat, President Assad's bloodthirsty brother. Following the first Hama massacre in the '80's when some 10,000 perished he was normally exiled in France but had returned to Syria for his mother's funeral. Ayman, who had been in the Syrian army during this time, knew his true reputation whereas we had no idea. Sheila should have twigged if she had noticed his entourage. They were all wearing Italian shoes, black leather jackets, with the giveaway bulge in the waistband of a hand gun, sure signs that they were guarding "Mr Big".

Damascus was for us the best overseas posting that we did. It was a combination of me enjoying my job supervising a Hungarian crewed small drilling rig used to repair non-functioning oil and gas wells. Each new work-over presented a unique set of problems. My job was to analyse the problem, decide upon the remedy, write a detailed repair programme and get all the other responsible parties to sign off to it. Then I supervised the execution of the programme from rig moving in to the well, doing the repair, and putting the well back on production. I should mention here one unforgettable experience. Whilst on site to supervise the first stainless steel dual completion to be run in Syria refusing to come out of the caravan until the temperature rose above - 10 degrees C. It gets very cold in the desert and we used to get snow in the winter. In my time in this job, with a repair typically taking 6 to 10 days, I wrote some +/- 90 programmes.

Meanwhile Sheila was able to visit a few of the over 5000 significant archaeological sites in Syria. South of Damascus there are the Roman ruins at Suweida, and the Roman theatre in Bosra. North there was Ma'aloula where they still spoke the language of Christ Aramaic. Further North, beyond the water wheels (norias) of Homs, was the Crusader castle Krak de Chevaliers. Going even further North there are the pillars at Ebla; Saladin's dramatic castle; Aleppo with its citadel, souk (now unfortunately recently burnt down), and the Baron Hotel once famous as a stop off for writers (Agatha Christy etc) and actors in the area. To the north of Aleppo there are the remains of the basilica built in honour of St Simeon and his feat of remaining atop a column. East of Damascus, heading out into the desert, you have Palmyra (already mentioned); Qasr al-Hayr al-Sharqi the earliest example of a khan – resting place for desert caravans; and then onto the fertile snake that is the Euphrates river. Here there were far too many, and mostly anonymous, ancient ruins to visit and clamber over to remember now. Along the way we visited Bedouin camp sites for coffee; apple orchards in the hills above the destroyed town of Qunaitra; chai (tea) with army boys who seemed to always be sitting on top of every hill; and kisses (for me not Sheila) from the mishmish (apricot) man. All these wonders were over and above the extraordinary sights and sounds of Damascus. A "Street Call Straight"; the Omayyed mosque; the Hamadeer souk; the Turkish Hamam (steam baths); and coming up to date the glass factory, the copper makers, the woodworkers, and all the other artisans who made up city life.

Our small but nationality diverse community proved to be a potent catalyst in evolving our Damascus Christmas tradition. As a joint, progressive, celebration we would join our Dutch friends Hank & Janet for Sinta Claus on the 5th December, Veronique and Steve for a French Christmas Eve, and our place for an English Christmas diner. Each event would observe, as best we could, the differing national traditions. There was always the re-enactment of the arrival of Sinta Clause's, accompanied by his Zware de Piets, in Holland. Integral with the evening's festivities was the tradition of giving and receiving parcels which were wrapped in the most devious ways imaginable. Also the recitation of poems which were the vehicle to give humorous feed-back on incidents from the preceding year were essential. A gentle means to remind each of us of our fallibilities. Christmas eve at Veronique's was naturally a very elegant event. Great food and good wine. For our part we did as traditional a British Christmas spread as Damascene ingredients would allow. Very happy days.

If you have made it this far please spend a reflective moment mourning what may well be the damage to many of these splendid sights. Even worse, for those who are still alive, is the ruin of their businesses. As such we fear for our shop keeper friend Nabil the butcher. News from inside Damascus / Syria (November 2012) is that many are ruined and penniless and some (far too many) may no longer be of this world. The Assad's butchery has reaped a terrible harvest.

Mayonnaise

Of the many things NOT available in Damascus Hellmann's real mayonnaise was but one. I include a photo to remind us of what we couldn't get. One other ingredient which was also unreliable was the electricity supply. Whilst we lived there we would have daily electricity and water cuts. In fact there was only a 3 hour window when we had both simultaneously available. You need the electricity to power the food processor as I don't recommend doing this by hand.

What we did have however were fresh eggs, excellent lemons, and good local olive oil. All that was missing was the expertise. One of Sheila's first shared cooking experiences after we settled into our house and started to understand the lie of the land was to teach some of our new friends how to make mayonnaise.

Ingredients

2 egg yolks
Salt and freshly ground black pepper
1 tblsp lemon juice
280 mls olive oil

1) Put the egg yolks, a pinch of salt, and the lemon juice into the bowl of your food processor. Whizz until the mixture turns pale and frothy.

2) With the processor running slowly add the olive oil in a steady continuous stream until you achieve a thick creamy mayonnaise consistency..

3) Taste for seasoning adding salt, pepper, and lemon juice as necessary.

Transfer to a sterilised jar if you are not going to consume it all immediately.

Beetroot, Tomato, & Basil Salad

The combination of the harsh living conditions, and a very small expat community, facilitated a wonderfully close and supportive relationship between those there at this time. We had arrived at the end of '89, survived the 1st Gulf war, accepted the travel limitations the Lebanese civil war and kidnappings imposed, and left as things started to improve in '93. Supplies were pretty limited & irregular, during our time. There were no 'supermarkets'. It was either the local shop or the 'smelly' souk. Even then everything was in short supply. Shell had advised us to include 4 years' worth of toilet paper, and dishwashing powder, with our normal arrival shipment.

The small expatriate community helped each other with the shopping. Whoever was first to discovered new stocks bought for all. This was also the Syrian way. You didn't buy by the kilo but by the box. Everyone would also share recipes to help consume these large purchases. Veronique was the source of this salad design ideal for the glut of beetroot that would inevitably hit the shops.

Ingredients - serves 4

4 - 6 beetroot
Virgin olive oil
6 large ripened in the sun tomatoes
A bunch of fresh basil
1 garlic clove crushed and finely chopped
Virgin olive oil
Good vinegar (ratio 1 of oil to 2 of vinegar)
1 Tps French mustard
Salt & Freshly ground black pepper

1) In Damascus I'm sure we used to cook the beetroot in the pressure cooker. A better method I'd suggest now is to bake them in the oven. Wash and trim each beetroot. Cut a suitably sized square of Aluminium foil to wrap the beet in. Add a dash of olive oil before twisting the top of the parcel closed. Bake in the oven for 1½ to 2 hour depending upon size. Test the beetroot are done by feel as you push a wooden cocktail stick into the beetroot. A little resistance means done.

2) Allow the beetroot to cool & then remove the outer skin. Slice into thin'ish discs. We could get field grown, sun ripened, tomatoes in Damascus. Often you would have to stop a lorry you'd spotted on the road, or at the traffic lights, and buy a 25 kg box. This allowed the repayment of previous favours. These tomatoes came as nature had shaped them and they needed a good wash. Then, as with the beets, thinly slice.

Combine tomato and beetroot slices in a nice big dish. Scatter with torn basil leaves and generously dress with the freshly made dressing.

Bosra (Made Up) Chutney

The abundance of seasonal ingredients and their availability, often times from road side sellers, meant we nearly always bought (in large quantities) before we knew we had the need or how we would prepare the purchase. This "Bosra" chutney was one such, very early on in our stay in Syria, example.

Work commitments, a 5 ½ day week and regular Drilling Department "duty" responsibilities outside normal office hours, meant I never made it to Bosra. The key attraction was the Roman amphitheatre. Sheila went twice. Once with Darron and Kevin during our first Christmas. Then with Veronique's (beetroot and basil recipe) father. We think the green tomatoes were purchased on the return trip to Damascus from the first

Ingredients

4 lbs green tomatoes (hopefully you can sell the rest to friends or family)
1 lb apples
1 ½ lbs onions or shallots
½ lb raisins
1 lb brown sugar
2 tblsp mixed pickle spice
½ oz grated ginger
1 pint of vinegar

1) Chop the green tomatoes, peel and chop the apples, and chop the onions or shallots if using.

2) Add these to a large saucepan and add the spices and vinegar. Bring to the boil and cook until the apples are soft. Add the sugar and continue to cook slowly until reduced and thickened.

3) Remove the saucepan from the heat and carefully ladle the chutney mixture into hot, sterile, jars. Seal the jars when cool.

4) Store in a dark cool place and mature for a minimum of 2 months.

Enjoy with cheese or cold meats.

Ku Ku (Koo Koo) – Iranian Frittata

The predictable weather, the fantastic scenery, and the possibility of travel meant we needed to expand our picnic food repertoire. This Iranian dish, ku ku, which is similar to a frittata, comes in many different varieties. Examples being; sabzi (herb); sibzammi (potato); morgh (chicken); or as in the recipe below, meat. I haven't found the Persian word for meat and having experienced country fare in the Middle East I expect because meat is such a rare and precious commodity. This ku ku is loosely based on Claudia Roden and Howard & Maschler versions. It incorporates the luxury western twist by using meat.

> I have learnt that a koo koo is not like an omelette where the eggs are complimented by the additions. Here the ingredients are bonded by the addition of the eggs. That's why it's good picnic food as it doesn't break up in transport. I've also seen that the 'real' Persian versions use saffron. Cheap in Iran but which in the west is more expensive than meat and therefore dropped.

Ingredients - serves 4 - 6

1 large onion finely chopped
Vegetable oil
1 large leek, or 4/6 spring onions chopped
500g minced beef or lamb
125g spinach
Salt and freshly ground black pepper
1 tblsp ground cinnamon
6 large eggs

1) Add a slug of vegetable oil to a heated, metal handled, frying pan. Fry the onion, leek or spring onions (we couldn't get leeks in Damascus), until translucent and soft. Add the beef (we used lamb, or more likely mutton, mince in Damascus as beef was a rarity) and cook through until it changes colour. Add the spinach, salt, pepper, and cinnamon and continue to cook gently. When the spinach has wilted down remove from the heat and allow to cool.

2) Into a large mixing bowl crack the 6 eggs & beat lightly. Add the meat mixture and fold in.

3) Re heat the frying pan adding another slug of oil. Pour the egg and meat into the pan and cook over a gentle heat for about 15 minutes until the eggs have set on the bottom and the koo koo is cooked over half way through.

4) Place under a hot grill, or in a medium oven, to cook until the top is golden.

Allow to cool as a koo koo is never served hot. Slice across wise into rectangular chunks. Eat by itself or accompanied with yoghurt.

Chicken with Olives, Capers, & Prunes

Chickens were one thing that were both good, and always available. Sheila used to buy our chickens, directed by Ayman our driver, in East Mezze from a shop which whilst in a street full of chicken and kebab rotisserie sellers only sold raw chicken. An often repeated favourite, adapted from "The Silver Palate Cookbook", was Chicken Marbella. Excellent olives and capers were one of the few things always available in Damascus. We did however have to import the prunes. We were introduced to this dish by Gilbert & Maurine of the Canadian Embassy. On asking what the recipe was after eating it at their apartment Maurine named this book. Sheila immediately realised we had our own copy but had never before done the recipe. Here is how you do it.

Ingredients - Serves 4

1 chicken (+ 1.2 kg) quartered
6 - 8 garlic cloves
1 tblsp dried oregano
Sea salt and freshly ground pepper to taste
2 tblsp red wine vinegar
2 tblsp good olive oil
½ cup pitted prunes
Handful of green olives
¼ cup capers
2 or 3 bay leaves
¼ cup brown sugar
1 glass white wine
½ cup of finely chopped fresh flat leaf parsley

1) In a large blow combine all the ingredients except the sugar, wine, and parsley. Cing film the bowl and marinate in the fridge overnight.

2) Pre heat the oven to 160 C.

3) Arrange the chicken in a single layer in a roasting dish spooning the remaining marinated over. Sprinkle the brown sugar over the chicken pieces and add the white wine.

4) Roast for 50 minutes to 1 hour whilst frequently basting with the cooking juices. The chicken is done if the thigh juices run clear when pricked (or meat temperature is +/- 85 C)

5) With a slotted spoon remove the chicken pieces to a hot serving plate. Spoon over the chicken some of the cooking juices (save any leftover juices to a sauce bowl) and generously garnish with the parsley or coriander.

Serve in shallow bowls with additional juice to taste. Accompany with a green salad. This dish is also excellent cold.

Cauliflower Romagna Style

The vegetable markets in Damascus, of necessity, where seasonal. That means as the year unfolded, and the crops came to season, a predictable sequence of oversupply of a single vegetable became that week's only choice. The cauliflowers where delicious but by the end of the season you did need to know recipes for a "hundred things to do" with them.

The other funny thing was that seller's would congregate in groups of road side stalls all selling identical produce. As we got used to what was possible we learned to compensate by either picking direct from the fields (potatoes from the fields around Qattinah lake) or stopping lorries on the road and buying from the driver. The other major source was sending Ayman, our driver, out in the hope that his comprehension of English vegetables names was up to the task.

Ingredients – serves 4

1 large cauliflower
1 oz of butter
3 tblsp olive oil
1 large garlic clove crushed
Bunch chopped parsley
Salt & Pepper
1 tblsp tomato puree
6 tblsp hot water
Grated parmesan

1) Divide cauliflower into roughly equal sized florets and wash. Thoroughly wash and drain.

2) Heat the butter and oil in a large sauce pan and fry the garlic and parsley for a few moments.

3) Add the cauliflower and stir and cook for 4 to 5 minutes. Now season with salt and pepper. Add the tomato puree dissolved in the hot water. Cover and cook over a low heat for a further 5 – 10 minutes until the cauliflower is just cooked through.

Turn into a serving dish, sprinkle with the parmesan cheese and serve hot.

Butterflied Leg of Lamb for the Barbeque

In all our overseas postings (with the exception of Oman to come) we always managed to find a house, worked hard to turn it into a home, and stayed in it until we left. It may seem strange to say this but it is surprising how many Shell'ies spent their time frequently moving trying to ascent some sort of house hierarchy. In Damascus we moved into a house which had been rejected by several other Shell staff. It was kind of half ground half first floor. It also had, a deciding factor, a large terrace. Later we were to realise it had a secret advantage – an important army (secret police?) General lived close by. We did not suffer too badly from the daily electric and water cuts that afflicted everyone else. We used to specialise in casual entertaining friends on our terrace inevitably by barbequing. This barbequed leg of lamb became a favourite.

Ingredients - 4 to 6

1 large leg of lamb de boned and butterflied
Several sprigs of rosemary
6 - 8 garlic cloves sliced into thin wedges
Olive oil
1 lemon
Salt and pepper

1) Ideally get your butcher to de bone the leg of lamb. To "butterfly" it lay it out, skin side down, spread apart with your hands and then depending upon the lie of the muscle make cuts half way through the thickness such that you can spread the meat out over a larger area. Turnover and using a small sharp knife make incisions in a regular pattern inserting a piece of garlic and some rosemary leaves into each.

2) Into a large plastic bag pour a good glug of olive oil, juice from half the lemon, and some freshly ground pepper. Now add the leg of lamb. Seal the top of the bag and allow the meat to marinate for a minimum of a couple of hours.

3) Get the BBQ fire well heated up and the coals glowing red. It will take about 15 minutes to cook the lamb. There will be quite an alarming build-up of charred meat but keep your nerve and turn several times.

Set the lamb aside to rest for 5 minutes. Carve into generously thick slices and serve with a gratin potatoes and or tomato salad.

Barbequed Red Peppers

This is another recipe which was inspired, and driven, by a seasonal abundance. Supported, in terms of frequency of cooking, by the number of times we fired up the trusty barbeque on our covered terrace. My technique was to put the peppers on the barbeque soon after lighting, you don't need to wait for the charcoal to burn down, as "burning" the skins is the whole point.

Having a beer close to hand as the 'process' of charring was at times rather speedy. As you can see you don't have to be too shy in showing the peppers some heat. I have also seen peppers 'charred' over a gas hob. My sense is that this misses a vital ingredient which is the smoky, charcoal, fragrance imparted by the real thing. Since Damascus we have cooked this almost every time we've had a barbeque.

Ingredients – serves 4

4 – 6 large red peppers
1 large zip lock plastic bag
1 beer for the cook

3 or 4 parts Virgin olive oil
1 part red wine vinegar
Two good pinches of dried mint
Pinch of sugar
Salt & Pepper to taste

1) With the barbeque lit scatter the peppers over the griddle. It will take a little while for the first side to char but once underway you will need to constantly turn them. They need to be charred fairly evenly on all sides.

2) Using tongs remove the peppers from the heat and drop into the zip lock plastic bag. Allow to cool and sweat.

3) Once thoroughly cool remove the peppers from the bag retaining the sweated juices. Now carefully peel the charred skin from the peppers and remove the stems and the seeds. Slice the pepper flesh into 1cm wide strips. Add to a bowl with the cooking juices.

4) Add to a 'shaker' the 3 to 4 parts olive oil, the vinegar, pinches of mint and sugar, and finally add a little at a time of salt and pepper. Shake well to amalgamate. Taste and adjust to your liking. Pour over the roasted peppers.

Allow some time for the tastes to combine. Eat with cheese, or add to a frittata.

Ayman's Mothers Green Bean Stew

Another classic, Damascus, shared dish. Shared because we had eaten this dish at our driver Ayman's fathers house, and would later on be given the recipe by our 'Syrian' family. And also shared because Sheila had bought, in the seasonal overabundance of beans, a huge quantity which we needed help to consume.

Having taken the amount we needed for us two the bulk of the purchase was given to the family. In return this was one of the first 'Syrian' dishes Sheila was introduced to by Ayman who had returned from delivering the beans with his Mother's recipe. The aroma of the cinnamon in the finalised dish is incredible.

Ingredients - serves 4

2 tblsp olive oil
*1 large onion chopped or 2 * medium shallots*
2 fat garlic cloves finely chopped or crushed
1 tsp of whole cumin seeds
*1 * 5 cm piece of cinnamon bark*
*400 g of large fresh sun ripened tomatoes or 1 * 400g tin of chopped tomatoes*
2 tsp - sun dried tomato paste.
450 g Green (French) Beans - trimmed & cut into 2 - 3 cm pieces
Salt and freshly ground black pepper

1) Pour a glug of olive oil into a gently heated pan. Add the onion / shallots and cook stirring occasionally until they start to sweat down. Add the garlic and continue to sweat off.

2) Add the cumin seeds and the stick of cinnamon bark. Continue to cook until you can smell the aroma of the herbs.

3) If using fresh tomatoes chop, remove the hard cores, and add to the pan. Continue to cook until they have broken down and form a thick sauce. If using tinned add in their place. Add the secret ingredient – sun dried tomato paste during this process.

4) Finally add the chopped green beans and cook until tender. Check for seasoning.

Serve in pasta bowls by themselves or accompanying a lamb dish.

Juniper & Gin Cabbage

This has become one of Sheila's 'signature' dishes having consistently served it in many of the locations we lived and over many years. It's origins we think are closely linked to the need to brighten up the anaemic cabbage which has become standard supermarket fare. The recipes inclusion in the Syrian section is a tribute to the pillow like size of the local produce.

> One of the most extraordinary aspects of the Damascus vegetable souk was the huge size of vegetable the Syrians preferred. In the UK or Holland we tend to think young and small is the taste preference. In Syria all vegetables were huge. Whether this was because it made preparation easies (large broad beans for example) or they had huge families to feed (Aymans Auntie had 22 children). This picture is from Turkey but you get the idea.

Ingredients - serves 4

1 * Large green cabbage (though perhaps not Syrian size) sliced
2 * garlic cloves finely chopped
12 juniper berries slightly crushed
A good "slosh" of Gin

1) Heat a knob of butter and a glug of olive oil in a large sauce pan. When hot add the garlic and the juniper berries. Cook for +/- 30 seconds.

2) Add the sliced cabbage and stir to coat with the garlic and juniper. Turn up the heat and add a ½ cup of water. Cover with a tight fitting lid on the pan and steam the cabbage. After 5 minutes check the water has not all evaporated. Continue to steam checking the cabbage to pick the point where it is just cooked.

3) Add the gin. Now turn up the heat and stir the cabbage as the alcohol evaporates.

Drain the cabbage and transfer to a heated serving dish.

Life on the Move

Below is an image of the article that inspired the writing of our story.

EX-PAT IN THE KITCHEN By Sheila Jenkins

Arriving in Damascus in September, 1989 and being shown the local supermarkets, I gazed with dismay at the half empty rows of shelves and thought what this place needs is a Commissariat.

Three and a half years on, not even an Albert Heijn or Waitrose can ever offer the wonderful fresh selection of seasonal fruits and vegetables found here. Cabbages the size of cushions, radishes as big as tennis balls - with no loss of flavour. Strawberries, cherries, apricots, peaches, grapes, figs, plums, apples, pears, melons, dates, quinces, oranges and lemons have never tasted this good.

My shelves groan with homemade preserves, chutney, jams, marmalades and bottled fruits I couldn't afford to make in Europe; never mind give away. Pickled walnuts, apricot and cherry jam made in the sun capturing all the flavour of the fresh fruits, without hours over a hot stove. Tomato puree done the same way adds a taste of sun ripe tomatoes to winter stews and sauces along with home dried herbs.

Unknown before, mulberries make sensational summer puddings as well as jam and jelly. But mulberry liqueur has to be my biggest success. I like to think I lifted the spirits of the men we left behind in the Gulf war with my home made liqueurs.

So now I wonder will I ever make my fig chutney again or sun dry tomatoes, now so fashionable in U.K. As I cure 20 kilos of Palmyra olives and grate enormous quinces for the last of this year's liqueurs.

I've had such fun discovering new and inventing different ways of preserving this glorious harvest. Damascus is said to be the Garden of Eden. It's certainly my idea of heaven on earth - I've never been so happy in my kitchen, I'm having the time of my life.

Travels With Our Kitchen

9.0 Sarawak - Back to the Jungle, Nov '93 – Sept '96

Returning to Sarawak, 25 km up the Borneo coast from Brunei, contained shades of a home coming. We knew the ropes and what to expect. This time we were not hosted, first night, as we had been in Brunei in the Company guest house. We immediately set up camp in the 'purple' palace. There were 21 coconut trees in the garden. These were to become immortalised by the search for the perfect "pinna colada" rum & coconut milk combination. Meal number one was barbequed king prawns (colour coded as to when ready to eat). I took on the heavy job of 'colada' taster. First we had to break into the coconuts through their heavy husks. A job that's never easy and one where the risks of serious injury increase exponentially as the drink tasting progressed. Luckily no injuries were inflicted but at a certain moment the lads were called to take over the barbeque and I fell over into bed. Another blessing was that on our first visit to the Miri boat club we met up with Rob and Eveline van Rijmsdijk, and their two boys, who we had known in Damascus. Now we really felt at home.

Work did not get off to the best of starts. As a department Head I was in line for a company car. With Sheila's back problems we thought it sensible to get an automatic so she could drive. The request was stonewalled. I felt there was some hidden agenda at play and was not much pleased. I immediately went into Miri town and bough the first automatic car, a Proton Saga, which I could find. We decided to only have one car and I would cycle to work. The second problem, all be it a little later on, was that having brought my bike from Damascus to cycle to work the 'speedometer' was stolen on the first day of use. At least I had the bike. Not for long. Whoever had the speedo came back the next day and stole the bike.

Another abiding memory was calling home (on the new-fangled "duty" mobile phone) from the fish market to check on the acceptability of whatever was the fresh fish catch of the day. Fouzia our amah (home help), who was a sea Dayak, used to hate duty weekends as it would often end with her feeling obliged to help prepare the 2 kg of baby squid I'd inevitably bought.

During our 3 year stay we developed the habit of when returning from UK leave to stop off in Kuching, the capital of Sarawak. We always stayed in the Holiday Inn but would eat out at the stalls or in Chinese restaurants. We also always visited, and inevitably buy from, Nelsons Gallery.

Here we are enjoying the company of Nelson owner of the gallery from which we acquired almost all our extensive collection of Iban artefacts. We have carved crocodiles; the front and back staircases from an elevated Iban long house; and I have the world's largest collection of tun-tuns (Iban hunting sticks). We also bought several contemporary paintings by Ramsey Ong and a small Iban blanket printed in the traditional way but done on silk.

As an aside we had always enjoyed eating at Far Eastern "stalls" - what is now known in the west as "street food". At the Miri stalls, just outside town and close to the beach, the purchasing, eating, and paying process went like this. Each stall would have on offer its particular speciality. For example "Singapore noodles", or one of our consistent favourites',

"Clam's in Black bean sauce", cooked by the most cheerful 'fat' momma. You ordered whatever combination your appetite desired stall by stall. This even extended to beer. There was a single 'beer' stall. The plates of food were delivered to your table, from each separate stall, as and when cooking was complete. The best bit was payment. The stall holders each had their own coloured plates. The stall holders calculated their share of the bill by adding up the number of their colour plates, blue, yellow, red, or whatever, you had on the table and charging pro rata.

I had been sent to Miri Shell to be Head of the Well Engineering department. Suddenly from being responsible only for myself in Syria here I had some 25 to 30 engineers to supervise. Two things helped me make the transition. By this time Drilling Engineers had morphed into Well Engineers and it was now much clearer what we were all supposed to do. All the engineering necessary to design, and drill oil, or gas, wells. The other aid was the engineers themselves. Several of them were always ready to help when I needed their support. During the second half of my 3 years I became involved in the re-engineering of the company forced on us by being technically bankrupt. I call it re-engineering because though we made lots of peoples jobs redundant, including my own, we had in fact to recruit some 600 new people because we didn't have the right skill profile in our staff for the stage of exploration and production operations we were in. Overall the company shrank from 4,500 down to 1,750. Luckily less than 70 people faced forced redundancy.

Living essentially "on the beach" meant that Sheila was quick to develop the habit of every morning walking along the beach for exercise. A variation of the Damascus stadium walks. Another continuation from Syria was chutney making. Miri was also memorable because Sheila was asked to contribute an article, **"Ex-Pat in the Kitchen"** to be included in a Shell publication **"Life On The Move"**. Shell wives memories of their experiences moving between assignments in different countries. This article, included in the Damascus chapter above, was to become the inspiration for this cook book. Sheila again made her own foodie luck and tracked down Benjamin, Chinese restaurant owner, who was prepared to run cookery courses. Somewhere in our travels we had lost our copy of the original recipe instructions. Luckily, Eveline who was on the course with Sheila did not lose hers. On a visit to us in Edinburgh in 2012 whilst this book was still under construction they very kindly gave us a copy. This allowed the inclusion of some of our favourite Miri dishes.

Less of a high light, but having a big impact upon our lives was the increasingly painful problems with Sheila's back. Having had a laminectomy in Edinburgh in 1968 she was lucky to escape the repercussions for so long. The first issue we faced was as she could not have an MRI scan in Sarawak where should we go? We chose Perth, Australia, on the basis that if the diagnosis was bad, and an operation was immediately necessary, having it done in a place where English was the native tongue was a good idea. As it turned out the problem was scar tissue, a bit like water pipes furring up in hard water areas, was limiting the sciatic nerves room to move and causing intense pain. She would eventually have the operation done, during special leave I'd taken from work, back in London in April 1996.

Having presented the final "re-engineering" report to the Shell directors in Kuala Lumpa in July '96, and gained their approval for our proposed reorganisation, we were given 3 months to implement it. Having eliminated my own job I knew this heralded my transfer to another operating company. Luckily I managed to find a job back in The Hague. We were on the move again.

Prawn Laksa

We discovered Laksa at a small restaurant called "21". In fact at one point it became a Saturday, after shopping, lunch time special. It is however very easy to knock up for yourself. The secret, we think, as with many other Eastern recipes is having good homemade chicken stock. Every time we have chicken we boil up the carcase with onion, carrots, celery, bay leaf, and a few pepper corns. Cover with water, bring to the boil, and simmer for 2 hours.

Ingredients - serves 2

50g medium rice noodles (we now use Amoy 'gluten' free)
2 - 3 tblsp laksa paste
*1 * 400g tin half fat coconut milk*
500ml chicken stock
150g large cooked prawns (you can of course cook these yourself)
Handful of bean sprouts
¼ cucumber seeds removed and sliced into match sticks
A bunch of coriander leaves to garnish

1) Put the noodles in a bowl and pour over boiling water. Leave to stand for 5 -6 minutes.

2) Heat a pan and add the laksa paste and a splash of coconut milk. Fry for 3 - 4 minutes then add the rest of the coconut milk and the stock. Bring to the boil, give it a stir, and simmer for 2 minutes.

3) Add the prawns to the mixture and allow to heat through. Finally stir in the bean sprouts.

4) Divide the noodles between two bowls (heated if in the West). Ladle over the soup sharing the prawns. Garnish with the coriander leaves and the cucumber matchsticks.

Saffron Rice

An essential addition to our diet especially in the Far East was rice. We started off with plain "boiled" rice as no doubt we had learnt from our parent's time in Singapore. Once you get into the swing you discover that there are of course many different varieties. Wikipedia quotes the number as being 40,000. Of these it lists some 80 varieties by name for Indonesia which would include Kalimantan, the southern half of Borneo. In addition a reference states that there are in total some 40 "wet", and 150 "dry", field varieties grown in Indonesia. Surprisingly Thailand, where rice is central to their diet and "kin khow" their version of bon appetite means eat rice, only has 6 varieties. With this vast choice there are many differing ways to cook it. Here is one method.

Ingredients - serves 4 to 6

2 oz butter
Seeds of 4 cardamoms
3 cloves
3 * 1 inch sticks cinnamon
1 onion finely chopped
12 oz long grained rice washed & soaked for 30 minutes
1 ¾ pints chicken stock
1 tsp salt
¾ tsp saffron crushed and soaked in 2 tblsp boiling water for 20 minutes

1) In a medium sized saucepan melt the butter and add the cardamom and the other spices and stir fry for 2 minutes until aromatic.

2) Add the onion and continue to cook for 8 to 10 minutes..

3) Now add the stock to the pan, with the salt, the saffron water, and the rice. Cover the pan and cook for 12 - 15 minutes until the rice is tender and all the liquid has been absorbed.

Remove from the heat, gently stir with a rice spoon, and transfer to a hot serving dish.

Saturday Morning Squid

When we were in Miri, unlike the early days in Brunei, cheaper air tickets meant more visitors. In one such period we had both Sheila's mother, and Tom a friend of Kevin's on his round the world "gap' trip who had arrived with a burst eardrum, staying. As mentioned before I used to buy squid on a Saturday morning coming home from having completed my drilling operations duty in the office. Having no doubt persuaded Fausia, our amah, to clean the squid we had Rob and Eveline with their two boys Floris and Maurits join us to help eat the results of our efforts. Eveline's presence was vital as she brought the old fashioned fat fryer. If you don't have an amah here's how to clean squid.

First you pull the head and tentacles away from the body of the squid. Then from the body you remove the thin quill and rinse out any guts. Take care as there will be an "ink" sack which if it bursts will blacken everything. The next job is peel off the coloured "skin" from the sack. This is easier the fresher the squid. Now cut the tentacles off from the head by cutting through just in-front of the eyes. Try not to rinse too much with water during this cleaning process.

Ingredients - serves 8

1 ½ kg baby squid - sacks cut into rings and the tentacles halved
1 ltr sunflower oil - for deep frying
1 cup of corn flour
Salt and pepper to season the flour
2 lemons quartered

1) Fill the deep fat fryer with oil and carefully begin to bring to heat.

2) Put the flour in a suitably sized plastic bag and lightly season with salt and pepper. Thoroughly mix together.

3) Add the quid to the flour mix and thoroughly coat by sealing the top and giving the bag a good shake.

4) With the oil to heat 180 C if you have a thermometer (or test using a small square of bread) cook the squid in several (say 3 or 4) batches by firstly shaking off any excess flour before frying until golden. This will only take a minute and you do not want to overcook. Remove from the fryer onto kitchen paper and keep hot. Continue until all the squid is cooked.

Divide among 8 bowls, squeeze over the lemon, and eat with your fingers.

Clam Chowder

Another example of how Sheila had to adapt to local availability was this chowder. It uses the ingredients that were available from the local Smarts supermarket. Tins of John West clams; Green Giant cans of sweet corn; frozen "blocks" of white fish (cod or haddock); and any kind of bacon we could source.

Ingredients - serves 2

Knob of butter
Small onion finely chopped
Bacon cut into small dice
2 medium potatoes peeled and cut into small cubes
250 ml Milk
250 ml stock (chicken or fish)
1 bay leaf
Frozen block of cod defrosted and cut into cubes
Small can of sweetcorn
400 ml tin of clams - drained juices retained
Freshly ground Sarawak black pepper & a little salt
A good a handful of chopped parsley

1) In a medium sized pan melt the butter. Add the chopped onions and gently sweat down until soft. Add the bacon dice and fry until just cooked through. Now add the chopped potatoes. Cover the vegetables with milk and stock, add the bay leaf, and slowly bring to boil. Simmer for +/- 15 minutes until the potato is just tender.

2) Drain the sweetcorn and add to the soup. Bring back to the boil and then add the cod cubes to the mixture and continue to simmer until the fish is almost done.

3) Add the drained clams to the soup and again bring back to the boil. Taste and check the seasoning. Fish out the bay leaf. Finally garnish with the chopped parsley and stir in to amalgamate the components.

Serve in warmed pastor dishes

Old English Pork Casserole

Regular visits to the early morning "pork" market, reliance upon Eveline's (who had trained to be a surgeon) anatomy knowledge, with subsequent selection and purchase demanded an extensive selection of pork recipes. This recipe is simple in its preparation but with good ingredients delicious in result.

Ingredients - serves 4

6 oz leeks
1 oz oil
1 ¾ lbs pork
2 oz seasoned flour
½ pint ale, or cider, or white wine
Dash Tabasco sauce
Piece of lemon peel
3 oz button mushrooms
Sprigs of Thyme, a bay leaf, and a handful of parsley
Salt and freshly ground Sarawak black pepper

1) Clean and thinly slice the leeks. In a suitably sized casserole add a splash of oil and sweat down the leeks on the hob over a medium heat.

2) Prepare the pork by cutting into nice bite sized chunks. In a plastic bag add the flour and season with pepper and salt. Add the pork chunks and shake to evenly cover all the meat.

3) Once the leeks are sweated down increase the heat and add the flour coated pork and fry, stirring to lightly brown all sides, for 5 minutes.

4) Add the ale (cider or wine dependent upon availability & taste), the dash of Tabasco, mushrooms, Thyme, bay leaf, and handful of parsley. Bring to a simmer, and check the seasoning.

5) Cover the casserole with a tightly fitting lid and place in a pre-heated oven 160 C and cook for 1 ½ hours. Take the casserole out and test that it is done.

Set aside to rest for 10 minutes. Serve with mashed potatoes and a green vegetable.

Barbecued Chinese Spareribs

One of the more intriguing issues raise by telling these stories has been "Where to include" some of our long standing favourites. These ribs whilst cooked in several places are included here to give expression to their "Chinese" style. It is also for sure that they were on the Sarawak menu and would have been barbequed there rather than the more European approach of 'oven' cooked.

Ingredients - serves 4

1.4 kg pork spare ribs
½ tsp each salt and freshly ground black pepper

Barbecue Sauce

2 tblsp light soy sauce
2 tblsp hoisin sauce
2 tblsp tomato puree
4 * large cloves garlic peeled
1 * thumb sized piece of fresh root ginger roughly chopped
2 tblsp Chinese rice wine
1 tblsp sugar
1 tblsp sesame oil
2 tsp chilli bean sauce

1) Skater the spare ribs in an oven proof dish in a single layer and evenly season with the salt and pepper. Place in a pre-heated oven, 140C, for 1 ½ hours. Set aside to cool as this should be done well in advance of the final cooking.

2) Add all the barbeque sauce ingredients to a bowl and whisk together to amalgamate.

3) For the final cooking again arrange the ribs in an oven proof dish as before and pour the barbecue sauce over them. Stir and turn the spare ribs until evenly coated in sauce.

4) Barbeque the ribs until nicely caramelised or place in a pre-heated oven, 180C, and cook the spareribs for 30 minutes.

Serve immediately accompanied with finger bowls as this is finger licking food. A salad on the side could be good as well.

Stir Fried Ginger Beef

This is an adaption of a "Benjamin" recipe. He used MSG in many of his recipes and Soda bicarbonate (meat tenderizer). We avoided both. Almost the best part of this revised recipe is eating the rice covered with the tasty ginger beef juices. Sheila's way with rice in given below.

Ingredients - serves 2

A) Marinade

50 mls water
1 egg
1 tblsp Oyster sauce
½ tsp light soy sauce
2 tblsp corn flour
3 tblsp sun flower oil
Dash sesame oil

B) Flavouring

2 tblsp sunflower oil
2 tblsp oyster sauce
½ tsp sugar
1 tsp light soy sauce
1 tsp dark soy sauce
pinch freshly ground black pepper
1 clove finely chopped garlic
1 cup of stock
1 tsp sesame oil
Corn flour to thicken

C) Ingredients

350 gm steak
1 large "thumb" of ginger very finely sliced
6 spring onions cut into 3 cm lengths
Extra ginger & spring onion to garnish (optional)

1) Cut the beef (steak) into long thin 'biting' slices and marinate in ingredients (A). Set aside, stirring occasionally, for at least 30 minutes.

2) Wash the rice and set to soak in a sieve in water. When ready drain the rice, add to the pan, and cover with water to a "finger" thickness depth. Place on the heat and bring to the boil. Cover and cook for 11 to 12 minutes. Set aside in a warm place.

3) Put the oil in a hot wok and stir fry the beef. Once just cooked remove the beef and drain. This may have to be done in two or more batches. Set aside and keep warm.

4) Add a little more oil and deep fry the ginger slices. Remove, drain, and set aside.

5) Add the garlic to the wok and fry until fragrant. Add the 'flavourings' (B) and let it simmer. Next add the 'ingredients' (C) and continue to stir fry.

6) When the mixture is boiling thicken with the corn flour dissolved in water.

Serve in attractive bowls with the rice. Garnish if doing with the ginger and spring onion matchsticks.

Stir Fried Salt & Pepper Squid with Chilli & Spring Onions

We always enjoyed eating salt and pepper squid or prawns at Benjamin's (he of the "Supreme Baking and Cooking Institute" - see below) restaurant. The recipe below seeks to recreate this treat with some twists that Rick Stein details in his Padstow Seafood School book **"Seafood"**. There are only two secrets with squid. One, the fresher the better. The ease of removing the purple membrane from the squid's body will let you know. Two, do not overcook. I've added the salad even though I know we couldn't get English 'watercress' in Sarawak but it is a great addition.

Ingredients - serves 4 as a starter

750 g squid (two small or one mid sized squid per person would be OK)
¼ tsp black peppercorns
¼ tsp Sichuan peppercorns
1 tsp Maldon salt
1 - 2 tblsp sunflower oil
1 medium hot chilli deseeded and finely sliced
3 spring onions nicely sliced on the diagonal

Salad

1/3 of a cucumber halved and deseeded
50g beansprouts
25g watercress
2 tsp dark soy sauce
2 tsp roasted sesame oil
1 pinch caster sugar
1 pinch salt

1) Remove the head and guts. Pull out the quill. Clean the squid using as little water as possible. Slice open the sack, remove any remaining guts. Score the inside with diagonal cuts which do not penetrate through the flesh.

2) Cut the cucumber into matchstick sized strips. Toss with the bean sprouts and watercress and set aside in the fridge. Whisk together the soy, sesame oil, sugar and salt.

3) In a small heavy bottomed frying pan, over a medium heat, carefully roast the black and Sichuan peppercorns until aromatic. Tip into a mortar and coarsely crush. Add the salt and stir in.

4) Bring a wok to a high heat. Add half the oil. Stir fry half the squid for +/- 2 minutes until it just starts to take colour. Tip onto a warm dish and repeat with remaining squid.

5) Return the first batch of squid to the wok and add 1 good teaspoon of the salt and pepper mix. Toss together to coat the squid for a few seconds. Now add the sliced chilli and the spring onions. Again toss together for a few moments.

Divide the squid between 4 bowls. Add the dressing to the salad mix and quickly toss together. Add the salad to the squid and serve immediately.

Travels With Our Kitchen

Benjamin's Cookery School - Miri 1994.

Sheila has managed in one way or another to attend a local/regional cookery school in most of our overseas assignments. Sometimes it has been thanks to the friends and acquaintances we have met in each area. At other times it has been more 'formal'. Such was the case in Miri. She attended, along with long term friend Evelien van Riemsdijk, who we have to thank for the copy of the course contents and recipes, Benjamin's grandly entitled:- ***"Supreme Baking and Cooking Institute"***. The 10 week, 10 day, programme is detailed below.

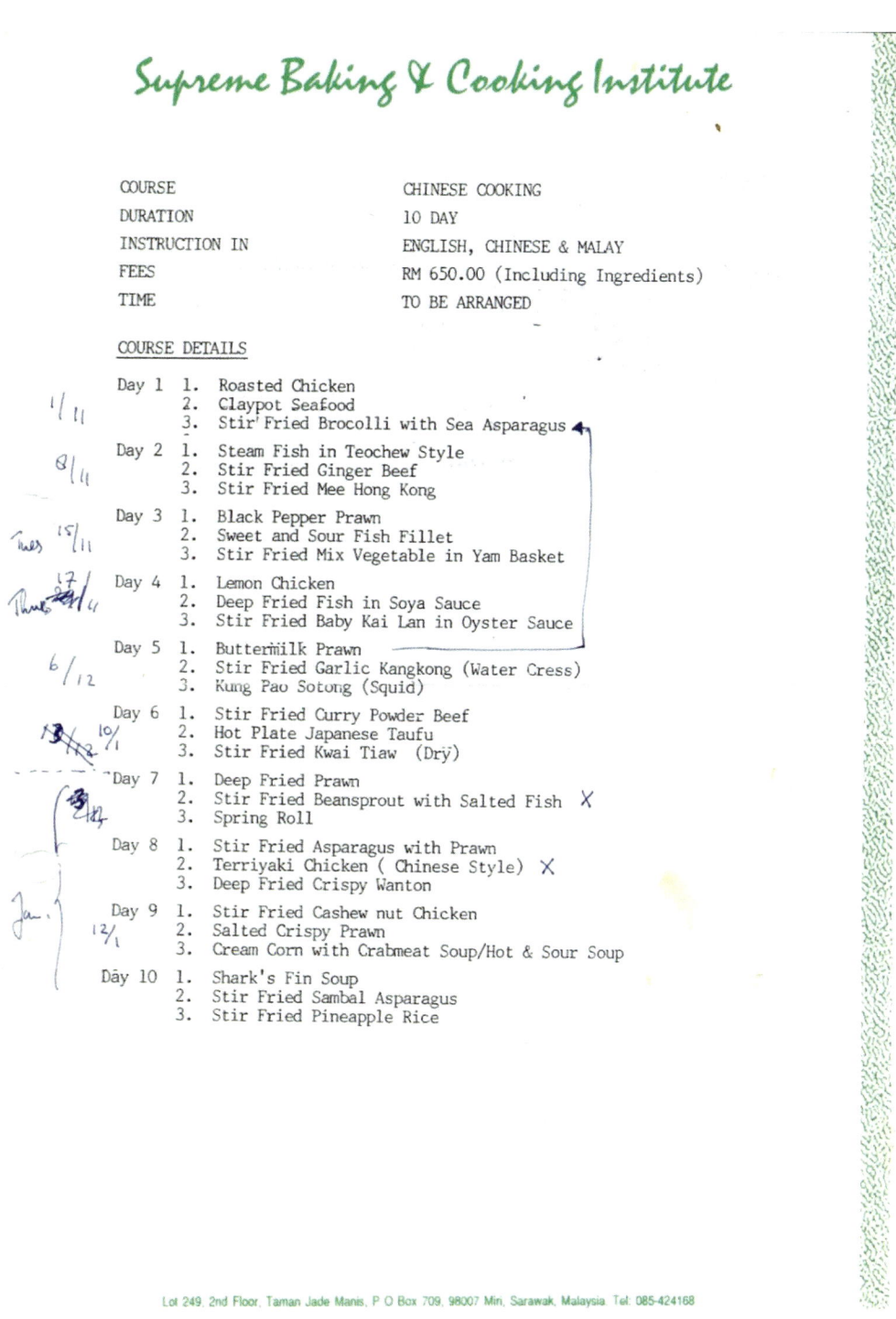

Supreme Baking & Cooking Institute

COURSE	CHINESE COOKING
DURATION	10 DAY
INSTRUCTION IN	ENGLISH, CHINESE & MALAY
FEES	RM 650.00 (Including Ingredients)
TIME	TO BE ARRANGED

COURSE DETAILS

Day 1
1. Roasted Chicken
2. Claypot Seafood
3. Stir Fried Brocolli with Sea Asparagus

Day 2
1. Steam Fish in Teochew Style
2. Stir Fried Ginger Beef
3. Stir Fried Mee Hong Kong

Day 3
1. Black Pepper Prawn
2. Sweet and Sour Fish Fillet
3. Stir Fried Mix Vegetable in Yam Basket

Day 4
1. Lemon Chicken
2. Deep Fried Fish in Soya Sauce
3. Stir Fried Baby Kai Lan in Oyster Sauce

Day 5
1. Buttermilk Prawn
2. Stir Fried Garlic Kangkong (Water Cress)
3. Kung Pao Sotong (Squid)

Day 6
1. Stir Fried Curry Powder Beef
2. Hot Plate Japanese Taufu
3. Stir Fried Kwai Tiaw (Dry)

Day 7
1. Deep Fried Prawn
2. Stir Fried Beansprout with Salted Fish
3. Spring Roll

Day 8
1. Stir Fried Asparagus with Prawn
2. Teriyaki Chicken (Chinese Style)
3. Deep Fried Crispy Wanton

Day 9
1. Stir Fried Cashew nut Chicken
2. Salted Crispy Prawn
3. Cream Corn with Crabmeat Soup/Hot & Sour Soup

Day 10
1. Shark's Fin Soup
2. Stir Fried Sambal Asparagus
3. Stir Fried Pineapple Rice

Lot 249, 2nd Floor, Taman Jade Manis, P O Box 709, 98007 Miri, Sarawak, Malaysia. Tel: 085-424168

Travels With Our Kitchen

Classes were run in the morning. Each of the 10, 1 per week, lessons was made up of a complete 3 course meal. The lessons end with eating the results for lunch.

> With us having been in Brunei, and Sheila having had a good exposure to Chinese / Indian cooking there her time at Benjamin's was more about refining techniques rather than learning new recipes. The more memorable and long lasting tips are given below:-

- Going to the Miri and Lutong vegetable markets and being given a tour by Benjamin in which he named, and explained the use, of the cultivated and wild vegetables available.

- Butchering a chicken. Benjamin boasted that he could feed 30 people from one whole, and complete (feet; liver; heart; & etc), chicken. This perhaps was a little exaggeration but it certainly contains a profound lesson.

- Cooking tips:- Blanch your vegetables before stir frying it helps retain their colour and their crunch. Sweet and sour prawns - coat with "Birds" custard powder for deep frying. Also Heinz tomato ketchup is good for additional sweetness. Egg white & corn flour is perfect for "velvetting" chicken and prawns (a version of light batter)

Supreme Baking & Cooking Institute

SALTED PRAWN — medium size.

Ingredients: A

Prawn	- 600 gms
Egg	- 1 No.
Tapioca Starch	- 3 Tbsp

Seasoning & Flavouring Ingredients: B

MSG	- 1 tsp
Salt	- 1 tsp
5 Spice	- 1 tsp

Garnishing Ingredients C

Spring Onion	- Some) Cut to fine pieces
Red Chilli	- 2 Nos)
Oil	- For deep frying

Methods:

1. Prepare, clean and devein the prawns. Wipe them dry. Add in the eggs and then coat them with the tapioca starch. Set aside.
2. In a heated wok, pour enough oil to deep fry the prawn till done. Dish out and set aside.
3. Pour the deep fried prawns to a wok and add in the B ingredients and then the C ingredients. Stir fry for a while until well mixed. Dish out and serve immediately.

> This recipe, perhaps more than any other, has gone through several evolutions and has been repeated, especially with squid ever since. A westernised version, much closer to how we would do it is given above

10.0 Den Haag – Dutch City Life, Oct '96 to Sept '99

The period of our departure from Sarawak, and arrival in Holland, was very rushed and highly stressful. I started work on the 1st October 10 days before the start of a training programme that I was to 'manage'. I imagine we first stayed in a hotel whist we house hunted but to be frank I cannot remember anything other than the trauma of my new job. There was also the on-going issue of Sheila's recuperation from her recent back surgery. To this was added the fact that, still in severe pain, she was referred to a 6 week "pain management" programme in the UK. During her period there I received the Miri shipment in our small apartment. When the shippers left there was only a small tunnel unoccupied by boxes connecting bedroom to toilet to front door. And that was with the garage filled. It was among the worst moments of my life.

Our second stay in Holland was to be very different from our first. Firstly we lived in Willems Park, on Zeestraat, in the very heart of Den Haag, close to the Peace Palace. Secondly we were, as in many cities, within walking distance of a village like area with its own specialist baker; multi lingual delicatessen; excellent wine shop; butchers that featured game; an excellent vegetable shop; and fishmongers.

These all offered a wide range of extremely high quality produce designed to tempt the many foreign diplomats who lived in this area. A far cry from the 'milkman's' van round we had relied upon in the North. Den Haag, the capital of the Netherlands, is a very easy place to enjoy life. It's easy to get out of the city. Ten, or max fifteen, minutes are all that's needed. Living in the centre of the city meant we could get every delicacy you need, and eat at any of the excellent restaurants, all within walking distance.

Our return to Holland meant we could again link up with Geraldine and John Rose who, after periods in Norway and Egypt, were again based in Germany. They would visit us and we would go through to them. In fact one of our first visits was to drive my newly acquired Ford Granada estate through to them with an ex Miri rattan couch on the roof, and the cushions and coffee table in the back. Gifts to help Lucas, and Katherine, Rose set up home and equally important help us downsize. These meeting arrangements were augmented by a variation – we would meet half way, at what we called the outback, for windsurfing and barbeques. There was a shallow meer (lake) close to the border which was just perfect to windsurf on. This satisfied one of my continuing sporting loves. The other, ice hockey, was also sorted by discovering a recreational team set up at the ice rink in Zoetemeer outside the Hague. Here after 11:00 at night a group of us would be put thorough ice skating drills for ½ an hour and then slit into 2 teams for a ½ hour knock about. Our coach was a Canadian who had once played for Holland. Our one big game, against a team of young college kids who being Dutch were all over 6 feet tall, was memorable for the margin by which we were beaten and also because I, selected to play offence, managed to score a goal.

Our Hague time was pretty difficult for Sheila. There was the continuing struggle to recuperate, and get strong again, after the back surgery. With the Shell families we knew being scattered all across The Hague, and its surroundings, there was little community spirit. It was quiet a lonely existence soon to be made worse by me working outside Holland for much of the last couple of years of our stay.

I had initially been transferred to Holland to be Shell's Head of Well Engineering Training working in the Leeuvenhorst Centre, in Nordwijk. I did not shine in this job. However it did keep me in touch with "learning" events (as they were called) across the several Shell Business Units. I was asked if I would be happy to help make up a guinea pig audience to assess a new 3 day workshop programme called the "Shell Leadership Challenge". I accepted and at the end of the trial programme I also volunteered to train to become a facilitator. After much seriously intense effort, and navigating the competency assessment conducted by Professor Rick Ross the programmes designer, I was one of the earliest people passed to deliver the workshop. We would run the programmes in the Royal Park Holiday Inn hotel, Soestduinen, in which Shell had influenced the design of the conference facilities to suit the presentation requirements of our programme. Very early on Sheila started joining me staying at the hotel during the 3 days of presentation. In fact she used to sit in and sometimes help out. When it was decided to do a special Leadership Challenge for the presenter's spouses she immediately signed up to attend.

This opportunity in turn led to me formally joining the LEAP (Leadership & Performance) Team in late 1997. This small team of some 40 people was tasked with changing the business culture within Shell and improving the company's return on capital invested. There were separate mini teams for each 'transformation' programme. I joined the Elite Team and we worked in support of the Exploration and Production business unit. I was to be involved in running learning workshops & providing consultancy services in the UK, Norway, Oman, Nigeria, Syria, and of course Holland. This job, and the nearly constant travel it entailed, in the last 18 months we were in Holland meant that Sheila spent many nights alone. This impacted out eating habits. When I was back in Willemspark, sometimes only for a day or two, we would eat out.

Now whilst the Dutch, as with the English, do not benefit from an instantaneously recognised gourmet reputation the reality on the ground can be stunning. We were surrounded by good restaurants. Excellent pizzas, Indonesian ricetaffle, and Singapore noodles, were available within easy walking distance. For fresh fish we used to go the short distance to Scheveningen harbour where the days catch was on sale. Scheveningen is also a great place for fish restaurants. My favourite dish became "kinder" fish and chips. The fish was a selection of off cuts from whatever was in supply deep fried. This delicacy was only available off the children's menu.

In mid-1999 the oil price dropped dramatically. Shell senior management, in spite of previous commitments to stick to the long term vision, panicked. Some 5,000 of the +/- 12,000 "International" staff were made redundant. I was lucky in that I had a choice. I could stay with LEAP and run a 12 - 18 month transformation programme in Nigeria or accept voluntary redundancy. We chose the latter. This meant we were on the move again. With no house in the UK we would have to head off to Limassol, Cyprus, and take up residence in our holiday home there. Before we go to the sun here are some of the Dutch based recipes we prepared during our stay.

Erwten Soup

There are some commercially prepared soups that taste better than all but their fine dining equivalents. One is the bottled "soup de poisson" we used to eat in the South of France. Another are the tins (blikjes) of Unox "Erwten Soep" we loved to eat on cold winter days. It takes 2 days to make and the key ingredient is the ham stock. As this is quite a process I'm not sure we made it when we lived in The Hague. Hence our normal reliance upon the tins.

Ingredients for the stock:-

3 lt water
1 ham hock
1 large Onion - chopped
2 big Carrots - chopped
2 Leeks - white parts sliced
1 stick celery chopped
6 Pepper corns
2 bay leaves

Ingredients for the soup

½ kg dry split green peas
½ kg dry split yellow peas
2 leeks - white and green parts sliced
1 medium sized celeriac peeled and diced into squares
1 stick celery sliced
2 medium carrots sliced
Chopped lovage leaves and parsley to garnish

1) Add the ham hock and 3lt water to a good sized sauce pan. Place on the heat and bring to the boil. Meanwhile wash the stock vegetables and chop / slice. Add the vegetables, the pepper corns, and the bay to the pan. Bring back to the boil and then gently simmer for 2 to 3 hours. Remove the ham hock and set aside. Drain the stock through a colander and discard the spent vegetables. Cover the stock and refrigerate along with the hock.

2) Soak both types of split pea overnight in cold water.

3) When ready to cook pour the stock into a large sauce pan. Drain the split peas and add to the stock. Place on the stove and slowly bring to a boil. Allow to cook at a simmer for 1 1/2 hours. Now add the leeks, celeriac, celery, and carrots. Continue to cook for another hour.

4) Ideally using a kitchen device, like a Kenwood mixer, in batches press the soup through a sieve. Once thick and smooth return to the saucepan re heat.

5) Take the ham hock and remove the meat from the bone tearing it into bite sized pieces. Add a good helping to the soup. Traditionally at this point Dutch smoked sausage is added. We not being too fond of this leave it out. Season to taste and bring back to a boil.

Serve in large bowls, garnished with the chopped lovage and parsley.

Fish Pie

A delight of living in the centre of Den Haag is the easy access to Scheveningen harbour and its fish restaurants. These, situated on the pier, often had a wet fish section. For a Saturday lunch my 'normal' choice was from the kinder (children's) menu. It was basically "fish and chips" but the deep fried fish was a range of whatever offcuts they had that day. Then after lunch we would buy whatever looked good and fresh on the slab. Fish pie became a favourite comfort dish.

Pie Ingredients - serves 4

Milk, bay leaf, 3 black pepper corns, mace 250g white, 250g smoked fish (prawns opt.)

For the white sauce
Knob butter, Corn flour
Generous handful of chopped parsley
Nutmeg, Salt and white pepper

Topping
4 large Floury Potatoes, tomatoes (optional), grated cheese

1) Lay the fish in a deep sided sauté pan and add enough milk to cover. Add the bay leaf, pepper corns, and mace. Bring slowly to the boil and cook the fish for 8 minutes. Remove from the heat and allow to cool. Remove the fish and retain the strained cooking milk.

2) Gently heat a sauce pan and add a good knob of butter and allow to melt. Now gently add the flour a little at a time until all the butter is absorbed. Now start adding the retained milk, mixing while you go, dissolving the flour and building a nice thick sauce. Add nutmeg, salt and pepper to taste. Finally stir in the chopped parsley.

3) Peel and $\frac{1}{4}$ the potatoes. Boil for 15 to 20 minutes until cooked. Mash adding a good knob of butter and season with salt and white pepper to taste.

4) Flake the fish into bite sized chunks and arrange in a layer in a shallow oven proof dish. Add the raw prawns if using. Pour the white sauce over the fish trying to cover every nook and cranny. If using tomatoes arrange the slices around the outside of the dish. Now using a fork carefully layer the mashed potato over the top of the fish. Using the forks prongs to tease up furrows in the top of the potato. Scatter over the grated cheese as this will brown up nicely when cooked.

5) Place the fish pie in the top of a hot 200 C preheated oven. Cook for +/- 40 minutes. Checking progress after 20 - 25 minutes to see if the sauce is bubbling over the sides of the dish. When cooked, and the potato ridges are golden brown, remove from the oven.

Allow to rest for +/- 5 minutes and slightly cool. Serve with peas or a nice green salad.

Bangers, Mash, & Onion Gravy

Bangers and mash had always been a poor man's stand-by. As such it went out of fashion in the '70's. The revival of the British 'banger' begun when we were in London and "Mr Parkinson", who I think lived in the West Indies, decided the only way to get a 'good un' was to make his own. The then famous "Porkinson Sausage". We used to bring them back with us after visits to the UK.

From here it migrated to up-market restaurants, for example where we eat it at "Langham's" in London. I suspect the real breakthrough was actually the addition of the onion gravy. I can assure you my Grandma had no truck with such fancifulness.

Ingredients - serves 4

For the Onion Gravy

4 medium onions cut in half and finely sliced
Small knob of butter and slash of cooking oil
1 tblsp flour
½ glass red wine
300 ml stock
1 tsp tomato puree
1 tsp English mustard
Dash Worcester sauce

For the Mash & Bangers

900 g floury potatoes
50g butter
Milk (optional)
Salt and pepper
Freshly ground nutmeg

8 best quality sausages
(meat content + 85%)

1) Heat the butter and oil in a hot saucepan and stir in the onions and cook for +/- 10minutes. Turn down the heat, season, cover the pan and cook for 30 minutes. Take off the lid, up the heat and boil off and juices. Sift the flour into the onions and then vigorously stir in the wine. When to a simmer add the tomato puree, mustard, Worcester sauce and cook for a couple of minutes. Pour into a heated sauce boat and keep hot.

2) Peel the potatoes and cut into reasonably even sized chunks. Cover with cold water and bring to the boil. Salt and cook for 15 to 20 minutes until done. Drain the potatoes, and return to the hot pan. Add the butter and thoroughly mash. Add some milk, the pepper, and the nutmeg. Beat in with a wooden spoon and taste. Adjust the seasoning. Set aside & keep hot.

3) While the potatoes are cooking lay the sausages out on an oven proof dish and cook for +/ 45 minutes in a very hot oven.

Serve the sausages with a generous helping of mashed potatoes and onion gravy.

Asparagus Risotto

We seldom made risottos before we moved to Den Haag. After eating risotto in a restaurant on Marylebone High Street, on a trip to London, Sheila became a real fan. In the early days she adapted Nigella Lawson's version from her book, *"How To Eat"*. We now know the real key to success is quality stock. It can be vegetable, chicken, or fish but ideally it should be homemade.

If the stock is good success is assured with some repeated, gentle, stirring. The other reason it became a favourite was that close by, in Piet Hendricks Straat, was an excellent Italian deli. Sheila bought her ingredients there. Risottos can be made with asparagus, mushrooms, prawns, or many other ingredients. The technique is the same. When cooking it now we happily follow our own instincts, and inspiration, in how we cook it.

Ingredients - serves 2

150 to 200 g English asparagus and extra stalks if you have them
1 ltr homemade chicken stock
Generous knob of butter
1 tblsp olive oil
2 leeks - the white part very finely sliced
3 generous handfuls of Arborio Risotto rice
1 glass white wine or vermouth
1 cup full of grated Parmesan cheese

1) Wash the asparagus and gently holding in both hands bend to snap off the tough bottom section of stalk. Cut of the spear leaving it whole, the cut the stem into 1 cm pieces. Retain the tough bottom stalks trimming off the dry bottom.

2) Add chicken stock to a sauce pan and bring to a boil. Blanch the tender asparagus pieces for +/- two minutes. Remove with a slotted spoon to a bowl of cold water. Now cook the tough stalks in the stock for 15 minutes. Drain the stalks returning the stock to the sauce pan.

3) Add the butter and oil to a hot sauté pan and gently sweat down the leek until soft but not coloured. Add the rice and thoroughly stir to coat each grain with butter and oil. Once achieved add the white wine / vermouth and let it bubble down until absorbed by the rice.

4) Now add two ladleful's of hot stock to the rice. Keep stirring until the liquid is absorbed. Continue adding a ladle full at a time, and then stirring until absorbed. Continue until the rice is just cooked al dente. This will take approximately 20 minutes. However the only way to properly judge if the rice is done is by frequently tasting.

5) Take the rice off the heat and stir in the asparagus tips. Return to the heat and reheat the asparagus. Stir in 2/3 rds of the grated parmesan cheese. Allow to 'rest' for a few minutes.

Serve in large bowls, garnish with the remaining parmesan. Accompany with a green salad.

Rabbit & Prunes

Ingredients - serves 4

2 lbs rabbit - jointed
3 rashers of bacon coarsely chopper
12 pieces dry prunes
4 tblsp brandy
3 medium sized onions finely chopped
1 glass of wine
Salt and freshly ground pepper
2 or 3 sprigs of Thyme (dried if you don't have fresh)

Gravy Browning

2 ½ tsp brown sugar
½ cups water
3 tblsp red wine vinegar
6 tblsp stock
Season to taste

1) Soak the prunes & raisins in 1 cup of water + the brandy for a minimum 2 hours.

2) Brown off the bacon in its own fat in a suitably sized casserole on a medium heat. Add the onions and sweat down. Place the rabbit joints in the casserole and add 1 cup of water, the prunes, and their liquor. Now season with salt & pepper and add the sprigs of Thyme.

3) Put the lid on the casserole and bring to the boil. Either continue to simmer on the stove, or place in a pre-heated oven 200 C or Gas mark 5, for 40 minutes. Check cooking status. Return to the oven / heat and cook for a final 20 minutes. Check the rabbit is cooked and seasoning is OK.

4) Add the brown sugar to a sauce pan over a medium heat and stir until melted. Remove from the heat. Continue to stir as you add the ½ cup water, the red wine vinegar, and 6 tablespoons of stock. Once amalgamated pour the stock over the cooked rabbit.

Serve with strong green vegetables and crusty bread.

Sheila's Fantastic Hamburgers

Sheila had for many years being treating us boys to her take on **Fay Maschler's** grilled hamburger recipe featured in her 1987 book *"Eating In"*. We didn't follow her salt-grilling method but simply oiled the burgers and fried them. This recipe, somewhat later, achieved the highest acclaim from our son Kevin. In the early 2000's **Jamie Oliver's Naked Chef** books had inspired lads to cook. Kevin, living in North London, took up a flat mates challenge to cook a better hamburger than his version of Janie's. He phoned us in Cyprus, at our expense, to demand this recipe. Fortunately for family pride he won. This is how it's done.

Ingredients - serves 2

250g good quality minced beef (not too lean)
1 shallot finely chopped
1 egg yolk
1 clove of garlic, crushed through a garlic press
1 tsp gluten free soy sauce or Worcester sauce
Freshly crushed black pepper corns – a good pinch
Sea salt – a generous pinch
Olive oil

1) Add all the ingredients, except the olive oil, to a mixing bowl. With your hand mash all the ingredients together until thoroughly mixed. Form the mixture into two evenly sized balls. Flatten each ball between your hands into your desired hamburger diameter / thickness. We normally go for a thickness of +/- 3cm. Transfer to a plate, cover with cling film, and place in the fridge

2) Place a heavy bottomed frying pan on a high heat and leave until very hot. In the meantime take the burgers from the fridge and brush both sides with olive oil. Season with a little sprinkle of salt and pepper.

3) When the frying pan is at heat carefully add the burgers to fry. Allow to fry for a couple of minute and then carefully flip to the other side. Now keep flipping the burgers every minute or so. The objective is to achieve a nice seared brown crust. This should take 4 to 6 minutes. Using a digital probe test the core temperature. The burgers will be medium rare at a temperature of about 68C.

4) Remove to a warm plate and rest for a couple of minutes.

Serve with chips, in our case with Sheila's gluten intolerance we miss out the buns, and add a mixed leaf green salad.

Sautéed Kidneys in Brandy and Orange Sauce

Kidneys have always been a favourite at our table. Normally in the places we were able to get kidneys the choice was lambs as we didn't buy pigs. In The Hague we were, thanks to the excellent butcher in Bankerstraat, able to get veal's kidney. Taking inspiration from Josceline Dimbelby's recipe in her book **"A Taste of Dreams"** we substituted veal for the lamb kidney specified for the original. Here is the method which will result in one of the most luxurious, tasty, suppers you can imagine.

Ingredients - serves 2

2 large red onions or 3 - 4 banana shallots halved and sliced
Butter and olive oil
1 veal kidney cored and sliced
1 tblsp oregano or rosemary
3 tblsp (+/-) plain flour seasoned with freshly crushed back pepper & a little salt
Juice of ½ a lemon
Juice of 1 orange (a carton of juice is OK)
2 tblsp brandy
4 - 5 floz single cream
A handful of flat leaf parsley chopped (garnish)

1) Add a knob of butter and a glug of olive oil to a pre heated, ideally heavy bottomed, frying pan. Carefully sweat down the onions until they are translucent but not coloured.

2) Dip the kidney slices in the seasoned flour and lightly coat. Add them to the onions and gently fry for 2 - 3 minutes. Stir in the herbs, lemon juice, and orange juice. Gently simmer, occasionally stirring, for another 2 - 3 minutes. Do not overcook. The kidney needs to be slightly pink in the middle.

3) Pour the brandy into the pan and when mixed in add the cream and stir in. Garnish the chopped flat leaf parsley.

Serve in large, hot, bowls poured over a pile of mashed potatoes with a green vegetable and or a green salad.

12.0 Cyrus - Life in the Holiday Home, Oct '99 to Jun '04

As a child I had lived in Cyprus for 6 months in 1956. My father had been stationed at RAF Fayed, on the edge of Egypt's Great Bitter Lake, and we had flown out to join him on the 5th July 1955. However after 4 or 5 months there, with Nasser coming to power, we were evacuated by troop ship to Cyprus. On arrival at Famagusta the brass band played as we transferred to busses to be driven through the night to a housing compound in Beringeria Village. My father was to be stationed at the newly set up Akrotiri air force base. The compound, which included a school and a cinema, and probably much else I can no longer remember was ringed by barbed wire and patrolled by the British army. The EOKA terrorist campaign for Enosis (independence) was in full swing and bombs used to be thrown over the wire every now and then. Of the few things I can recall one of the most vivid is crawling through the barbed wire to get to the adjacent river bed and shoot rocky lizards with my catapult.

Later in life in London we were to meet Chris, and Nana, Themistoclaus. He was born in Limassol and still had most of his family there. Soon after our arrival in Damascus, Syria, we heard they were visiting Limassol. Sheila flew over to meet up with them. This was to prove very fortuitous because the deal with Al Furat for the Shell secondi's like myself was that we would work 3 months (6 days a week) and then get a short break. This was followed by another 3 months and a half year leave. Then 3 months' work, short break, and finally an end of year proper vacation. As we had rented out our Kenilworth Court, Putney, apartment we needed another bolt hole for these short breaks. We chose to go to Cyprus.

At that time (end '89) Syria was in desperate shape. Limited food was imported. All local produce was strictly "seasonal" and variable in supply. Plus the use of "night soil" and the prevalence of disease meant that to stay healthy uncooked vegetables were a no-no. As eating camel or goat did not come naturally we were also pretty restricted as to our protein intake. Visiting Cyprus, which at that time still followed its age old traditions re the supply, and preparation of, its Greek cuisine was for us a food paradise. To help supplement the Syrian fare we soon purchased a large Coleman, steel framed, cool box. This we would load with goodies and ship back to Damascus. At times this weighed over 30 kg and the Customs lady at Larnaca airport came to recognise us. The final twist was in order to dissuade the Syrian customs from too close an examination we used to say the contents were "haram" (forbidden for Muslims)

Later in 1997 whilst living in The Hague, in combination with Chris and Nana, we were to buy a holiday property in Limassol. Chris heard of 2 apartments (1st and 3rd floor) which had never been lived in which were for sale. If both were bought together the price dropped to the very attractive. We jumped at the chance and also signed up for Chris's renovation plans. This subsequently became our second home.

We (well certainly not me) had never imagined that I'd be in a position that "accepting redundancy" from Shell was to be our reality. If the job provides the house - redundancy is two losses, income and the roof over our heads. As Cyprus at the time was the only home we had that was where we went. When we moved there full time we brought with us many previously acquired preconceptions to our full time retirement in 2000. Our memories were of sunny days, long lunches, cheap and rustic vegetables and fruit, and delicious calamari & chips at the BEMAS 'club'. Some things remained unchanged but much was completely changed and not always for the better. We started off well enough. We soon got the apartment sorted out with the arrival of our shipment from Holland. I assumed I would easily get another job so set to writing "application" letters. This it would transpire was not about to immediately come to pass. Meanwhile we joined the local Limassol Hash and through this started to meet other expats.

I started to recycle masonry from old buildings and built a garden on the patch of land beside our building. Sheila organised a birthday party for me with the instruction that if guests wanted to give a present then something to grow would be much appreciated. We eventually had three olive trees, a lemon, and a pomegranate tree. We also grew a selection of herbs and cacti.

Another route we pursued to meet new people was to join, at the invitation of some fellow Hashers, Toastmasters. This was a partial success. As with the folks from the Hash we had a mixed reception with the toastmaster's members. At issue was the fact that many expats had sold up in the UK, when they moved to Cyprus. Over time they were confronted by a constantly rising cost of living. With UK house prices now far exceeding Cypriot ones they could not afford to return home. In a sense they were financially trapped. As we had a Shell pension, our flat in Edinburgh, and two cars we experienced for the first time in our lives how corrosive jealousy could be. On a positive note Cyprus was an ideal place for outdoor activities. I bought a bike; the windsurfing on Akotiri beach was excellent; and with snow on Troodos mountain in the winter I taught myself to snowboard. Sheila did lots of cooking for the Hash; enjoyed walking the Limassol beach 'walk' way across the road from the flat; and continued to make plenty of chutneys. We also introduced the idea of retirement "away days". We would go off for picnic's or barbecues on deserted beaches; visit Roman ruins; visit the Turkish North when the border opened; or just go off and try new faraway restaurants.

On the eating out scene all the traditional fare was still just available, all be it in fatal decline. A few traditional tavernas still remained where the food was good. We also liked the "Famagusta" restaurant on Avdimou beach. However the food was steak pie, or fish and chips, rather than Greek. On the whole the Limassol hotels, and restaurant's, were disappointing. Expensive and debased by the knowledge that tourists, unlikely to return, could be palmed off with plenty of cheap wine and mediocre fare. One favourite restaurant from the early days was never visited again after our attempt to have a quiet night out was ruined by them catering for coach loads of tourist. There was one other issue that only became obvious with full time residency. In the winter restaurants' were in general unheated, and therefore extremely cold. The prospect of eating rapidly chilling food whilst frozen did not encourage us to extensive winter time eating out. Finally the hotels, even the supposedly 5 star ones, failed to inspire. Perhaps it was because in Cyprus the 5 stars were awarded for "room size" rather than quality.

There was one new arrival that was a notable exception. "Little Plates" offered a Greek related, but heavily international influenced, cuisine. Roddy, who was a South African Cypriot, had run a large restaurant there before coming to Cyprus. Little Plates made reference to a menu that consisted of some 25 to 30 small, meze style, dishes. Deep fried celery leaves were a particular favourite. Once he was established he ran cookery lessons to which Sheila naturally signed up for. A flavour of this experience is given at the end of this section.

My first retirement project was to write a review, "The Transformed Shell", of my last few years work in Shell helping to reorganise Sarawak Shell, and then later on my experiences in the LEAP Team. Then through an acquaintance I was asked to do some consultancy work for a small Limassol company - Audah Group. They wanted a job ranking, and performance assessment, system designed for them. After this I decided to try and get additional work. This led to me working through another small Cypriot based company, ORCA Ltd, writing and delivering 2 or 3 day workshops on a whole range of subjects to clients in Quatar, and Abu Dhabi. Ultimately it was to be through this company that I bid on, and won, a contract to do consultancy work on the implementation of a Balanced Scorecard for Oman Refinery.

The developing reality on the ground in Cyprus was not improving. Under the emotional leadership of a newly elected, ex EOKA terrorist, President Tassos Papadopoulos the Greek South rejected the prospect of "unifying" with the Turkish North of the island. In spite of reneging on an agreed deal to reunite the island Cyprus's entry to the EU went ahead. That was marginally OK but of course it went hand in hand with extortionate, escalating prices. Given subsequent events they may have been better off being refused entry. Some things remained in spite of the creeping invasion of a multitude of cheap concrete buildings; and increasing waves of "personal space" unaware Russians. There was still the Limassol market; it was possible to buy tomatoes that were field grown & ripened in the sun; and the calamari & chips at the BEMAS club, close to where we lived, was excellent. However we were becoming increasingly aware of the limitations imposed upon us of a continuing divided island, a sharply rising cost of living, and rubbing along with ever more miserable, hard pressed, UK expats. When the opportunity of doing some consultancy work in Oman materialised we jumped at the chance. To close the story when the 3 month Oman assignment morphed into a full time job we decided in 2007 to sell flat 101, Green Valley. It was bought by an acquaintance who had been renting it from us. With all the subsequent problems there are many the occasion when we thank our lucky stars we are out of there. Below are the recipe equivalents to some of the highlights of our stay.

Elisabeth's (Liz's) Pate

We had not appreciated it when we just "holidayed" in Cyprus but full time living revealed just what a small, and limited, expat community there was in Limassol. In our Shell life, particularly when overseas where the host Governments insist on higher qualifications (often a degree) before a Work Permit will be granted, we had unconsciously got used to well-educated, and worldly, acquaintances. In Limassol we met, and rubbed along with, for the most part regular people. Football, horses, and the price of Cypriot brandy, were the things of their daily lives. I for one missed the 'intellectual' challenge of a good discussion. It was however available at Liz's dinner parties. In a previous life she, and her husband of the time, ran a restaurant on Crete. So you knew the food would be good. She was also a formidable intellect, and sought out similarly endowed guests. With the discussions always came Liz's pate. Both were invariably extraordinarily enjoyable.

Ingredients - serves 4

1 kg pork - ½ belly and ½ lean
1 kg chicken livers
100 g chopped onions
225 g butter
5 cloves garlic very finely chopped
30 g salt
Pepper to taste
1 Cyprus whole bunch (very good handful) parsley roughly chopped
Streaky bacon to line the baking tin and cover the top of the pate

1) In a heavy bottomed pan cook the onions, garlic, and parsley in butter until soft. Remove to the food processor bowl.

2) In the same pan cook the livers until they just begin to take on a little colour. Add to the processor bowl and process until a fine mouse consistency is reached.

3) Mince the pork twice if not already done by the butcher. Mix into the mouse and season with the salt and pepper. Fry off a small sample and check the taste. Re season as necessary.

4) Line a large pate terrine with the streaky bacon rashers with each rasher being stretched and flattened using the back of a knife. Carefully add the pate mix on top of the bacon until the terrine is nearly full. Cover the top of the pate with the remaining streaky bacon rashers.

5) Cover the top of the terrine with a double layer of aluminium foil carefully crimping the edges to form a good seal.

6) Place in a bain marie and add water to a level half way up the side of the terrine. Cook in a pre-heated oven at 180 to 200 for 1 to 2 hours. The time variation depends upon how shallow the terrine is. In a shallow dish it will cook faster. Test using a clean skewer. When it exits the pate "dry" it is cooked. Set the pate aside to cool.

Refrigerate. The pate will keep for up to 3 weeks if kept refrigerated.

Baked Fish with Fennel & Rosemary

This approach to baking a whole, if you're lucky decently sized, fish was inspired by a Nigel Slater recipe included in the *"Marie Clair Cookbook"* for whom he wrote.

In the original recipe Nigel uses red snapper. A fantastic choice if you have it. Otherwise you may have to fall back on, as we did in Cyprus, the more humble species, and fish farmed at that, bass or bream. Whatever this cooking method keeps the fish moist and the fennel and herbs add a wonderful fragrance.

Ingredients   Serves 2

1 medium whole fish (bream, red snapper, sea bass) scaled and gutted
2 large bulbs fennel
2 medium red onions
4 cloves garlic
1 lime or lemon
1 tblsp fennel seeds
4 small sprigs of rosemary
Parsley
1 bay leaf
4 tblsp virgin olive oil
Green pepper corns
Salt and freshly ground pepper

1) Pre heat the oven to 190 C. Clean and thinly slice the fennel bulbs. Place the fish on top of the sliced fennel in a shallow baking dish. Peel and slice the onions and add to the dish.

2) Crush the garlic with the flat of a knife and add to the dish along with the lime, or lemon, thinly sliced. Scatter over the fennel seeds, and the bay leaf. Finally add the chopped parsley, and fennel fond if available.

3) Pour over the olive oil and season with ground pepper, salt, and green pepper corns. Cover with aluminium foil and bake for 25 minutes until the fennel and onion are tender.

Set aside to rest for a few moments. Serve with a mixed leaf salad and crusty bread.

Imam Bayildi (The Imam Swooned)

Over the several years we had visited Cyprus I had dutifully bought beautiful dark, purple, smooth, shiny skinned, aubergines every time they were in season. These would be proudly brought home, shown off to Sheila, and then refrigerated. After a couple of weeks, and much failed inspirational talk about how to cook them, they would be thrown out with a heavy sense of guilt. This year I vowed to finally do it, cook Imam Bayildi. And cook this dish I did. It wasn't necessarily a pretty sight and at one point I was asked, "Are you putting a lot of love into your cooking?" At that moment NO I WAS NOT. I had lost my house keys on returning from the local kiosk (paper shop) via the garden where I did a spot of impromptu weeding. Skinning the tomatoes was not going well. A combination of poor eye sight; forgetting to cut crosses in the bottom of each tomato; and probably not leaving them in the boiling water long enough. And my excuse, "It's the tomatoes they are too new / unripe / old / wrong sort / etc..." Anyway I struggled through this minor crisis and went on to cook my dish. There was one further cause of extreme stress that at a certain moment nearly led to the ingredients being dumped in the bin. I was trying to cook using the most interesting parts of THREE recipes. The spices from Sarah Woodward **"The Classic Mediterranean Cook Book"**; the preparation of the aubergines from **"The Real Greek"**; and not bothering with salting the aubergines from Alistair Little's **"Food of the Sun"**. End result huge confusion for significant lengths of time. However, the end result was extremely tasty, and well worth the effort. It provided excellent fodder at the picnic after the weekly Sunday run on the HASH, and for Tuesday lunch. Eaten cool, or room temperature, the paprika and the ground allspice really combine in a splendid extra dimension to the taste. I didn't swoon but the end result was worth the earlier humour failure.

Ingredients   Serves 6

4 - 6 medium, shinny skinned, aubergines
1 - 1.5 kg plum tomatoes skinned & chopped
2 onions peeled & finely sliced
3 - 4 cloves garlic crushed & chopped
1 spoonful magic ingredient (sun dried tomato paste)
1 tsp sweet paprika
1 tsp ground allspice
Salt & freshly ground black pepper to taste
Large handful finely chopped parsley (keep some back for garnish)

1) Wash the aubergines and chop off their tops. With a sharp potato peeler cut strips of skin off top to toe to leave alternating strips skin on - skin off. Don't bother salting. Best buy really bright fresh plump medium sized aubergines. Cut a deep slash in each aubergine that will be the pocket for the other ingredients when baking. Place the aubergines in a bowl and micro wave for 5 minutes on high. Remove and leave to stand draining off any excess liquids.

2) In a medium hot, oiled, frying pan sweat down the sliced onions and garlic. Whilst this is underway pour boiling water over your tomatoes not forgetting to cut crosses on the bottom of each one. After 2 minutes in the water remove and skin. Be patient & don't lose your temper. Once the onions are translucent add the tomatoes which you have by now cut into chunks. Add also the dried tomato paste; the sweet paprika; the ground allspice; and a good part of the chopped parsley. Bring to a slow bubble and cook for 15 minutes stirring regularly.

3) Take the partially cooked, and now cool enough to handle, aubergines and carefully prise open the cut pocket. Place them in an oven proof dish into which they just neatly fit. Pour the tomato & onions into and over the aubergines. Bake for 40 minutes in a 190 C / Gas 5 oven.

4) Reward yourself with a drink. My recommendation would be Kasara Arak from the Lebanon if you can get it. After the cooking time is up, and assuming the aubergines are now very soft and tender, set aside to cool.

5) Sprinkle the remaining parsley over and eat at mid-day temperature (remember this could be anything from 25 C to 45 C and if hotter you shouldn't be cooking !!!) with pita bread.

Travels With Our Kitchen

Cyprus Village Salad

I don't really know why but salads have always proved a daunting task for me. Quite early on in my kitchen life I became a 'wizz' at creating salad dressings. Feeling at ease, and creative, with the crinkly green stuff was to take many more years. As I think about it I find it difficult to put my finger on just what the blocker was. What unblocked it is much more easily recalled. This was learning that a Cyprus village salad had in it what vegetable / salad things you had in the fridge. Simple as that. Don't worry if the ingredients are 'supposed' to go together. Only ensure that the building blocks are fresh and clean. Then once assembled add virgin olive oil and if you like a good squeeze of lemon juice.

One other tip. It is possible to buy very good, and sometimes quite fiery, rocket nearly all year in Cyprus. We are not talking tidily little leaves that here in the UK are called 'wild' and cost a fortune. We are talking large dark green leaves where it is the taste that is wild not the price. Salad items in Cyprus are sold all at one price. Anything between 15, and 25, cents each. (say 20 - 30p UK). Lettuce; spring onions; rocket; radishes; parsley; coriander; dill; and lambs lettuce; all fall into this one price fits all category. As an example of quantity forget UK supermarket little triangular packets and think more of a bunch of parsley that is so large you can just about get your hand around the stalks.

This is not a recipe but more an idea of what you could do with the leaves you have in the fridge.

Garlic cracked & rubbed around the bowl or for a special dressing
A lettuce - in the UK we find the "Little Gem" variety excellent
1 bunch of rocket (in Cyprus the leaves are very large so need to be made bite sized - I tended to chop not tear so that the leaves didn't bruise)
Spring onions
Several tomatoes (if you like you could skin & chop them into small squares)
Cucumber de-seeded and chopped into small squares
Selection of herbs based upon availability
Celery
Lambs Lettuce (small plump light green leaves that worked as a laxative very well)
A cabbage - good in winter very finely sliced as a lettuce substitute

1) Carefully wash any muddy salad ingredients and spin dry in a salad spinner.

2) Start by gently cracking a fresh garlic clove by bashing with the flat of a knife. Then cut it in half and rub the cut side around the inside your chosen salad bowl. Now tear up some lettuce leaves and place in the bottom of the salad bowl.

3) Next align all the rocket leaves with the stalks all at one end and with a sharp knife slice diagonally starting with the top of the longest leaves and working all the way down to your fingers holding just the end of the stems. Sprinkle over the lettuce.

4) Next add spring onion. One, or two, large ones or if you have smaller ones use 3, or 4. Again slice on the diagonal starting at the white, bulb, end and working up into the green leaves. You don't need too much of the green.

5) Now add the chopped tomatoes as much for the colour as anything else and the chopped cucumber.

6) Finally chopped the available herbs (parsley, chives,

7) Good additional possibilities are celery, especially the tender leaves. Another favourite is radishes. One caution here if you have plenty of fiery rocket then cut back on the quantity especially if the radishes are 'mind blowers'.

8) If you want to be fancy and create a Greek salad then add broken lumps of feta and a few black, smoked, olives.

Baked Sea Bass

An island should have fish. Well not Cyprus. Every restaurant is offering fish, or fish meze's, but if you ask "Where is the fish market?" you get a blank look. Well we know where the fish market is. It's in the 'Old (just recently very ably re furbished) Limassol Market. And we now know that the identically sized Sea Bream, and Sea Bass, are farmed just off shore. Also we accept that the squid comes frozen. What may come from the sea are the few sad immature, pre breeding, random fish species occasionally seen. Little hope here of a fishing revival. However if the storm is severe enough it disrupts the fish farms and the fish escape. Being naive they are easily caught and were in good supply. If you go up the coast and your timing is right there are buckets full to be had. Now all you need to do is scale and gut them. Cut off the fins with a good pair of scissors. De scale with the back of a knife. Then degut by going in at the bum with a sharp knife and cutting up the gut until just under the jaw. Pull out the guts and quickly rinse.

Here's our favourite ways to cook them. Its inspiration was a recipe in the Good Housekeeping, taken from the **"River Café Cook Book Easy"**. Adapted in time estimates because of the time it takes me to de scale and gut the fish and their small size. Also because we grow our thyme in a window box (as well as the wild Cyrus thyme taken from the hills and replanted in our 'bit of dirt') you don't need to bother stripping the leaves from the small branches. Just bung in a whole handful of tender thyme and knock some leaves off over the dish after cooking.

Ingredients   Serves 2

2 equally sized Sea bass - scaled and gutted
½ kg medium waxy peeled potatoes
50 g (good sprinkling) black olives I like the wrinkly smoked ones
Similar amount of caper berries rinsed
Good slug (glassful) dry white wine
Handful fresh thyme sprigs
Extra virgin olive oil (Uncle Bambos's olive oil, which when we got it had a very misty look to it, had now settled to a beautiful deep green colour and was excellent. The fact I helped pick the olives has no influence on my unreserved recommendation of it)

1) Boil the potatoes in salted water until just cooked. Cut lengthways into 1 cm slices. Line a roasting tin with baking parchment and drizzle with olive oil. Lay out the potato slices in the bottom of the tin. Add the fish on top and salt and pepper, put some of the thyme in its belly and lay the rest on top. Scatter over the olives and capers.

2) Put into the pre heated oven (200 C) for 5 minutes. Now pour the wine over the fish and drizzle with a little more oil. Bake for a further 15 - 20 minutes, depending on fish size, until cooked. Take out of the oven and lift the fish out. My experience, especially with smaller fish is that you need to skin them and cut the fillets off the bones. This is not an elegant, or easy, task. However if done reasonably well it pays dividends as when eating you won't be fighting the bones that whole time.

3) Place the potatoes on a warm plate and pile the fish on top. De leaf some of the sprigs of thyme and pour the juices from the pan over the lot. Eat well.

Black Virgin Olive Oil

There was still one place, undeterred by HSE restrictions, which still made virgin olive oil in the old traditional way. This is not really a recipe but homage to the olive and a record of our privilege attending this ritual on several occasions. The first year in Cyprus I had volunteered to help Uncles Odysseus, and Bambos, picking olives. In fact you don't pick you place netting on the floor and "rake" the olives from the tree. In this day and age you take your harvest to the local 'factory'. There they are transformed into olive oil with I guess that you are taking away the oil from some of your olives as well as the neighbour ahead and behind in the queue. Below are the photo's & brief descriptions of how in every village across the island it used to be done.

Step 1, OK after the real step 1 which is harvest your olives from the tree, is to 'crack' the olives. As you'll see from the picture this is really the work of 'donkeys', or if it's during the school holidays, and only for a few minutes children. I think this was one of the last, outside, stone wheels in Cyprus.

The olives, now cracked, were loaded into the flat woven baskets. Here three are loaded into the press. The screw of the press is then tightened down onto the olive laden baskets. Here the children are again the 'motive' force. However the shear effort to squeeze the last drops of oil requires heavy force to the wooden handle slotted into the square base of the threaded press.

The virgin, cold press, olive oil now drains off to be collected in a large pottery bowl. This is not the end of the process however. The pressure on the olive filled basket is released and boiling water is pored over the 1st pressed olives and then they are pressed again. The result is still "virgin" olive oil but not cold pressed and now you need to separate off the water.

Ingredients

Fresh cold press Virgin olive oil
Toasted Cypriot village bread

1) Take a slice of freshly made warm toast. Gently pour olive oil over the toast. Eat.

Prawn Saganaki

Of the recipes that were included in the "Little Plates" cookery school demonstration this meze dish was one of Sheila's favourites. When referring to the handout that Roddy prepared to support the cooking demonstration Sheila remembered that some of the ladies did have some issues with how they were written. The origin of this was probably that Roddy was "thinking" about the cooking in a restaurant style environment. Also he was writing in what was for him a foreign language. The recipe below whilst true to the original has some home cooking modifications.

Ingredients - serves 4 small plates

Olive oil
1 large onion finely chopped
1 tsp dry oregano
1 * generous glass white wine
2 * large, ripe, tomatoes grated
2 tblsp tomato paste
1/2 ltr water
A pinch of sugar
Salt and freshly ground black pepper
200 g uncooked prawns (or mussels see below)
100g Feta cheese coarsely crumbled

1) Sauté the onions and oregano in a little olive oil until translucent

2) Add all the other ingredients except the sea food into a sauce pan and bring to a boil and allow to simmer for approximately 30 minutes or until the sauce becomes rich and aromatic. Season to taste.

3) If making the prawn version now sauté them in a non-stick pan with a little oil until they begin to colour pink. Then add them to the sauce. Allow to simmer for a few minutes.

4) In the original Roddy does suggest that you could use mussels in place of prawns. If so they would have to be cleaned and de-bearded discarding any that refuse to close if tapped. They could then be added to the sauce, brought to the boil, and stirring occasionally simmered until mussels opened.

5) Finally crumble the Feta cheese into the seafood sauce gently stirring it in and allow to simmer for a few moments.

Serve on small plates as a starter.

Little Plates (Roddy's) Cooking Lessons

Roddy, who was a South African Cypriot, arrived in Limassol soon after we moved there on our first "go" at retiring. Southern Cyprus was at a 'transitional' stage where it was shedding its traditions and getting ready to become "European". Strangely this hollowed out the dining out options. There was still a few, actually very few, places like the BEMA club where you could still get honest 'peasant' food. The so called 5 star hotels where expensive and not an attractive proposition if you were a resident. Also the vast bulk of restaurants catered for the "tourists" where there was no need to take too much effort because they probably wouldn't come back and anyway all the rival restaurants where happily ripping them off to.

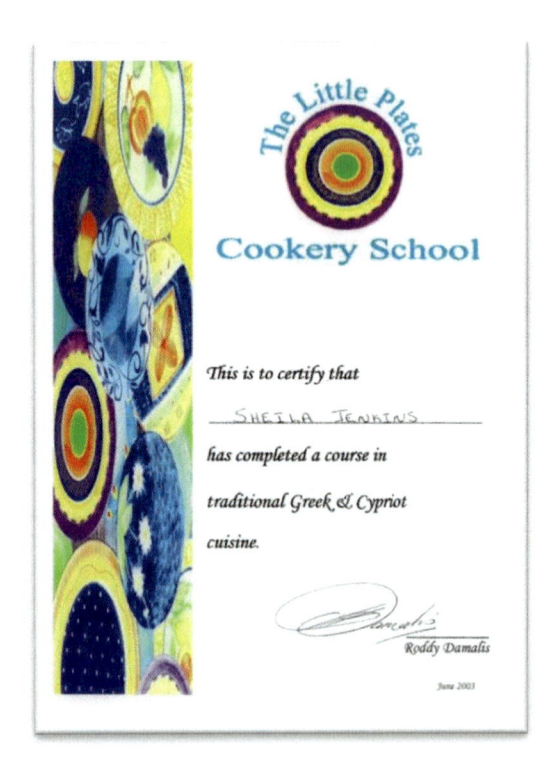

Little Plates was a real breath of fresh air. Quite small with a menu that comprised, as the name dictates, a large and diverse selection of I guess you would say 'meze' / starters. Rather than order starters, main course, and pudding you ordered say 3 or 4 meze dishes> Each person choose to their fancy and then you all shared by tasting a bit of everything that was brought to table. Particularly memorable for me was his "deep fried celery leaves". The Cooking lessons, June 2003, got going about a year or 18 months after the restaurant became established. His lessons which covered everything from starters to filo pastry ran over a 10 week period. Below are the happy students having eaten their best efforts.

Travels With Our Kitchen

12.0 Oman - 3 Months Become 7 Years, June '04 to Sept '11

Through a Cyprus based company I bid on, and won, a 3 month contract to do some consultancy work for the Oman Refinery Company (ORC), Muscat. As Sheila & I had enjoyed our previous visits to Oman we naturally planned to go together. The plan being for me to go first, sort out a place to stay, then Sheila would join me. I found a serviced apartment in the Safir Hotel. This consisted of a bedroom, bathroom, and small kitchen. This, unknown to us at the time, was to be our base for 6 months. Round the corner from the hotel was a small, Indian run, food shop. This was our initial source of most of our fare. Slowly with the car hire sorted, and our memories refreshed as to the location of supermarkets, we expanded our food sources.

A new colleague at ORC, and someone who was to make our Oman stay (eventually stretching to 7 years) beyond memorable, was Faisal Al Riyami. He introduced us to the PDO Club fishing competition. This was held on +/- 9 Thursday mornings a year (once a month except for high summer) and ran from 06:00 am to 12:00. There were several 'prize' categories. Bottom fish, & trawling, where only 5 of each species could be weighed. Also "Catch of the Day" - the heaviest fish. And finally an overall winner - the person credited with landing the heaviest total catch.

As my job at the 'Refinery ended just prior to Christmas we packed our suitcases and returned to Cyprus. No sooner had we got home than the phone rang - Oman Gas Company who I had talked to when in Oman wanted me to join them and to do the same +/- 6 month 'consultancy'. A new contract was drawn up and I flew out before New Year. I had hoped to stay again at the Safia apartments but they were full. Instead I found a small top floor flat to rent. Once set up and sorted Sheila joined me. Working essentially for myself I did not have a work permit. I would get a 1 month visa on arrival which could be extended for a further month. Then you had to leave the country. The job with Oman Gas was not as enjoyable as working in the 'Refinery' but the time soon passed and again our minds turned to "what next"? I had been talking to Petroleum Development Oman (Shell) in the hope of getting some work. The lady I met directed me to Gary Plank who worked for a company called IPEDEX. He needed somebody to do a 3 month assignment in PDO Contracts Department. He also offered us the use of a flat for a couple of months. We accepted the job and the flat. No sooner had I started this job than Gary told me about another job. An Omani company, Shaleem Petroleum LCC, had been awarded a 5 year contract to provide 5 small drilling rigs to work repairing existing PDO oil wells. They needed an Operations Manager. I accepted the job and for a couple of weeks managed to work both in PDO, and for Sheikh Abdul Aziz Al Mahri Chairman of Shaleem. I stayed for just short of 18 months working for Shaleem. I helped them mobilise 2 new rigs from Italy and build up the company from +/- 50 staff to over 180. There were some issues though. The way they executed the work for PDO broke many of the fundamental rules of 'best oil field practice'. We started to have an ever increasing number of 'lost time' injuries. I was unable to change the way the Sheikh worked. We also had huge "cash flow" problems and had essentially fraudulently increased our loan facilities through a local bank.

Travels With Our Kitchen

We did manage to pay the salaries on time but suppliers were left to try to get their bills paid. The Sheikh was related to the Sultan of Oman's family and few where prepared to challenge him. He therefore sought to maximise this advantage. Meanwhile angry service providers where chasing me around super markets screaming demands for their overdue bills to be paid. The final straw was one of our rig workers losing his thumb in an accident that happened completely due to company negligence.

We again started to pack the bags in preparation of leaving. However IPEDEX, now renamed SPIE Oil & Gas Services, won a 5 year Manpower Supply Contract to provide staff to Occidental Petroleum's Safah, and Mukhaizna, onshore oil fields. They needed a Contract Manager. I eagerly accepted. The real clincher in the decision was Town House #7 that came with the job.

It was an upside down house. Being built on a pretty steep hill the living area was at street level at the front and the bedrooms were downstairs at the back. We had a small garden where the two original mature date palms were joined by three lime trees and a range of exotic grasses that we planted and tended. Fresh limes just off the tree are a sheer joy. There was also the basil, which grew, and a number of other herbs that were decidedly iff'y.

Once I had a proper job I was able to get an Oman Work Permit. Only with this could you open a bank account; get a driving license; buy a car; and absolutely vital get a Royal Oman Police "Liquor Permit". The license allowed the purchase of a fixed, Rials Omani (OMR 100.00), amount of booze a month if bought through one of the official liquor stores. This new sense of permanence encouraged us to regularly enjoy the Oman fine dining scene. The Mumtaz Indian Restaurant in the whole time we were there never disappointed and introduced us, and a group of visiting French colleagues, to Indian wine. The main hotels, The Hilton, Al Bustal Hotel (managed by the Intercontinental Group), and the Chedi, all had excellent restaurants. Of particular note, and included at the end of this section, the Al Bustan Hotal had for too short a period hosted Shannon Bennet's "Vue" restaurant. A real joy after the privations of Cyprus.

A big feature of our life in Oman was Hashing, and Camping. Both posed different but interesting food challenges. Sheila would often take popcorn for the kids and dips for the adults to the regular Saturday (first day of the working week) Hashes. Camping especially in the summer with temperatures in excess of 45 C posed different demands. A ready prepared meal for the first night which could be eaten only after the tents was up, and the fire was lit. One standard food offering was frittata; anther was Ku Ku, an Iranian version of a frittata. Breakfast tended to be very traditional, bacon, Sheila's pre-cooked tomatoes, and eggs (we can't agree on baked beans but I know we did them) all done over the open fire. Breakfast was my job. We always insisted on making real coffee our preferred brand of pre ground being the Dutch Douwe Egberts, vacuum packed, filter blend.

Travels With Our Kitchen

During our 7 years in Oman naturally much changed. When we first arrived most trips outside Muscat, say to Seifa beach, or up Jabal Tanuf, involved serious off road driving. By the time we left almost all corners of the country were connected by new highways. As with the roads the food supply infrastructure was updated and expanded. The small, Indian run, corner shops which once were the source of much everyday food virtually disappeared by the time we left. The traditional fish, and vegetable, markets in Mutrah however continued as they had done possibly for hundreds of years. The fish market in particular, especially after the cruise ships started docking regularly, seemed to be on the "tourist" agenda. Best to be avoided on those days. However on any normal day it was the most fascinating of places. Half of the market was taken up displaying a wonderful array of freshly landed, whole, fish. The other part was taken up by the fish scalers, and gutters. Once you had bought your fish they prepared it. The adjoining vegetable market was also a joy. Garlic from Al Jabal Al Akhdar; bananas from Salalah, dates from Nizwa, oranges from I know not where; and an array of local herbs. Another source was of course the modern, new, supermarkets that had joined the existing Al Fair shops. Much of their food was imported. Fresh beef from Australia; frozen pork from Brazil; and lamb from among other places Pakistan. Oman produce included fruit and vegetables; it provided the fish, and the chicken (two standard sizes) and eggs (which seemed to last forever).

Lastly our Oman Christmas celebrations, and accompanying Christmas dinner, became an annual, shared, special event. One of the local supermarkets, Al Fair, flew in most of the traditional Christmas dinner ingredients. That fixed the menu. The other very important element was the repeat presence of special guest Faisal Al Ryami. I had met Faisal at Oman Refinery soon after I first arrived. In time he became our source of fresh fish following his usual success in the monthly fishing competitions. He was born, and brought up, in Portsmouth in the UK. His parents had been evacuated from Zanzibar when Tanzania, formed a year earlier, introduced one party socialist rule in 1962. He was brought up knowing all about, and enjoying, the traditional English Christmas festivities. From our second Christmas onwards we always invited Faisal to join us and always prepared a Christmas stocking for him. We in turn enjoyed the great privilege of being invited to his parents' house to share with the extended family Eid festivities. This always featured a sumptuous spread of goat, chicken and potato curry, biryani, with red and green chillies, followed by bought in ice cream. Once our attendance became regular Sheila took over providing home-made, Al Jabal Al Akhdar (Green Mountain) sourced pomegranate, ice cream. This gave us a very special insight into Oman family life.

Basil Pesto

The super markets in Oman imported herbs from Holland on a regular basis. We tried to grow, and keep alive, all the available varieties. We enjoyed very mixed success. Sage was the most consistent disaster. Rosemary, thyme, and oregano were pretty hit and miss always ending in miss. Basil was the only consistent success. It seemed to evolve from a frail Dutch green house plant to the rough, tough, version illustrated that was able to withstand + 40C with some success. Hence we had big pots of it that seemed to be able to re seed themselves.

There are 2 main things to do with excess basil. One is to add to beetroot and tomato salad, and the other is to make pesto. This is the pesto recipe.

Ingredients – to make about 4 small jars

150 g of basil leaves
150 g parmesan
100 g on pine nuts (snoba in Arabic)
2 cloves garlic
Good virgin olive oil
Season to taste.

1) Weigh out your ingredients and set aside in individual small bowls. Grate the parmesan cheese.

2) Roughly chop the garlic.

3) Set up your blender and add the basil leaves, parmesan, and pine nuts. Give a quick 'blitz'.

4) With the blender running slowly add the virgin olive oil until you achieve the paste consistency you find most attractive.

5) Taste and season until you have a strong fresh combination that complements the ingredients.

Salad Nicoise

Of the early and consistent pleasures we enjoyed during our 7 years in Oman was attending, at Faisal Riyamis invitation, the Petroleum Development Oman club fishing competitions.

If there was an increasing sadness over the years it was that tuna, such as you see Faisal proudly showing, just about disappeared and are no longer landed. I should add that even this nice specimen is tiny compared to some we saw caught in the early days. The Korean industrial fishing fleets allowed into Omani waters by the Government 'hoovered' up everything.

Tuna, as fresh as this, can be eaten raw. I also seem to recall that Faisal saved the livers of tuna when he gutted them. For the recipe below all you need is a couple of nice chunky steaks. One last acknowledgement – Yun Tanaka in his book **"Simple to Sensational"** includes his version of Salad Nicoise. The simple one I'd say is what we all know using tinned tuna. In his 'sensational' version he doesn't mix the ingredients but plates up leaving the fresh cooked tuna steaks whole. My take is a variation on the simple but with ample access to good quality tuna steaks they are cooked and flaked.

Ingredients - serves 4

*2 * good Tuna steaks - fresh and deep red in colour*
*4 * organic hard boiled eggs*
*8 * small new potatoes cooked*
Bunch baby tomatoes quartered
Cos lettuce leaves (heart)
Mixed salad leaves
*12 * good quality anchovy fillets*
12 – 16 pitted black (Greek) olives
Handful of green French beans cooked & cut into 4cm lengths
Virgin olive oil
Salt & freshly crushed black pepper
Lemon juice
French mustard for the salad dressing

1) To cook the tuna first oil the steaks. Heat a heavy pan to medium / high heat. Carefully lay the steaks in the pan. Watch the side of the steaks. As they cook you will notice a colour change. Turn the steaks over as you see it cooking a little way toward the middle of the

steak. Repeating this process on the second side which will take less time. With the centre still red remove from the pan and allow to cool.

2) Put the mixed salad leaves and the coz lettuce hearts into a large salad bowl. Flake the tuna into bite sized chunks and scatter over the leaves. Quarter the eggs, tomatoes, and potatoes and add to the bowl. Add the anchovy fillets on top of the egg quarters. Finally scatter the beans, and pitted black olives.

3) For the vinaigrette dressing mix 1 part lemon juice to 3 parts virgin olive oil. Add a spoon full of Dijon mustards and salt and crushed black pepper. Thoroughly mix (shake) to amalgamate into a stable emulsion. Taste for seasoning. Spoon over the salad.

Very carefully toss the salad nicoise and serve in large pasta bowls.

Travels With Our Kitchen

My variation on "Jamie's" Chorizo & Tomato Salad.

In the intro mention was made of the differing 'ingredients' we could get here in Oman. In this recipe instead of the Spanish olive oil I used Palestinian, and the wine vinegar was from the Lebanon. An observation - many less than well-known places produce really excellent ingredients.

> This combination of support for the Palestinian people, and the idea that high air miles are in general bad, was a winning incentive to buy as local as possible. It also introduced you to some sources you would not otherwise try. The ripe tomatoes were from Oman, as was the flat leaf parsley, even if the excellent baby tomatoes were from Holland

Ingredients   - serves 4

1 raw chorizo sausage (+/- 250 g) sliced/chopped into mouth sized chunks
3 or 4 large, ripe, tomatoes roughly chopped
Roughly equal amount of 'cherry' tomatoes
3 spring onions finely sliced on the diagonal
Sea salt & freshly crushed pepper (bash in the pestle)
Extra virgin olive oil (here from Palestine with that nutty, silky, taste that tells you a 'person' harvested these and was there when the oil was produced)
Vinegar - I uses wine vinegar from the Lebanon. Their cuisine is French/Turkish and they know a thing or 2 about good ingredients.
Hand-full of flat leaved parsley - copped
2 cloves of garlic   -   I used local El Jebel el Aktar garlic pungent, and 10 times better than the Chinese stuff that goes for garlic in the UK
Arabic flat bread

Method

1) Fry the chopped chorizo in a small pan with a glug of olive oil over a medium heat. Keep an eye on it and stir as needed.

2) Chop up your tomatoes as appropriate to their size. Add to a bowl. Slice the spring onions and add to the tomatoes. Season with a good pinch of sea salt, and pepper, add a glug of olive oil & a splash of vinegar. Chop the parsley and sprinkle into the bowl. Carefully toss, amalgamate, the ingredients and set aside.

3) Back to the Chorizo, which you have not forgotten to occasionally stir, and into which you are now going to add the finely sliced/chopped garlic. Once you sense the garlic cooking down add a splash of vinegar and take off the heat.

4) Spoon the chorizo and oily juices into the salad. Toss all the ingredients together and serve immediately. Accompany with the Arabic flat bread.

Masala Omelette

In my Oman job I used to travel to the interior to attend HSE meetings at Occidentals Safah oil field. As it was over 5 hours drive away I would normally stay in the "camp". All the staff worked on rotation, 12 hour shifts days and nights. The camp was a collection of port-a-cabins fitted out as 2 man accommodation. Occasionally I would have to stay in the nearest town, Ibri, some 85 km away down an unmade road. The Ibri Hotel was someway outside town on the main road to Abu Dhabi. It had AC, the sheets were clean, and evening super, always an Indian inspired minimal buffet, cost the equivalent to GBP 2.50. Breakfast was "Masala Omelette". The first serious drive we did after we bought the Range Rover Sport was a round trip Muscat, Nizwa, Ibri via the new 'mountain route. The return route was the old road to Nizwa, and then the new highway back to Muscat. An 850 km round trip. Sheila had "Masala Omelette" for the first time on this trip. The recipe below benefits from the influence of Madhir Jaffery and her book, *"Simple Indian Cookery"*. It is now a firm favourite. If you like a chilli kick this is a good way to start the day.

Ingredients – serves 2

1 big or 2 regular spring onions sliced
1 red pepper sliced up
1 large red chilli finely sliced / chopped (save some for extra garnish)
6 small tomatoes sliced in half
4 large or 6 medium eggs
½ tspn cumin seed
½ tspn cumin powder
½ tspn coriander powder
¼ tspn turmeric
A good helping of coriander leaves (garnish)
Salt and pepper to taste
Small bunch of fresh coriander leaves chopped

1) Bring a medium sized, metal handled, frying pan to heat and add a small slug of oil. Then add the dry the spices – cumin, coriander, and turmeric. Fry for a few seconds until they release their aromas.

2) Add the spring onions, red pepper, chopped chilli, and tomatoes. Fry off until soft. Toward the end of this process carefully season with salt and pepper to lift the flavour.

3) Meanwhile crack the eggs into a bowl and gently whisk,

4) When the vegetables are softened add the egg mixture and gently amalgamate. Continue to cook until the bottom and edges are cooked and firm.

5) Place the frying pan under the grill or in a preheated oven and cook off until the top is firm and the omelette cooked through.

Bring to the table and serve with garnished with chopped coriander and/or extra chilli if you like some heat.

Barbequed Yabbies - Moreton Bay Bugs

In Oman they called Moreton Bay Bugs "Oman Lobster Tails". We knew them from Sarawak. The difference in Oman was that they were I guess seasonal, never in abundant supply, and always sold whole. As you can see it is easy to understand why they are called "bugs"..

Whenever I saw them for sale, usually in the supermarket in the Sultan Centre, I would buy. I always tried to buy similar sized ones and avoided those carrying roe. In Oman they were never alive and you had to be quiet careful that they were fresh. General condition and smell were the best indicators.

Ingredients

6 - 8 Yabbies (if you can try and get even sized ones - they are +/- hand sized across their heads.

Cooking

Get the coals burnt down to a solid red glow. Place the bigger yabbies' (whole heads on) on the griddle top side (hard shell side) down. Arrange the smaller ones around the bigger ones in an effort to get them to cook at the same time. Ideally keep the tails flat. When the underside starts to bubble, and the hard outer shells have now turned dark red, they are pretty well done. Another couple of minute's bottom side down will do the trick.

Serving

Turn the cooked yabbies' onto their back. With a sharp knife cut through the membrane that connects the head to the tail very carefully. You just want to cut the flexible membrane enough to allow the tails to be pulled off. Then cut down the centre of the tail as you would a lobster tail. Break the halves open and extract the delicious, white, tail meat. Eat accompanied with a fresh salad, bread, mayonnaise, new potatoes, & etc, and a glass of chilled white wine.

Thai Chicken & Noodle Picnic Salad

This was an on the moment "made up" dish. We needed to make a picnic for 6 people and it needed to have a tasty chilli "kick" for the two Thai ladies. We had a couple of pots of (small) crayfish tails; and the other ingredients were all to hand.

The intense Oman sun is such that when you go to the beach you take your own shade. Our preferred equipment was an "Easy-Up" which saved our skin on many occasions. This is on Seifa beach to the south east of Muscat about a 1½ hour drive away. When we first arrived in Oman you had to travel a really adventurous off road route to get there. When we left there was a hard top road, a marina, a posh hotel and a golf course there.

Ingredients   - serves 4

2 Pots crayfish tails
2 hot red chilli - deseeded & finely chopped
2 or 4 spring onions finally sliced
2 clove of garlic finely chopped
1 generous handful coriander - chopped
A couple of generous pinches roasted, plain, pea nuts coarsely bashed
2 bundles Rice noodles soaked.

For the sauce

6 tbls fresh lime juice;
4 tbls Thai fish sauce;
2 tbl soft brown sugar.

1) Cook rice noodles for 1 - 2 minutes in boiling water. Drain and set aside to cool.

2) Prepare all the vegetables.

3) Put noodles & vegetables in separate containers

4) Add all the sauce ingredients to a small jar & give an initial shake.

5) Drive to picnic site, put up the "easy up", and open bottle nice dry white wine.

6) Add vegetables, and crayfish tails to the noodles and mix in gently with a fork. Give the sauce another shake and pour over the salad.

Serve and enjoy.

Lobster Tails in Prawn Sauce

The food supply chain in Oman, as noted elsewhere, was a little erratic. The upshot is if you see something new you buy regardless of price and without any idea of a recipe. Such was my purchase of 2 frozen lobster tails. Now we knew they wouldn't rival their Scottish, cooked from live, cousins. What was called for here was a 'strong' tasty sauce. So we bought a pack of frozen Tiger prawns. Should be straight forward now?

Ingredients

1 pack (2) frozen lobster tails (probably only 400 g between them)
1 kg pack frozen Tiger prawns (or fresh)
1 medium onion chopped
1 garlic - chopped
1 tin Cherry tomatoes
A good pinch of cayenne pepper
A nob of butter
Sugar
Salt & pepper
Slug of dry Martini
Flat leaf parsley to garnish

1) Defrost the prawns. Pull off their heads, and remove the legs / scales and reserve. Put the pealed prawns aside and keep.
2) Melt butter in a large pan and add the chopped onions and garlic. Sweat down.
3) Add the prawn heads, legs, and tails. Stir as they start to take colour. Add the tin of tomatoes and bring back to the boil.
4) Now add the cinnamon, rosemary, sugar, salt and pepper, and 2 teaspoons of sun dried tomato paste, and simmer for 30 minutes.
5) While the heads / shells are cooking down slice the prawns along their back and devein.
6) Bring a large sauce pan of salted water to the boil. Add the prawns and cook for a couple of minutes. Prawns are colour coded - pink / red = done. Remove with a slotted spoon.
7) In the same water cook the lobster tails also for 2 minutes or until pink. Remove.
8) After 30 minutes remove the prawn stock from the heat and using a ladle transfer some of the heads and shells to a conical sieve. Squeeze out all the juices into a bowl. Repeat until all the heads etc have been used.
9) Return the juices to the prawn stock and bring to a simmer. Add the Martini (Brandy would be better but we didn't have any) and cream. Stir and allow to rest.
10) Put the pre washed rice on and cook for 15 minutes lid on. Leave to rest for a couple of minutes.
11) Slice the lobster tails into medallions and add to the prawn stock. Return to the heat for a minute or so.
12) Serve in pasta bowls. First the rice and then the lobster and prawn sauce on the top. Garnish with the chopped flat leaf parsley

One of the lobster tails didn't look very good so we now had the most spoilt Omani cats in the world.

Jamie's Curry for Fish / Chicken / Veg

The smell of curry leaves will be a lasting memory of our time in Oman. The small Indian / Pakistani shops smelt of them as did the vegetable sections of the major stores. Making the curry paste below gave us a good reason to buy. This recipe is based on one in Jamie Oliver's ***"Happy Days with the Naked Chef"***. As with Thai cooking prepare and measure out all the ingredients before you start.

Ingredients - serves 4

5 tblsp vegetable oil
2 tsp mustard seeds
1 tsp fenugreek seeds
3 * fresh green chillies - deseeds and thinly sliced
1 handful curry leaves
2 thumb sized pieces of fresh ginger peeled & coarsely grated
3 * onions peeled and finely chopped or pulse in a food processor
1 tsp chilli powder
1 tsp turmeric
6 * tomatoes chopped in a food processor
1 * 400 ml can of coconut milk
Salt

1) Heat the oil in a pan and when hot add the mustard seeds. When they start to pop add the fenugreek seeds, fresh green chillies, curry leaves, and the ginger. Stir fry for a few minutes until fragrant.

2) Tip your onions into a food processor and blitz. Add to the spices and cook until the onions start to take on some colour and soften. Add the chilli powder and the turmeric.

3) Blitz the tomatoes in the processor and add to the pan. Cook for a further two minutes than add 2 wine glasses of water and the coconut milk. Bring to heat and simmer for about 5 minutes until it reaches the consistency of double cream. Taste a small sample carefully adding salt as necessary.

This curry sauce can be used in for vegetable, fish, or chicken curries. For a vegetable version add some 800 gram of mixed vegetables to the sauce, bring back to a boil, and simmer the vegies until cooked. Similarly for the fish curry (see the next recipe). For the chicken it is best to first stir fry the chicken pieces with some crushed coriander seeds until they take some colour. Now add to the sauce and cook for a further 8 to 12 minutes.

Fish of The Day Curry

As mentioned above we were blessed with an on-going invitation to attend, especially after SPIE the company I managed provided sponsorship, the PDO club fishing competitions. Faisal, who was a very serious fisherman having competed in International events, used to spoil us by giving us some of his catch. Often his "catch of the day". With a steady supply of super fresh fish, but highly variable in terms of species, the challenge was always "How to cook them?"

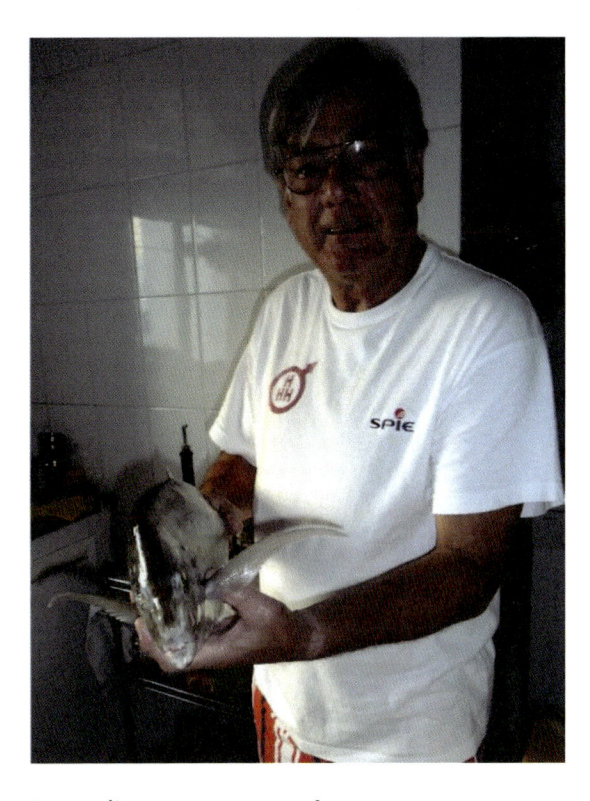

A typical fishing competition haul would include hamour (grouper); mahi mahi (dolfino); barracuda; kharodail (cutlass fish); shark; trevally; Sultan fish (goatfish); tuna; raheesa (pompano); and others species unknown to us. What we did quickly learn was that the firm fleshed fish, barracuda being a good example, were good in a curry. Now we have a chance to put Jamie's curry sauce to its intended use

Ingredients - serves 4

Pre prepared Jamie Curry Base (recipe above)
800g firm fleshed white fish (monk fish cheeks, haddock or hake if in the UK) in mouth sized chunks.
1 tsp tamarind paste
1 large handful spinach or pak choi
1 handful of coriander chopped

1) Gently heat through the pre prepared Jamie curry base until it begins to simmer.

2) Add the chunks of fish and the tamarind paste and continue to simmer for +/- 6 minutes checking to make sure the fish chunks are cook through.

3) At the end of cooking add the spinach or pak choi and chopped coriander and stir in. Keep on the heat until the spinach begins to wilt.

Serve with rice in bowls with nan bread or chapattis.

Chilli Jam

After a false start we were blessed to have as our maid (non live in I should point out) Arlene. She was from the Philippines. Before leaving home, and coming to Oman, she had been a student at an agricultural college. Probably being a maid in Oman she had better prospects than staying in the Philippines. In her time in Oman she had saved enough to buy a house and was saving with the idea of buying a minivan to rent out as a taxi on her return.

Arlene being intelligent, and sensible with money, was for the most part a joy, and a great help to us, especially as she had learnt Arabic when working in the isolated south of the country. There was however one interesting issue that earned her scorn. The prices we were prepared to pay for vegetables. I'm afraid we, who regarded the price as hopefully an indicator that it might be OK to consume, used to take the prices off before we got home. This particularly applied to the red peppers necessary for this chilli jam recipe. As she was the head 'dicer and chopper' we used to give her a jar every time we made it. We suspect once she recognised this the "chilli" hit scale was ramped up closer to her preference.

Ingredients

8 red peppers deseeded and roughly chopped
10 red chillies - depending on the chilli strength deseed as appropriate
A good thumb sized piece of fresh ginger peeled and roughly chopped
8 cloves of garlic chopped
400 g can of cherry tomatoes
750 g golden caster sugar
250 g red wine vinegar

1) Tip the chopped peppers, chillies (with or without seeds as discussed above) and the garlic into a food processor and whizz until finely chopped.

2) Scrape all of this mixture into a heavy bottomed sauce pan. Add the tomatoes, sugar, and vinegar and bring to the boil. Skim off any scum that comes to the surface. Adjust the heat such that the mixture simmers and cook for about 50 minutes stirring occasionally

3) Once the jam becomes sticky continue to cook for a further 15 minutes stirring frequently to avoid sticking. The aim is to achieve the look of bubbling larva.

4) Remove from the heat and transfer to sterilized jars. Screw on the jar tops and set aside to cool completely.

The jam will keep for up to 3 months. It should be refrigerated once opened.

Thai Pomelo Salad with Prawns

This recipe is based upon one by Ken Hom from his book *"Simple Thai Cookery"*; modified by our learning from cookery lessons in the Oriental hotel in Bangkok; and most important of all the authentic Thai help, and guidance, from Angkana. It initially came about thanks to the occasional availability in Oman of Waitrose, sustainable, north Atlantic prawns. Pomelo, imported I imagine, was in reasonably regular supply from the Sultan Centre supermarket.

The kitchen in Oman was pretty small, old fashioned, and not particularly well equipped with cupboard space. We did however have a very large fridge (cheap in Oman) and until the glass door exploded a very reliable cooker. This I must add was almost a first in our travels. In most other previous places ovens had been a serious challenge. Here Angkana, who had worked in restaurants, demonstrates the subtleties of Thai wok frying.

Ingredients   -   serves 4

1 Large Pomelo
2 medium shallots finely sliced
4 garlic cloves (more or less if you like) finely chopped
2 medium chillies - seeded and finely chopped (extra in soy sauce if you like heat)
2 spring onions nicely sliced on an angle
250 g cooked prawns (as mentioned we used smallish north Atlantic ones)
Roasted, plain, pea nuts coarsely chopped or bashed in a mortar
Juice of 1 lime
1 tblsp fish sauce (nam pla)
1 tblsp sugar
1 handful (generous) of fresh coriander leaves
Vegetable oil

Method

1) Cut off the top of the pomelo a slice at a time until the segments are revealed. The peal the skin away top to bottom. Separate the segments and remove the membrane releasing the 'tear drop' shaped fruit elements

2) Heat a splash of oil in the wok until very hot. Add the shallots and garlic and stir fry keeping everything moving until the garlic begins to brown. Turn out onto kitchen paper.

3) Flake the pomelo into a suitably sized bowl. Add the chopped chilly, sliced spring onion, crushed pea nuts, the prawns, and the fried onions and garlic. Gently amalgamate.

4) There is a possible "secret ingredient" that could be added now. This is what one version of Thai Shrimp Powder looks like

5) Now combine the lime juice, fish sauce, and sugar in a small bowl. Pour over the salad and toss gently. Garnish with the coriander leaves and you are ready to serve.

Hamour – Two Tasty Alternatives

First catch your hamour. A nice 5 kg job, see below, is good for a start. Oman does have a tremendous history / reputation for its sailors and their journeys. This tradition is kept alive by among others the fishermen. And if you're extremely lucky you may be blessed to know one who is prepared to share, after the fishing competition, 'catch of the day'.

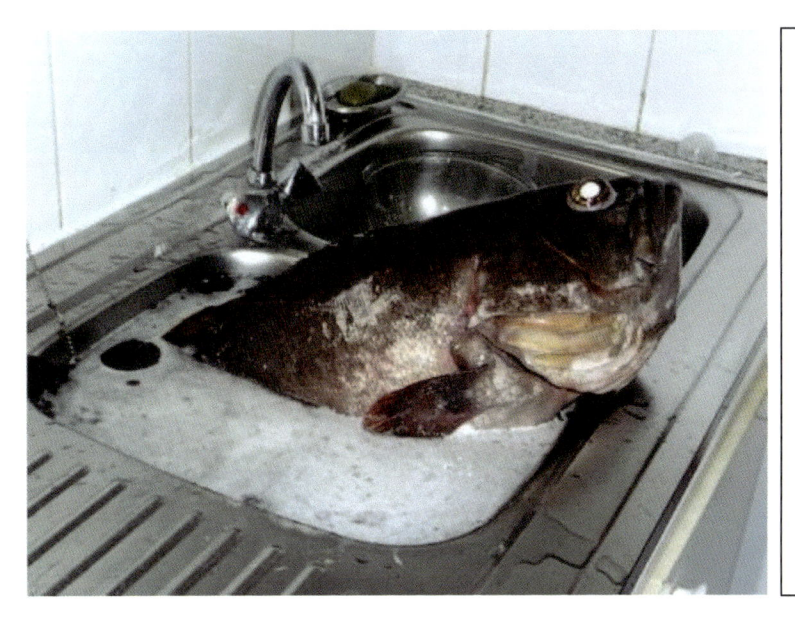

> This is what a 5 kg, 'catch of the day' Hamour skin on, guts inside, with fins to rip your fingers, looks like. It more than fills a kitchen sink. For us there was no "ask your fish monger to prepare". When you handle it is surprisingly heavy and very difficult to get a grip of. First cut off the fins with tough scissors. Then de-scale. A tip is to do this with the fish inside a dustbin bag by 'feel' to stop the scales from flying everywhere.

Next gut the fish. Insert a very sharp knife in the anus and cut up the stomach until the blade is between the lower jaw bones. Pull out all the guts. You can now either cut off the head, or cut out the gills. The gills are also surprisingly sharp so take care. Now for the last surprise. It is really difficult to make the first cut through the skin as you set about starting the filleting. Great force, and an equal amount of care for your fingers, is needed. Just get brave. Slice in at the side where the upper dorsal fin was. Once you have a big enough incision you'll be able to feel / see the bone structure. Slowly making sweeping cuts, keeping the blade aligned with the back bone & rib cage, cut off your first fillet. Turnover and repeat. It's going to look / be a bit scruffy. Tidy the fillets up knowing there will be no waste as it will go into the stock. Cut the tidied fillets into "serving" sized chinks. We used to freeze the cut offs, and any bits you can't immediately eat, to make 'Thai fish cakes' .

Hamour Steaks - serves 4

4 large streaks (skin on) cut from your 5 kg fresh Omani Hamour
Olive oil
Sea salt
Crushed black pepper

Put a heavy bottomed frying pan (or griddle) on the heat and allow it to come to a good temperature. Oil and salt the Hamour steaks. Place the steaks skin side down in the pan and cook. Watch the side of the steaks as they cook. As they cook you will see a colour change taking place and slowly moving up the side of the steak. After 5 – 8 minutes (depends upon thickness) turn over and continue to cook. After 3 to 5 minutes turn over and test by pressing a finger gently onto the steak. Like cooking cod you want the 'flakes' of flesh easily parting. Set on warm plates and serve with vegetables, and potatoes, of your choice.

Thai Fish Cakes with Cucumber Sauce

For the Cucumber Sauce
1 large cucumber
3 tblsp Thai fish sauce (nam pla)
3 tbsp lime juice
2 tblsp sugar
1 large red chilli deseeded and finely chopped
2 or 3 small shallots finely chopped
3 tblsp water

For the fish Cakes
450 g of the skinless Hamour off cuts / small steaks
2 eggs beaten
50g green beans chopped
½ tspn freshly ground white pepper
1 tblsp Thai red curry paste
3 Kaffir lime leaves shredded (place leaves on top of each other – fold in half and thinly slice)
2 tblsp Thai fish sauce (nam pla)
1 tblsp corn flour
2 tsp sugar
Bunch of fresh coriander leaves chopped
450ml ground nut oil for frying

1) Peel the cucumber, cut in half, and de seed with a teaspoon. Cut into thin diagonal slices.

2) In a bowl combine the fish sauce, lime juice, sugar, and water and stir until the sugar dissolves. Add the cucumber, chilli, and shallots and mix well. Leave to stand for 20 minutes.

3) Cut the fish into small chunks. Put the fish, eggs, white pepper, and curry paste into a food processor. Pulse into a smooth but not mushy paste.

4) Scrape the fish mixture into a large bowl and fold in the shredded lime leaves, fish sauce, corn flour, sugar, coriander, and the sliced green beans. With your hands amalgamate the ingredients such that all the elements are well mixed through.

5) Turn out the mixture onto a floured surface and divide the mixture into however many +/- 6 cm patties you can make.

6) Heat the wok to a high heat and add the oil. When very hot and smoking add 3 – 4 fish cakes a batch at a time and deep fry for +/- 3 minutes or until golden brown. Remove, drain on kitchen paper, and set aside to keep hot. Cook the remaining cakes in the same way.

Serve with the dipping sauce.

Thrice Cooked Chips

Potatoes were a problem in Oman. Either they were Saudi, large and sweet through old age, or they were from the USA in which case they are small and sweet through old age. There were a few occasions when we could get Lebanese potatoes. Not necessarily brilliant but good enough to make do.

For the purists I don't know the starch % - when we need chips we go with the flow. You do need a few hours to do this - it is after all a Heston Blumenthal recipe - so start well before you need to eat. The aim is to reach chip perfection. Crisp on the outside, but still soft on the inside. To keep things simple we don't go with the "pickled onion" spray but do feel free to add if you like.

Ingredients

4 - 6 potatoes
Sun Flower oil
Salt - quiet a lot and the best quality you have
A good book to read as this has quite a bit of 'down' time.

Method

1) Wash and peel the potatoes. Cut into chunky sized chips without being too fussy about equality of size/thickness. Rinse under running cold water. This was a problem in an Oman summer as with temperatures of 45 C +++ the cold water runs hot. Luckily our kitchen had an old fashioned wall mounted heater tank (turned off), its water was colder than the cold.

2) Put chips into a large sauce pan cover with water and bring to the boil. Simmer until the outside of the chips begin to almost crumble. Remove the pan from the heat and very carefully take the chips out using a slotted spoon / spatula. Gently place on a baking rack and once they are cool place in the fridge, or freezer for an hour to dry.

3) Fill the deep fat fryer with sun flower oil & heat to 130 C. Carefully lower the chips into the oil and let them cook until they take on a dry appearance with a slight colouring (6 - 8 minutes). Remove and drain off the oil. Turn them onto a cake tray and allow to cool. Return them to the fridge/freezer until cold and dry. If cooking a quantity it is best to do the frying in smallish batches.

4) Reheat the oil to 180 C. Carefully lower the chips into the oil and cook until golden brown. This will take 3 - 6 minutes. Remove from the oil onto kitchen paper to absorb any excess oil. Tip into a pre-warmed dish and generously sprinkle with sea salt.

Naturally they are wonderful with deep fried battered fish, but also great with steak.

Travels With Our Kitchen

Roast Chicken – Working with the Omani Chuck.

Every cookery magazine/cook book explains at great length the gastronomic advantages of using organic, free range, chickens that have been lovingly reared and humanely slaughtered. In the real world, the 85% not imagined in the Western conscious, the chicken reality is different, and possibly best not thought about too much.

Strangely in Oman the eggs had a shelf life of + 3 months, and the milk did not go off. The chickens seemed to have been 'treated' too. When butchered, they had strangely coloured joints. They also come in only 2 sizes. They were 800, or 1,100 grams. They were factory reared and I suspect full of growth hormones and other chemical unmentionables. But we still have to eat to live so we accept, and adapt, to what was available.

Actually, and perhaps thankfully, chickens are not 'free range' in Oman. Why? Because with summer temperatures at 45C, and over, the out of doors, wander about, chicken would be cooked before you bought it. So the challenge is what to do to make the factory chuck to help it taste good? The answer is be generous with onions, fresh lemons, and herbs.

Ingredients - serves 4

1 * 1.1 kg fresh Omani chicken (2 choices, from Salalah in the South, or Soha in the North - pick the one that looks closest to your idea of an appropriate carcase)
2 red onions - 1 sliced, 1 quartered
½ a lemon, or 2 limes picked from the garden (yes we grow our own)
A (large) bunch of herbs - I now am in a Tarragon period but it will change
Olive oil
Sea salt and freshly crushed black pepper

1) Cut off the 'gland' in the parson's nose. Remove excess fat from the cavity and stuff with onion, lemon or lime, and the herbs.
2) Light the oven and turn to 'high'.
3) Slice one of the onions into rings and put them in your chosen roasting dish.
4) Oil and then season the chicken with salt and pepper rubbing it in with your hands. Sit the chicken on the onions in the roasting dish and put in the oven. Cook for either 20 minutes per pound + 20, or until a temperature gauge gives a reading from the thickest part of 75 C.
5) Set the chicken aside and allow to 'rest' for a minimum of 10 minutes.
6) Whilst this is going on you have prepared and cooked your choice of potatoes and veg.
7) Deglaze the roasting pan with a combination of the water the veg was cooked in, and some form (white wine / dry Vermouth) of alcohol. Stir and release all the taste from the bottom of the pan. Pour through a sieve and add to a small pan. Bring back to the boil and reduce.
8) Carve the chicken onto plates, and serve with a generous poring of juice.

Um Ali - Omani Bread & Butter Pudding

At the end 2009 Astrid (Silins), daughter Clea, and father André, visited us in Oman. By this time we had developed a very enjoyable, Oman tourist freindly, introduction to the sights.

This featured a "round trip" drive out to the Wahiba Sands; an overnight stay at an upmarket (glamping) desert camp timed to see the sunset over the desert; and next day returning via Sur, and up the new coast road to Qurayyat, before heading back to Muscat. Mountains, desert, sea, all the key features of the beautiful Oman scenery in one two day

Having enjoyed this for our pudding Astrid asked if she could have the recipe. Sous Chef, Saman Premadasa, sat up half the night carefully composing the recipe below in his English for her.

Ingredients - serves lots

15 croissant or puff pastry shells
1 litre fresh milk
150g sugar
2 or 3 cardamom pods
1 bay leaf or cinnamon leaf
10g each cashew nuts, almonds, hazel nuts, pine nuts
25g mixed peel

1) Boil milk sugar cardamom bay leaf for 5 minutes until the froth comes out. Stair gradually.
2) Croissants or puff pastry shells cut and arrange neatly in an oven proof dish.
3) Pour the milk over the top of the puff pastry shells.
4) Add the nuts on top with mix peel. Bake in an oven 150C for 10 to 15 minutes until the crust brown colour.
5) Optionally you can add some wipe cream for an enhanced the flavour

Vue Cookery Class – Al Bustan Hotel

During our time in Oman we gravitated toward only eating out in places "that could cook better than Sheila". This after much trial and error and some spectacularly unappetising meals narrowed down the choice. By our final days it was one Indian restaurant, the Mumtaz, and two hotels. These were the Chedi Hotel, and the Vue restaurant in the Al Bustan Hotel. This later, French style restaurant had as proprietor / chef Shannon Bennett. He was an Australian chef, trained in the UK and France, with an established reputation. There were no menus as such. You could have a 3 course or 5 course meal. Sheila and her friend Hillary discovered very soon after the restaurant opened that a 3 course 'lunch' represented really good value. The evening offering proved a little more expensive as the Al Bustan is some little way outside Muscat so the choice was taxi or stay overnight. We found the latter option a great treat. When we found out that Shannon was to run a cookery class one Thursday morning we immediately signed up.

> A few words about the Al Bustan Hotel. It had initially been built to host a GCC (Gulf Countries Council) meeting. In our time it had been refurbished again, no expense spared, and had reopened for a GCC Summit in 2008. The facings of the floors looking into the central atrium were done in natural timber and in the Omani style. Very elegant and very impressive.

Back to the cookery programme. It included breakfast in the Al Bustan atrium; a visit to the Mutrah fish and vegetable markets; back to the kitchen to cook what had been bought; and finally to sit down in the Vue restaurant and eat the results of their efforts.

We, unlike many of the cooking students, had been to the fish market many times before. However this was the most interesting visit. Shannon and Josh were frequent (daily) buyers at the market so were well known and I expect their business was keenly sought. Below are my notes on the experience:-

Travels With Our Kitchen

Vue – Al Bustan Cookery Class 7th Oct '10

Who were the Chef's ?
- Shannon Bennet
- Josh

What was the Programme ?
- Breakfast
- Visit the Mutrah Fish Market - Bought – prawns, sardines, snapper
- Visit adjoining Veg Market - Bought - rocket, beetroot, spring onions, bananas

What did we Learn ?

In the Fish Market

- Prawns - fresh equals heads firmly on, legs and whiskers undamaged
- Squid/cuttel fish - should be translucent, if really fresh will change their colour to background
- Sardines - no sign of 'leakage' from anus/belly; no smell; fresh eyes
- Snapper - check gills both sides dark red, bright eyes, smell of the sea, feel first (very firm)

In the restaurant.

- Scale fish either under water or inside a dustbin bag working by 'feel', as much as anything, keeping the scales inside.
- Use strong scissors to remove fins.
- You can de vein a prawn (once shelled) by using a toothpick.
- Easiest way to prepare sardines cut off the head, then cut a triangle - anus to rib cage / back bone.
- Aluminium foil has a shiny side and a dull side - in making your foil bags double layers dull side out. Seal sides pop in ingredients seal top.
- Chocolate pudding - calorie control the end result and keep the taste. Use high % coca dark chocolate

This was a great day.

13.0 Thailand - Many Visits & Now Family

We first visited Thailand/Bangkok in December 1979. We were en-route to Brunei. Sheila wanted to stay in all the old "classic" oriental hotels: the Oriental, Thailand; Raffles', Singapore; Repulse Bay, Hong Kong. We therefore stayed in the Oriental Hotel. This was our first "tourist" regime visit in that we did the day tours and watched the "cultural" shows. We had realised without this imposed rigour we would not see very much in our short stay. In addition I don't think we could have possibly foreseen that we would visit many more times over the years.

In '79 we did 2 serious, and essential, touristy trips. One is the culture show at the Rose Garden an institution that is still going strong. We visited again in March 2011 as it was the preferred venue for Kevin and Wanvisa's wedding later in the year. Unfortunately that autumn was very wet in Thailand and much of the country, and some of Bangkok, was flooded. We had to go to Pataya. The second essential trip is up the river to the old capital Ayutthaya.

Remembering this, our first Bangkok visit, has refreshed memories of past food hang-ups until now buried, and ignored. I at that time was no fan of coriander. I'm not absolutely sure I was OK with really spicy, chilli laced, food either. The Oriental at that time had several restaurants each with its own dress code. The code spanned from almost beach ware on the terrace, through smart casual in the Italian, all the way to formal jacket & tie in Lord Jim's the upstairs fish restaurant. We were not all that adventurous and ate several times on the river side terrace, and as a special treat we had a sea food basket at Lord Jims. Memories are of a huge pile of sea food served in a rattan basket along with plastic bibs to protect us from the inevitable mess.

Our second trip in 1981 was also whilst based in Brunei. Somewhat wiser to the Shell expat ways we learnt to refine our yearly holiday timing, and schedule. We aimed to take annual leave every 10 months (the minimum stay allowed between leaves) starting at the school Easter holiday break. This meant that Darron and Kevin could visit over Christmas, and be there during the summer months to benefit from all the activities organised for the visiting boarding school pupils. The other trick was at the start of the vacation to travel directly back to the UK. On the return we would arrange to visit India, Thailand, Hong Kong, or Singapore, before the return to work. We therefore acclimatised slowly and returned reasonably well rested. On this particular stay at the Oriental we were greeted as "retuning" guests and whisked straight to our room. We felt very privileged.

Our third trip, and the first of 3 from Oman, many, many, years later was in October 2008. We again stayed at the Oriental. Darron had moved to Thailand and was teaching English as a foreign language. He was based in Ayutthaya, the old capital on the river. We could only manage a short stay but it gave us the chance to attend the hotel's Thai cooking class. We had several years earlier listened to Jim Kempston talking about how much he had enjoyed attending. The details of our lessons are set out at the end of this chapter.

Travels With Our Kitchen

The Oriental, dwarfed by the new high rises all around it, still retains the original "old" hotel building. The main hotel is now a new building with a waterfront terrace. The cookery school, gym, and Thai themed restaurant are on the other side of the Chao Phraya River. Small wooden ferries, flying the Oriental Hotel flag, carried you back and forth between the two.

After the cookery lessons we had arranged for Darron to come down from Ayutthaya and stay for a couple of nights in the hotel. That saved us the hassle of having to organise travel. He could come down on the train to Bangkok and then get a taxi to the hotel. During this visit there may have been mention by Darron that he had met someone. The 'official' announcement, as Darron was later to explain, could only happen after they had successfully "made-up" after their first argument. This he obviously felt was the tipping point in their relationship.

Our 2nd trip from Oman (4th in total) in December 2009 also took us back to stay in the Oriental. This time instead of Darron coming to visit us in the hotel we travelled up to Ayutthaya to meet Angkana. We stayed in a very nice Thai guest house with the luxury of AC and clean sheets. What more could you want.

We revisited the remains of the old city, now a World Heritage Site. It is just staggering in its extent and beauty. The famous photo is of the Buddhist head which over the years has become entwined in the roots of a tree. This is however just one of a multitude of complete statues, decapitated heads and body parts, scattered amung the red brick remains of the main temples and buildings.

Sheila had done some research prior to our arrival. We knew we had to try an outside restaurant highly recommended in the "Lonely Planet" guide. Their Thai pork and noodles was rated among the best there was. I have to say as much as we did enjoy it, and the accompanying dishes, I can't honestly remember the details of the other dishes we ate.

Travels With Our Kitchen

Visiting the rented house where Darron, and Angkana, stayed we had our first experience of her excellent cooking. The barbeque was lit and she cooked fish encased with salt. She prepared what we now call "Angkana's Sweet & Sour". And just in case we had large appetites she prepared another dish, deep fried spicy fish, as well as the obligatory khou (fragrant Thai rice). Visiting them gave us a chance to see Thailand from a slightly more realistic vantage point than the Oriental's riverside terrace. For example on a visit to the market to buy vegetables we were instructed to remain out of the stall holder's sight. If she had seen us 'falanges' (foreigners) the price of the vegetables would have increased dramatically.

Our next trip in March 2011 was to visit them after they had visited Oman and got married in the Thai embassy, in Muscat. Darron had moved to a new job, still teaching English, in Hua Hin. This town is some 120 km south of Bangkok on the Western side of the bay and is where the Thai Royal family traditionally went for their sea side holidays. It is a little "touristy" but without the excesses of say Pattaya. They quickly found a small house to rent. We did not immediately go there to visit them. Their marriage had to be blessed by Buddhist Monks as is the tradition at Angkana's mothers village up country from Trat in the Eastern half of Thailand.

Angkana's mother's house was decorated in preparation. Early on the day (3am) the noise of chopping indicated that preparation of the food had started. People started to gather and around 07:00 the Monks arrived. The blessing, with chanting, and the bride and groom being tied together with string, commenced. On completion the Monks were fed. Following this the audience was blessed by the monk flicking holy water at them and then they were finished.

We all, with the exception of Angkana, then set off to the temple. When everyone was gathered, Anganna's mother, family and relations, plus the drummers and the single ladies, we all marched back in a column to the house. At 9 minutes past 9 Darron was allowed to pay those protecting entry to the house with a silver, and a gold, belt to enter and await his bride. Once reunited all was deemed well. We could now eat, rest up, and prepare for the celebration party that night. The next day, after the celebrations, we flew back to Bangkok from Trat. We then took a taxi down the other side of the country to Hau Hin where we had booked into the Station Hotel. Darron meanwhile drove back to Hau Hin as he had to be back at work.

The house they had rented was really too small for Angkana's children, Kane, Jerry (their nick names) and Noey (her Thai name) to come over from Trat. Whilst we were there we looked at houses inland from Hau Hin with the thought of purchase. We now headed back to Oman as I to had to work. After a false start Darron and Angkana were able to find a suitable house. It was close to a village style school she felt was suitable for the children. They bought it and moved in in mid-2011. In November 2011, following my retirement we visited again. This time of course to see D & A and the family but also to import some of our possessions to furnish the annex as a "granny flat" and to be there for Kevins and Wanvisa's wedding and Buddhist blessing. They had initially planned to hold the ceremony at the Rose Garden but the flooding around Bangkok forced its relocation to Nog Noosh, outside Pattaya. We, based with Darron and Angkana, decided that the best way for us to attend was to hire a taxi and get driven there. First though we had to set up the granny flat such that we could move in. This achieved we were ready for the 6 hour drive and all excited in anticipation of the big occasion.

Their Thai blessing followed pretty much the same format we had enjoyed with D & A. The big difference was Kevin arriving on an elephant and the rather exotic surroundings of the Noch Noosh gardens. The column of marchers were headed by drummers and dancing girls. We had an 'interpreter' which was a great help for the friends of Kevin's, and ourselves, in reaching some understanding of what was going on.

That evening, just as in Trat, we were to have a big party. Highlights included good food, exotic drinks, a live Thai band, and the ritual of releasing paper, fire powered, lanterns to float up, and off, into the night sky. The next day we and Piyapon, Wan's mother, joined Kevin and Wanvisa in a villa they had rented. They then headed south for their "honeymoon". Piyapon and we taxi'd up to Bangkok where we stayed with her. There we were royally entertained with the first meal being a barbeque on her terrace. With our strong links to Thailand now cemented we have unconsciously incorporated more and more Thai food into our everyday diet. To this has been added a further Thai dimension. Clarissa Dickson-Wright, famous as one of the "Two Fat Ladies" TV cookery series, lived in Musselburgh, just outside Edinburgh. She maintains that Mr Clarks Fish Shop is the "best in the world". Naturally after we retired to Edinburgh we sought it out. Indeed it is fabulous. Most wet fish shops in the UK present their fish "heads off". From our Faisal "fish of the day" experience we prefer heads on. That's what you get at Mr Clarks. It also happens that Mrs Noey Clark is Thai. We discovered when Piyapon stayed with us that they are from villages quiet close together. With the relationship that close we now only buy fish there.

Finally we have now enjoyed two extended stays at Darron and Angkana's in Hua Hin. We stayed for 2 months in early 2013, and 3 months in early 2014. This last stay included looking after the grandchildren Kane, Jerry, and Noey, for a couple of weeks. Angkana, who is an excellent cook, enjoyed the challenge of cooking for us once she realised we were up for trying new ingredients. From the 2013 stay I have photo's of over 25 different dishes she cooked for us. From the 2014 trip I have photo's of some +/- 45 herbs, vegetables, and fruit which were completely new to us. Phak-chee-farang, saw toothed coriander; kra-chai, wild ginger; phak-bung Thai, swamp cabbage; and ma-prang, there isn't an English name for these fruit which are part of the mango family. I'll stop there. Enough to say that below are some of the Thai flavours that now regularly feature in our diet.

Phad Thai - Cookery Lesson

We had travelled to Trat on the Eastern side of Thailand to travel up toward the Cambodian border to reach Angkana's mothers village. The Thai family didn't believe the marrage in Oman was a valid wedding. For them a full Thai Buddhist blessing was necessary for the union of Darron & Angkana to be valid. Following the blessing, we needed to eat. It was time for Angkana's sister Dum, the best Phad Thai exponent in the extended family, to cook us lunch.

Once we had said yes we would love Phad Thai a motor bike was summoned and a person sent to market to buy the fresh ingredients. The next point of note is that most recipes will suggest 'soaking' the dry flat rice noodles in warm water for +/- 25 minutes. Cooking outside and behind the house a large amount of oil was added to a big wok and once to high heat the dry noodles were just added. Not a technique for the average Western domestic setting. I must say we were privileged to be so well catered for and the result was extremely tasty.

The recipe below is closer to a John Torode version, printed in the BBC Good Food magazine, than the technique and ingredients enjoyed above. One key tip ahead of cooking. We have a selection of differing sized, tiny, small, and medium stainless dishes. You add the pre prepared ingredients to an appropriately sized dish and then line them up in the order in which they are to be added. Now you can't go wrong.

Ingredients - serves 4

225 g dried rice noodles
3 tblsp vegetable oil
4 cloves garlic finely chopped
Stems of the coriander garnish chopped up
250 g raw prawns shelled and de veined
1 tsp sugar
2 eggs beaten
2 tblsp Thai fish sauce (nam pla)
2 tblsp oyster sauce

175 g bean sprouts
Juice of one lime
4 spring onions sliced on the diagonal
100 g coarsely crushed plain roasted peanuts.
3 large (medium) red chillies sliced in half lengthways, de seeded, and then finely chopped
To garnish:- lime wedges, good handful chopped fresh coriander, 3 / 4 spring unions cut into 5cm match sticks,

1) Soak the noodles as per the instructions on the package. Drain in a colander

2) Heat a wok over a high heat and add 1 tblsp vegetable oil. When very hot add the garlic and chopped coriander stems. Stir for a few moments taking care not to burn the garlic. Add the prawns and stir fry for 30 seconds then add the sugar, the noodles and stir for a minute or so gently mixing everything together. Now add the eggs and cook for a further 2 minutes.

3) Pour in the oyster, and fish, sauces followed by the bean sprouts and lime juice, the diagonally sliced spring onion, ¾ of the peanuts, and the chopped chilli.

4) Continue to stir fry turning gently for a further 2 or 3 minutes.

Turn out into serving bowls and garnish with the remaining peanuts, chopped coriander, and spring onion matchsticks. Finally place a lime wedge on the side of each bowl.

Travels With Our Kitchen

Angkana's Pineapple, Cucumber, and Prawn

When you have the privilege of eating with a Thai family expect two surprises. Number 1 - not all Thai food is 'Richter Scale' HOT. Thais know we 'Brit's' exist on bland, boring, food. They therefore prepare, for example, a sweet and sour, no chilly, dish. They also like to tease our palette. Expect a hot dish, with additional chillies on side, to explore what you're made of.

Angkana's first meal for us featured this spectacular sweet & sour dish. It is wonderfully colourful with the combination of the fruit and the vegetables. In general Thai's shop every day and normally go to the markets very early in the morning to get the best on offer that day. No wonder the meal tasted very fresh with crunchy vegetables. Fantastic.

Ingredients - Serves 2

2 garlic cloves smashed and chopped
150g raw king prawns (large)
½ a (UK) cucumber cut into same sized chunks
¼ fresh pineapple - cut into chunks
1 red pepper cut into mouth sized chunks
1 tblsp Oyster sauce
½ cup chicken stock
1 tblsp Fish sauce / tomato ketchup
1 onion cut into small pieces
8 cherry tomatoes cut in half

1) Add a splash of oil to a wok, medium heat, and fry garlic till golden. Then add the king (large) prawns and fry off until they begin to colour. If you only have small prawns add in step 3.

2) Then add the cucumber and pineapple and carefully stir to heat evenly. Now add the oyster sauce, and chicken stock. Continue to slowly turn and heat through

3) Add fish sauce & tomato ketchup to taste / colour. Finally add the onion and the tomatoes. Continue to gently stir and cook.

4) Taste for 'sweetness'. Adjust as necessary with more fish sauce or ketchup.

Serve in generous sized bowls with Thai sticky / fragrant rice (your choice)

Barbecue Salted Whole Fish

The fish that Angkana prepared for the barbecue looked very like the bottom right hand corner ones in the photo. I imagine that in a Thai market your fish, just as in Oman's Mutrah market, comes guts included. You will need to gut the fish if this is the case.

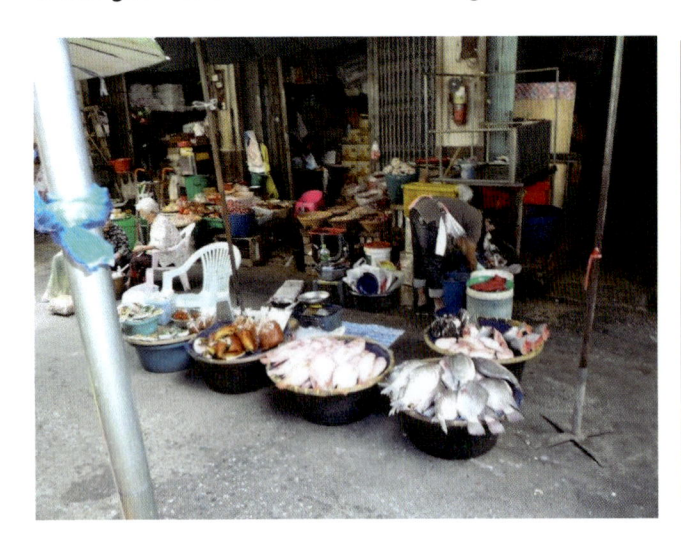

Ingredients

- *1 whole fish (such as a snapper or a good sized bream)*
- *2/3 sticks lemon grass outer course layers removed & bashed with the back of a knife*
- *Kafir lime leaves either side peeled away from the central vein*

1) Gut the fish leaving its head on but removing the gills. Try and keep rinsing the fish in water to a minimum. I would also tend to cut the fins off using a good sharp & strong pair of scissors.

2) Tuck the bashed lemons grass sticks, cut in half, and the Kafir lime leaves into the cavity. Place the fish onto a plate, slightly dampen the upper side if dry and coat with the good layer of salt. You are going to cook this side of the fish first so you need the salt to stay on.

3) Carefully place the fish, salt side down on the barbecue and cook for 5 / 10 minutes depending upon the heat of the BBQ and the fish size.

4) Now cover the upper side of the fish with salt. When you have a good coating carefully turn over and cook the other side. There are a few ways to test if the fish is done. Use a temperature probe (55c); you can use a tooth pick, a good tip from Vue restaurant, as it doesn't damage the fish too much; or like Angkana have years of experience and just "know".

Remove the fish and knock off any remaining salt. Unzip down the middle of the fish along the line in the skin and peel the skin off. Serve the chunks of moist, fragrant fish with Thai sticky rice and dipping sauce if desired.

Thai Chicken Soup for the SOUL (Khou Tom)

This is our take, from Angkena's first visit with us in Oman, on her everyday Thai breakfast. Reference is also due to Ken Hom, *"Simple Thai Cookery"*, (BBC Books), for his "Savoury Rice Soup". When Angkana cooked this the first time with us she said the secret was to cook the rice in the chicken stock. Having now done this several times with some adaptions I think there are two key elements in this recipe. The first is really good 'chicken' stock. We always make our own using chicken carcases. The second is getting the 'match' stick/shredded ginger, chillies and spring onions, all beautifully identically sized.

Ingredients - Serves two

100 grams of cooked free range chicken
Cooked prawns if using
1½ lt Good chicken stock
2 sticks of Lemon grass - bashed to release the flavour
4 Khafir lime leaves - central stem (vein) removed
3 table spoons Fish sauce
Freshly bashed black pepper corns (to taste)
2 handfuls (+/- 100g) of good quality Thai rice (rinsed in cold water)
2 cloves of garlic finely chopped

Garnish

1 generous sized "thumb" of ginger sliced into thin matchsticks
2 red & 2 green chilies deseeded and sliced into matchsticks (slice with the inside uppermost this way the knife gets a better grip)
2 spring onions sliced into matchsticks
1 large handful of coriander leaves

1) In a saucepan bring the stock, with lemon grass, lime leaves, fish sauce, & pepper to the boil.

2) Add the rinsed Thai rice. Bring back to the boil & part cook the rice. Add ½ the garnish ingredients (except the coriander) and continue to simmer until the rice is cooked through.

3) Whilst the rice is cooking fry the chopped garlic with a glug of oil in a small heavy bottomed frying pan. Take care to avoid burning the smallest garlic pieces. When done turn out onto a small plate covered with kitchen paper to absorb the excess oil.

4) With the rice cooked add the chicken (and prawns if feeling extravagant) and bring to the boil to reheat the chicken / cook the prawns. Stir in the fried garlic (with or without the cooking oil). Serve in large bowls topping each with a helping of the remaining garnish and the coriander leaves.

Squid stuffed with Pork

After we got home to Edinburgh, and being reminded of this dish whilst going through the holiday photo's, I decided to seek out the recipe. You get an amazing amount of information (too much ???) by doing an internet search. Some of it quiet fascinating. I found a Gordon Ramsey version; a claim that it is in fact not a Thai recipe but Vietnamese; but none that seemed close to how Angkana cooked it.

Then Sheila remembered "Vatch's Thai Cook Book" a recent addition to our book collection but in fact first published in 1994. We had been reminded of it as we had seen a copy on a visit to our Dutch friends the van Riimsdijks. With help from this source (though he steams the squid), combined with the web info, and the photo of Angkana's dish, we have reconstructed how we think Angkana cooked it.

Ingredients

6 baby, or 4 medium, squid carefully cleaned (keep the tentacles)
A knob of coconut oil
2 cloves garlic finely chopped
2 red chilli's deseeded and finely chopped
2 large shallots chopped
250g pork mince
2 tblsp fish sauce
1 tblsp palm sugar
1 lime juiced
1 generous handful of chopped coriander

1) Add the coconut oil to a medium hot wok, When melted add the garlic and chilli. Stir fry for 1 – 2 minutes making sure you don't burn the garlic. Add the shallots and stir fry until soft.

2) Add the pork mince, shrimp paste if using, fish sauce, palm sugar, and half the lime juice. Press and stir to break up and cook the pork mince. Add as required some water or chicken stock to loosen the mixture. Taste and adjust seasoning with black pepper/fish sauce/lime juice as needed. Near the end of cooking stir in the coriander. Set aside to cool.

3) Divide the pork mixture into 6 equal (4 if medium squid) portions. Carefully stuff each squid with the mixture sealing the end with a tooth pick.

4) There are several cooking options. The stuffed squid could be barbecued; they could be cooked under a grill; or they could be wok fried. Whichever method do not overcook. They will only take a couple of minutes.

Serve up and hope the kids like them.

Pork Burgers – For the Grandchildren

The first thing Darron and Angkana did after getting married, and moving to Hua Hin, was to ship her children (Kain, Jerry, and Noey) from Trat to come and live with them. When looking for the house they wanted to be near to a village, rather than a city, school. Something more like the school they were attending up in the jungle. They found a house in a new development with 3 bed rooms, a swimming pool, and what we now call a 'granny' flat (probably the maids quarters). They bought in mid 2011, and we visited and set up the Granny flat in November 2011. Once settled in Sheila decided the children need to be introduced to "spiced" English food.

We had seen the looks of astonishment and suspicion on the children's faces when viewing Western dishes Angkana made for us. We also knew that Thais cannot believe foreigners can cook Thai. Therefore the big question was "where to start?" After some thought Sheila decided that spicy pork burgers had to be a winner. We could get excellent pork, and Angkana we knew had all the spices we needed to hand.

Ingredients - serves 3 hungry young Thai's

1 kg Pork mince
Good handful coriander – roughly chopped
5 cm chubby thumb of galangal or fresh ginger
4 hot red chillies (de-seed if not Thai)
4 garlic cloves finely chopped
Glug of oil
Salt and pepper to taste

1) Combine all the ingredients together in a bowl and allow to stand for +/- ½ hour for the flavours to amalgamate.

2) Heat the oil in a frying pan or wok. When the pan is at a good heat cook off a small sample of the burger mix. Taste for seasoning. Adjust as necessary.

3) Make into equal sized burgers. By using a large ladle as a measure you can be pretty consistent with the burger sizing.

4) Bring the pan / wok back to a good heat and cook the burgers in batches for +/- 4 minutes a side ensuring that the burgers take on a nice colour.

Serve up and hope the kids like them.

Mussaman Beef Curry

This recipe is added a little bit as a "last minute" effort. Firstly because I realised that we were missing a "curry" recipe, and secondly because this is one of Darron's favourite meals. For reference I consulted *"a little taste of Thailand"*, with recipes by Oi Cheepchaiissara, which we bought on our first extended visit to Hua Hin.

Serves 4

2 pieces of cinnamon stick
10 cardamom seeds
5 cloves
2 tblsp vegetable oil
2 tblsp Mussaman curry paste
800 g stewing beef cut into 5cm (2in) cubes.
410 ml coconut milk
250 ml beef stock
2 or 3 medium potatoes cut into 2.5 cm squares
Large thumb ginger shredded into matchstick sized strips
3 tblsp fish sauce
3 tblsp palm sugar
110 g roasted salted peanuts lightly pounded
3 tblsp tamarind puree

1) Dry fry the cinnamon stick, cardamom seeds, and cloves in a wok over a low heat. Stir all the ingredients around for 2 to 3 minutes until they become fragrant. Remove and set aside.

2) Heat the oil in the wok and then stir fry the Mussaman paste over a medium heat for 2 minutes until fragrant.

3) Add the beef to the pan and stir fry for 5 minutes browning all sides. Add the coconut milk, beef stock, potatoes, shredded ginger, fish sauce, palm sugar, ¾ of the peanuts, tamarind puree and the dry fried spices.

4) Reduce the heat and simmer occasionally stirring for 50 to 60 minutes until the meat and potatoes are just cooked. Taste and adjust seasoning as necessary.

Serve in bowls garnished with the remaining peanuts accompanied with rice.

Note:- You can easily make your own Mussaman paste. In a pestle and mortar blend 10 long dried, red chillies, de-seeded and chopped; 1 tablespoon of ground coriander seed; 1 teaspoon each of ground cumin, cinnamon, cardamom, and white pepper; and 1 or 2 star anise. Once suitably pounded and mixed add one at a time about 6 chopped shallots, 6 or 7 garlic cloves chopped, a thumb of chopped galangal, 1 tablespoon Kaffir zest or finely chopped leaves, and lastly a tablespoon each of shrimp paste and salt. Pound together until you have a smooth paste. I have read that you should pound for a minimum of 20 minutes. On the other hand you could use a blender.

Thai Mussels (Hoi Malaeng Pho) and Gourd (Fug Kheaw) & Pork Ball Soup

On our early 2013, 2 month, visit to Hua Hin, just after Darron started his British Council job in Malaysia, we were thoroughly spoilt by Angkana and her consistently excellent, and oft time new for us, Thai cuisine. In the whole time of our stay we hardly ate the same meal twice.

Spoilt for choice it was difficult to pick a single recipe to include at the last moment. After a little refection we chose Thai mussels. Firstly the dish looked, and tasted, wonderful. Secondly it is the only shell fish recipe in the book. To complete the story I should also mention that she cooked us Thai 'cockles', and Thai 'clams', both of which were excellent eating.

All Angkana's meals came with at least 2 different dishes and of course Khaow (rice). She is very particular about the type, and quality, of the rice she buys and when she does buy it is by the 15kg sack. Enough, along with the 1kg of dried red peppers, to last the family for 2 weeks. Here we had Cucumber Soup with pork Meat Balls, and rice, with our mussels.

Serves 4

1 ½ kg fresh Thai mussels
3 sticks of lemon grass - bashed
Generous handful of Holy Basil leaves

1) Rinse the mussels thoroughly under cold running water scraping off any barnacles, pulling off any "beards', and discarding any mussels that don't close on being tapped.

2) Put the mussels in a heavy based pan or wok over high heat and add the lemon grass and basil leaves. Cover with a lid and cook. Shake the pan carefully several times during cooking to ensure even cooking and that the juices, lemon glass, and leaves are spread over every mussel. Continue to cook for 5 – 8 minutes until all the mussels are "open".

3) Ladle into a serving dish discarding any mussels that do not open.

Serve in bowls accompanied, if you wish, with a Thai dipping sauce.

Neua Yang Nam Tok (Waterfall Beef Salad)

I think this may have been one of the first dishes that Angkana cooked for us using Thai mint. It seemed a slightly strange idea at the time as we tend to think of mint as in mint sauce with lamb, or perhaps more exotically mint tea, as the more natural uses of mint.

The other interesting thing at the time we ate it was that we knew the meaning of "nam tok". The village Angkana comes from, close to the Cambodian border, has a water fall – nam tok – the children used to play in. The dish gets its name from the juices that ooze from the meat and run down the plate like a water fall. A very tasty waterfall. It also uses dry fried rice which is coarsely pounded in a mortar as a very characteristic garnish.

Ingredients - Serves 4
½ kg good quality, thick cut, beef steak

For the Marinade
1 tsp fish sauce (nam pla)
1 tsp tamarind paste + 3 tsp water
1 tblsp lime juice
1 tblsp chopped chilli (deseeded if you like it slightly less hot)

For the stir fry
1/3 cup fish sauce
1/3 cup lime juice
2 - 3 tblsp chopped shallots
2 - 3 tblsp chopped coriander (roots included if you can get them)

Garnish
2 tblsp khou koor (coarsely ground dry fried rice)
A healthy hand full of mint leaves

1) Combine all the marinade ingredients then thoroughly coat the steak. Leave to marinade for at least 3 hours.

2) Remove the steak from the marinade and either barbeque, or grill till rare. Set aside to rest. When cool enough to handle slice thinly and then cut into bite sized pieces.

3) Bring a little oil to medium high heat and add the sliced steak and the stir fry ingredients. Fry whilst stirring to heat evenly through (+/- 2 minutes). Take off the heat.

4) Add the khao koor, and the mint leaves, and gently amalgamate. Transfer to a serving bowl.

Serve with Thai fragrant rice.

Poo Jaa (Thai Crab Cakes)

This recipe was inspired by several Thai experiences. Firstly Anganna's wonderful cooking, and the extensive range of different dishes she made for us, during our visits in 2013, and '14. The other influence was the Oriental Hotel - Cookery School version we learnt on our visit to Bangkok in 2008 (See below).

Crab Cake Ingredients

- *75g minced chicken breast*
- *18 gms garlic & coriander root finely chopped*
- *2 tblsp light Soy sauce*
- *¾ tsp ground pepper*
- *1 small egg*
- *150g (Scottish) crab meat*
- *2 spring onions sliced*
- *Ground nut oil*

Ingredients - Cucumber dipping sauce

4 tblsp rice vinegar
3 tblsp sugar
1 tsp salt
½ a medium cucumber cubed into dolly mixture sized pieces
1 small shallot finely chopped
1 Thai medium chilli deseeded and finely sliced
Fish sauce (naam pla) to taste

1) Boil the sugar, vinigar, and salt in a sauce pan for 3 to 4 minutes stirring to disolve the sugar. Set aside to completely cool.

2) Mix the cucumber, shallot, and chilli in a serving bowl. Pour the vinigar/sugar mix over to just cover the cucumber.

3) In a mixing bowl combine the chicken, garlic, coriander, egg, soy sauce, and the pepper. Mix together by hand until the ingredients are evenly distributed.

4) Add the crab meat & the spring onions and knead until you have a sticky mix.

5) Form into 4 or 6 evenly sized patties you could put them in the fridge to firm up if you have time.

6) Add a slug of ground nut oil to a hot wok or frying pan and deep fry until crispy on both sides. Don't over-load the pan so cook in two batches if necessary.

Serve accompanied with the cucumber dipping sauce.

Travels With Our Kitchen

Oriental Hotel Cookery School - 3rd October 2008.

We remembered from some time past Jim Kempston's praise for the Oriental Hotel's Cooks School. Our first trip from Oman, many years later, was in October 2008. Coming to Bangkok to visit Darron gave us every excuse to stay at the Oriental. A major attraction being the chance to attend the hotel's Thai cooking class. Immediately after we checked in we looked up the possibilities offered by the cooks school. There were differing menus, and specific techniques, on different days. We chose our day on the basis that the menu, especially the crab cakes, appealed to our taste. Luckily we were able to book a place. The 'cooks school' is on the other side of the Chao Phraya river (river of Kings) from the old Oriental hotel building.

On the morning of our lessons we breakfasted on the terrace overlooking the river. In good time we took the ferry across the river to join our class mates for the lesson. We were given hand-outs that contained photos of the different, for us unusual, ingredients, vegetables, spices, etc., with their Thai & English names. It also included the recipes we were to cook Poo Jaa (Crab Cakes in Shells); Khao Ob Supparoat (Fried rice with Prawns, Chinese Sausages & Pineapple); Green Curry; and Khanom Gluay (Steamed Banana Pudding). The lessons were to be very hands on. We were to chop, grate, peel, mix, cook and finally eat the result of our efforts. Fortunately it was tasty.

It turned out to be a small class which was good because you could easily cluster around the chef to watch what he was doing. We had a little advantage compared with others in the class in that from our time in the Far East we could identify some of the ingredients.

Looking back at my notes I'm embarrassed to say they don't seem to throw a lot of light upon what we learnt. They do include the fact that Thai's believe the number 9 to be lucky. And the vital information that palm sugar is collected like rubber and then boiled. Not in the notes but remembered, probably because we bought cooking spoons made from coconut shells to use with our wok, was the Chef's mantra when stir frying "Press and Stir".

The Poo Jaa (Crab Cakes in Shells) recipe, complete with Sheila's notes, is given below.

The Thai Cooking School
at The Oriental

Poo Jaa
Crab Cakes in Shells

Serves 4, 1 shell per serving

Ingredients

75	grams	(½ cup)	chicken breast, minced
18	grams	(2½ tablespoons)	garlic and coriander roots, finely chopped
22	grams	(2 tablespoons)	~~white~~ soy sauce
3	grams	(¾ teaspoon)	ground pepper
60	grams	(1) + 1	egg *beaten well*
150	grams	(2 cups)	crab meat
5	grams	(2 tablespoons)	spring onion, sliced
4			crab shells

wet hands
& fill well - plump.

1 egg beaten.

Sauce Good with Salt

Preparation

1. In a mixing bowl, mix chicken together with garlic and coriander roots. Add soy sauce and pepper and egg, mix well.

2. Add crab meat and (spring onions) continue to knead until sticky. *press & slice* *add onion last.*

3. Put the mixture into crab shells and steam for 4-5 minutes until just 80% cooked. *Cut in half easy when cold.*

4. Just right before serving, dip the crab cakes in shells in beaten egg then deep-fry until golden brown. Serve with cucumber relish.

Ingredients for cucumber relish

500	grams	(3¼ cups)	white sugar
300	grams	(1½ cups) *rice*	vinegar
18	grams	(1 tablespoon)	salt
120	grams	(1 cup)	cucumbers, sliced
30	grams	(3 tablespoons)	shallots, slivered & *mix* *
30	grams	(3 tablespoons)	Thai red and/or orange chillies, sliced

* to brighten

Preparation

1. Boil sugar, vinegar and salt in a saucepan for 3 minutes. Leave to cool completely.

2. Mix cucumber, shallot and chillies in a serving bowl. Pour the vinegar minutes over the vegetables until they are just covered.

Friday 3

Travels With Our Kitchen

14.0 Edinburgh - Final Retirement, Nov '11.

Having prematurely retired to Cyprus in 1999, and at the time not owning a house in the UK, the first priority was to buy somewhere. With no close family left to be a focus of our house hunting, and Darron at that time working in my old university town Edinburgh, we thought this would make a good starting place.

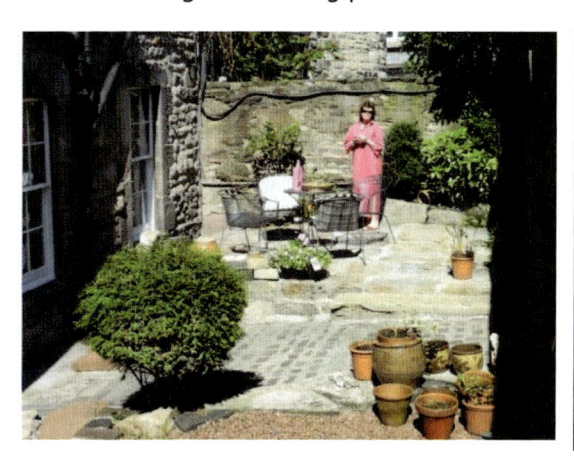

After a false start or two we eventually bought 17A Union Street in early 2000. During the next 10 years we did several 'holiday' stays but we never really lived there. At first we lived in the Cyprus flat. Then after June 2004 we lived in various flats, and houses, in Muscat, Oman. Real Edinburgh life only started, arriving back from Thailand having setup the granny flat in Hua Hin, and attended Kevin and Wanvisa's Buddhist blessing, with full time retirement in November 2011.

The first challenge was combining, and downsizing, the equipment from three kitchens into one. Which sauce pans to keep, what to do with the 2 extra whizzers? In theory this should be dead easy. In practice it is very seriously difficult and emotional. We can't get rid of that butter dish we had it in Edinburgh student days. That's my favourite knife I can't give that to a charity shop. Sometimes technology did help if in not quiet the intended way. The toaster blew up. Sheila melted a "beanie" bag in the micro wave. That said the cellars are still full, and between us Sheila has a choice of 8 different Japanese "Globe" knives, and I have a collection of 10 from different places, and episodes, of our lives. As you can tell we like kitchen stuff. Not least the collection of hand carved spoons from Scotland, Syria, China, Kenya, Morocco, and Thailand. We can't persuade ourselves that we can give these things away and not lose part of our personal history. To end on a success story we have downsized the cookery book collection. It now only numbers some 335 volumes, and counting.

The other challenge, anticipated in a minor way though nothing like as great as the real thing, we had to face was being a foreigner in our own country. This was particularly acute with regard to food shopping. In the 22 years we had lived outside the UK a shopping revolution had taken place. We were used to being able to choose from 2 sorts of eggs - big or little. We were also used to "buying" in bulk when an item was available because if we didn't we knew we'd never see it again. The choice overload that greets the shopper at any contemporary UK supermarket still causes panic attacks. All be it this was easy compared to the issues at the petrol station. In my years abroad I had become used to an attendant filling the car with petrol; they would also cleaned the windscreen; and take the money. Now back on home territory I was mortified by the idea of "paying the pump'.

What was a wondrous change was the spread of 'farmers' markets / shops; really world class specialist retailers. "Something Fishy", and Mr Clarkes the Musselburgh fishmongers; Craigies farm shop; Chinese supermarkets; award winning butchers; Polish corner shops; and one that we have enjoyed over the years, probably the best vegetable shop in the world, "Tatty Shaws".

From having tried 'retirement' before we knew that from Day 1 we would have to be explicit about the rules. The first rule was - "No alcohol (wine) at lunch time during the week unless it was a very special occasion, or we had visitors. There was also a 2nd rule - "No cleaning lady". I would do the hoovering and the money saved would be spent eating out once a month at "Michelin" star restaurants. This worked for a while but fell into disuse on the basis of a rule we'd had for years - "Restaurant food was only good (worth it) if it was cooked better than I could manage, or if it was something that Sheila wouldn't / couldn't cook". We were soon to discover that some very upmarket Edinburgh restaurants could not match this criterion. Not only that but this was combined with prices in excess of £85 per head. The old faithful such as Fishers in Leith, and new discoveries like The Wee Restaurant, continued to impress with their honest sumptuous offerings. Some we judged way off the mark. Now this may sound pretentious but remember on Gordon Ramsey's "Kitchens from Hell" TV programme, when tested, several supposedly professional chefs were unable to make an omelette. Knowledge and real culinary skill matter.

As for "eating in" we immediately sought ingredients and produce that were not available in Oman. We had the time, fresh ingredients, and enthusiasm to raise our gastronomic sights. Simon & Sarah Richards, with whom we shared our first retirement Hogmanay, gave me a large one day, one page, diary. This became our project book. In this all manner of things were recorded including the entire extra special, and successful, meals we cooked in our first year back in Edinburgh. There are over 80 references to recipes which we had cooked. Not only old favourites but also new, and exciting, cooking challenges. Some worked, and were delicious, and some (my pea soup) on being incorrectly reheated produced very unpleasant after effects. Included below are a selection of the more successful recipes.

Christmas Goose al la Raymond Blank

Since our return to Edinburgh we have been blessed by Christmas visits of Kevin, Wan, and latterly Milo. Wan joined her mother in England when she was 12 years old. As her Thai upbringing until then did not feature Christmas celebrations she never really acquired a taste for the typical English festive spread. For her first visit we upped the Thai element and played down the normal festive fare. Since then we have slowly reintroduced the traditional elements and lowered the Thai. Now, as I detail below, she has become quite a fan.

Our excellent local butchers, Crombie's, operates a very slick Christmas order and collect system. They are our first choice to supply top quality ingredients for the Christmas table. We, over the years, have gravitated to goose being our preferred option. This quality was soon to be even further enhanced by a cooking method witnessed on a TV show which featured Raymond Blanc's favourite cooking method. In brief it is remove the bag of giblets, then butcher the goose to remove the neck, excess carcase and fat, the wings and legs to leave a "crown". Setting aside the legs, and the crown, you brown the remainder in its own fat before adding your vegetables. Then you add the legs to the pan and cover with foil and cook in the oven. After an hour you add the crown suitably seasoned. When the crown breast reaches a temperature of 55C remove, wrap tightly in foil, and allow to "rest" for ½ hour. During this resting period return the legs to the oven and continue to cook. They are then removed and allowed to rest whilst you make the jus. This way you achieve nicely cooked legs, moist breast, and a years' worth of goose fat. Perfection, and now a firm favourite with the whole family, when accompanied by gluten free chipolatas wrapped in streaky bacon; roast potatoes and parsnips; stuffing; bread sauce;

and the jus. There is one vegetable that remains a step too far for a Thai palette. Brussel sprouts. In future years we will have to continue to work on this.

One last note of explanation. The recipes below may well read as incorporating expensive ingredients. They may also be a tad more complex, and time consuming, to prepare and this is probably true. These are the joys that a pension, combined with being time rich, in retirement provides. We do however pride ourselves on hunting down bargains. Best by dates ensure there is a ready supply of price reductions from supermarkets. The other advantage is that you are tempted to buy items that would normally not feature in your diet. Maybe this was what helped drive the number of different dishes we ate in our first year to over 80. However we did not forget any of the more humble of our favourites' that we had enjoyed on our travels. They still feature regularly in our diet. Enjoy.

Heston Blumenthal's Pea & Ham Soup.

Christmas 2011 I was gifted a fairly substantial, 397 page, cook book - **"Heston Blumenthal at Home"**. I think the concept was that the recipes be more accessible for the amateur cook. However some of the dishes, thrice cooked chips for example, take just as long as the **"In Search of Perfection"** versions. Anyway it only took a month or so after settling in, whilst looking after Megs (Simon & Sarah's rather old wire haired terrier) we decided to have a go at Heston's Pea & Ham soup recipe.

This the first time we made it we followed the instruction to the letter and strained the 'liquidized' peas (900g of them) "through a fine sieve, pressing through as many solids as possible". This is an extremely physical, time consuming, activity. The resultant soup was very smooth. For subsequent versions we used the Kenwood sieve attachment. The result may not be quiet as smooth but the arms don't ache as much!

HB recommends drizzling the served soup with "mint" oil. We did this but perhaps because of the exhaustion didn't think it did much. To round things off we topped with torn ham, some whole peas, and mint leaves.

Ingredients - Serves four

1 * small (+/- 750g) boneless gammon (though we used a shank - bone in)
1 union finely sliced
1 leek, white part only, cleaned and sliced
1 carrot peeled and sliced
900g of frozen peas
50 g unsalted butter
1 banana shallot peeled and diced
1 clove garlic finely chopped
160g unsmoked bacon cut into 'lardons' (we used a supermarket pac of chopped pancetta)
Salt & freshly bashed black pepper
Sprig of fresh mint

1) Put the gammon (ham shank) in an ovenproof saucepan with the onion, leek, and carrot. Cover with cold water. Bring to a simmer on the stove and then place in a preheated oven (100C) for 5 hours.

2) Whilst the stock is cooking take a large roasting tin, line with a double layer of kitchen paper, and empty your 900g of frozen peas into it. Allow to de frost checking the wetness of

the paper. Once saturated remove and repeat the drying process. You want the peas to be dry and at room temperature before using.

3) Allow the stock to cool. Remove the gammon (ham shank) from the stock and strain the liquid, discarding the cooked vegetables, through a large sieve lined with muslin.

4) Melt half the butter in a saucepan and add the shallot, garlic, and bacon (pancetta). Cook over a medium heat until soft but not coloured. Now add 750 ml of your stock and bring to the boil. Simmer for 5 minutes. Finally add all but 50g of the peas. Immediately remove from the heat.

5) Liquidise the mixture in batches. Once all done fit the finest mesh disc to the Kenwood sieve and again in batches strain the mixture discarding the fibrous residue. (You could do this manually with a sieve & muslin if you like). Pour the soup into a clean pan. Season with salt and pepper and gently bring to heat.

6) Flake the cooked ham and select some 150g of bite sixed pieces. Ladle the soup into 4 pre warmed soup bowls. Divide the ham in 4 and place in the centre of each bowl. Carefully scatter a ¼ of the reserved, whole, peas on the ham. Finally add your sprig of mint.

Poached Seafood Ragout

This I cooked on Valentine's Day 2012 after we had finally located Mr Clark's, the highly acclaimed Musselburgh, wet fish shop.

We had eaten at Tom Kitchin's restaurant but did not think it rivalled many of the fine dining experiences we had had in Oman, Thailand, France, or for that matter other Michelin starred restaurants in Edinburgh. He writes inspiring recipes though. Here is our take on one from the Scotsman on Sunday. This, given the occasion, is naturally for only two people.

1 carrot, thinly sliced
½ leek, thinly sliced
1 courgette, thinly sliced
4 oysters
25ml white wine
1 shallot, finely chopped
200ml whipping cream
20 mussels, washed and cleaned
4 large langoustines
2 hand-dived scallops
10g butter
1 tbsp chopped mixed herbs (chives, dill, chervil)
½ glass of champagne

1) Heat a non-stick frying pan and add splash of oil. Add the carrot and leek to the pan, then sweat gently for one or two minutes. Add the courgette and let it sweat for a further couple of minutes. Season with salt and, once cooked, set aside.

2) Open the oysters, placing the juice from the shellfish into a saucepan, and then set the oysters aside. Add the white wine to the oyster juices, then add the finely chopped shallots. Cook on a medium heat to reduce the liquid.

3) Once reduced, add the whipping cream and bring to the boil. Add the mussels (washed and cleaned) and gently cook until they open. Add the langoustines and poach gently for a minute.

4) Add the scallops and poach for a further two minutes.

5) Add the butter and the cooked vegetables, then add the oysters and gently warm through.

6) Finally, add the chopped herbs and half a glass of champagne to the pan.

Serve in large, attractive bowls, and enjoy with the rest of the champagne.

Arbroath Smokies Dauphine

Returning from a visit to Simon and Sarah's (Larachhmor, Strachen, Aberdeenshire) we did the longer coastal route. This allowed a small side trip to Johnshaven where we bought a large crab and extra claws. Also included, a first for us, was a stop in Arbroath. You can't visit this town and leave without having bought some of the now EU Protected Geographical Indication, world renowned, Arbroath smokies. The photo below comes from Iain R Spink's website as I didn't have the presence of mind to photo the ones we bought.

Smokies can only be produced from haddock. After being caught they are gutted, washed, and boxed at sea. Once ashore they are headed, and cleaned, prior to being dry salted. This helps firm up the fish by reducing their moisture content. After washing the salt off they are now ready to be smoked. This is traditionally done using a half whiskey barrel over a hard wood fire. Smoking takes between 30 and 50 minutes depending upon the weather.

The best way to eat smokies is straight off the barrel when just smoked. It is possible to do this without going to Arbroath as Sheila discovered when she had Spink's smokies at the Royal Highland Show. If you can't get them this way try them grilled. Backbone removed and into a medium oven for 3 minutes. They also make a delicious supper following the method below.

Ingredients (4 people)

Smokies come in "pairs" they also still have their back bones intact
1 large onion finely chopped
2 cloves of garlic finely chopped
¼ pint milk and a ¼ pint cream
4 small baking potatoes – peeled and thinly sliced
Nutmeg - 74 grinds
*2 * 6 vine tomatoes*
Pepper and Salt

1) To cook the smokies place under a reasonably hot grill and cook for only +/- 3 minutes until heated through. Set aside and when cool enough to handle remove the back bone and flake.

2) Add the onion and garlic to a sauce pan with a splash of oil and start to sweat down. Add the milk and cream to the pan and bring to the boil. Add the potatoes and cook until just turning soft. Remove the potatoes and keep the milk / cream mixture.

3) In a shallow, oven proof, dish layer up with alternate flaked smokie, and potatoes. Once complete add nutmeg to the milk/cream to taste and pour over.

4) Place in a medium oven and bake for 20mins until the top takes colour and the juices bubble.

   Serve with baked vine tomatoes.

Goose Egg Tortilla (Spanish Omelette)

Our friend Sarah keeps geese in the extensive garden of their Larachmhor home. Occasionally, depending upon their productivity, we are treated to a delivery of goose eggs. On the first delivery our question was "What would be the best way to cook them?" Whilst in Sarawak Sheila had given lessons to Miri Women's Guild expat ladies on "How to cook an Iranian omelette (Kuku)". A Spanish lady member returned the favour and taught Sheila how to cook a proper Tortilla. Or perhaps, more accurately, "her" personal version of a Tortilla. The secret she said was to use only 5 ingredients. This we agreed was the way for us to go with our goose eggs.

Makes 2 omelettes enough for 4 people

2 large potatoes
1 medium onion - finely chopped
1 large clove garlic - skinned and cracked under a knife blade
Olive and sunflower oil (to cover the potatoes and onion)
3 Goose eggs
Salt & Pepper

1) Peel the potatoes and cut into small squares, finely chop the onion, then add to a heavy bottomed pan. Pour the combined oils to just cover the potatoes. Now gently bring to a simmer and comfit the potatoes. Remove from the heat. Using a perforated spoon separate the potatoes and onions from the oil and allow to cool.

2) Crack the goose eggs into a bowl and very gently whisk to amalgamate. Add the cooled potato and onions to the eggs and gently stir to combine the mix.

3) Add a knob of butter to a small frying pan and melt. Add ½ the egg mix to the pan. The aim here is to create a "pillow" shaped omelette some 3 to 4 cm deep. As the eggs cook using a non-stick spatula carefully work around the pan rounding the omelette edge.

4) With the omelette cooking and the bottom firm and taking on some colour place a suitable sized plate on top of the pan. Invert catching the omelette cooked side up. Return to the pan and complete the cooking.

5) Remove the omelette and if intending to eat hot transfer to a warm plate and keep hot. Repeat the exercise with the remaining egg mix.

Serve with a salad. We did a version of Jamie Oliver's fennel and radish salad.

Thai Squid Salad (Yam Pla-muk)

Ankanna had prepared a squid salad for us during our extended stay in Hua Hin. There she cooked the squid by simply pouring boiling water over it. I imagine the lime in the sauce she dressed the salad with also helped the cooking process. Back home we tend to stick to boiling for a minute or so in flavoured water.

> I'm not sure everyone will agree but for my taste you cannot beat fresh North Sea squid. It must have something to do with the cold water. I think they are sweeter than those from warmer waters. It will come as no surprise but we source ours when Mrs Clark's answer to the question is:- "They are good, and fresh in this morning".

Ingredients - serves 4

400g cleaned squid cut into fine rings & tentacles halved
1 stick lemon grass
2 kafir lime leaves
2 tblsp Fish Sauce (Nam Pla)
2 tsp Palm sugar
2 tblsp Lime juice
2 fresh red chilli's deseeded and finely sliced
¾ cucumber - peeled, deseeded, and sliced
1 red bell pepper quartered and diagonally sliced
Good handful of fresh mint leaves roughly torn
1 small sweet red onion halved and very finely sliced
A good sprinkling of toasted dry peanuts

1) Bring a sauce pan of water to the boil. Add a stick of lemon grass and two lime leaves. Now add the prepared squid and cook for 1 minute. Remove with a slotted spoon. Set aside to cool

2) To make the dressing in a small bowl add the fish sauce, palm sugar, and lime juice. Stir until the sugar has dissolved. Now stir in the sliced red chilli.

3) Pat the squid dry if necessary and transfer to a serving bowl. Add the cucumber, mint leaves, and sliced onion. Pour the dressing over and gently stir to combine all the ingredients.

4) Sprinkle over the dry roasted pea nuts.

Baked Beetroot with Feta & Thyme

An early, and continuing, joy of returning to live in the UK is the quality & consistency of the supermarkets offerings. Beetroot, leaves still on, was one of the first such experiences. The inspiration for this recipe was from Lucas Hollweg writing in the Sunday Times. The first variation we applied was to the cooking method of the beetroot. Rather than boil we wrap in aluminium foil parcels, having added a little oil, and roast in the oven. You can test the beets to see if they are done by using a wooden cocktail stick and sensing how easily it sticks into the beet. A little resistance equals done. This dish also works without the addition of the Feta. It depends upon how you intend to serve. For a main course it would need the feta.

Ingredients - Serves four

6 * medium sized beetroots (+/- 800g)
A splash of oil (olive or rapeseed) for each foil parcel
1 red union finely chopped
2 cloves of garlic finely chopped
150g Feta
200ml single cream or crème fresh diluted with milk
Thyme - 8 bushy sprigs finely chopped & 2 bushy sprigs to garnish
Salt & freshly bashed black pepper

1) To cook the beetroot we bake them in foil with a little olive oil. Wash and trim the beetroot. Cut suitably sized aluminium foil squares to wrap the beet. Before closing the top drizzle a little olive oil into the parcel. Twist the top closed.

2) Bake in a hot oven for 60 to 90 minutes depending upon size. Test whether the beets are done by pushing a cocktail stick through the foil into the beet and sensing the resistance. A slight resistance indicates 'done'.

3) Take the beets out of the oven and set aside. While they cool heat a slug of olive oil in a frying pan over a medium heat and sweat off the onion and garlic. When they are soft and sweet remove from the heat and stir in the chopped thyme leaves. With the beets now cool enough to handle take out of the parcel, top and tail, and remove the skin. Thinly slice all the beets.

4) Lay half the beet slices, slightly overlapping, in a single layer in the bottom of a buttered gratin dish. Season well and sprinkle with the onion mix and half the feta.

5) Then top off with another layer of beetroot. Season again and pour the cream over the top. Scatter the remaining feta and the extra thyme leaves over the top.

6) Bake in the pre heated oven (200 C / Gas mark 6) for about 40 minutes or until the top is bubbling and the sides are turning brown.

Fresh "Johnshaven" Brown Crabs

Permanently back home in Edinburgh, and continuing the visits to our friend the Richards in Larachmhor, we exploit the chance to detour to Johnshaven the fishing harbour south of Aberdeen. Family business Murry McBay continues to supply live lobsters, and crabs, to all corners of the globe. On a recent visit they were shipping to Norway, France, and Greece. They have two large, shallow sea water tanks. One for the lobsters and one for the brown crabs. You lean over, size them up, and one of the brothers will pick your choice from the tank. As you are going to have to recover the One other t

- **Ingredients**

- *1 large (+/- 1 kg) live crab preferably with the claws bound*

- *Ample boiling water*

- *Enough salt to make the water "sea" salty (a lot)*

1) The first issue is how to 'humanely' kill the crab. I prefer to speedily immerse the crab in a very large sauce pan of fiercely boiling water. Other techniques include leaving them for an hour or so in the freezer prior to cooking. Also I have read that crabs can be humanely killed using a sharp skewer inserted first between the eyes then into the body via the tail flap.

2) The water which you are going to bring to a fierce boil needs to be as salty as sea water. Holding the crab from the back, fingers on top and thumb underneath, plunge into the boiling water. The water will initially go off the boil. Bring it back to a rolling boil. Then turn off the heat and cover the pan.

3) Leave for 14 to 15 minutes. Then using tongs lift the crab out and set aside the rest and cool to room temperature.

4) Place the crab on a board on its back and break off the main claws using a twisting motion. Of late I have started to use the point of a knife to prise the claws/legs off. Then break off the legs making sure to remove the knuckle joint close to the body.

5) Now lift up and break off the tail flap. Using a large strong knife work the point between the back of the shell (where the flap was) and the lower body. Twist to crack the body from the shell. Now using your thumbs push the body out of the shell.

6) Remove the dead men's fingers (the grey furry gills) and discard. Cut the central body section in half and winkle out the white meat and save in a bowl. We use a purpose designed crab/lobster fork. One end has bent 'prongs' and the other end is a narrow spoon.

7) With the crabs shell on its back, eyes facing you, break out the mouth part and the attached stomach. Everything in the shell is now edible. Spoon out into a second bowl.

8) Now turn to the claws. Break off the lower joints. Hold the claw securely down on the board and using the back of your heavy knife crack the claw shell. Remove the white meat from the claws.

9) Finally if you have the energy & enthusiasm you can get a little, very sweet, meat from the legs.

10) You'll now have two bowls with delicious white and brown meat.

Enjoy any way you wish but with mustard mayonnaise, a fragrant salad, and crunchy bread takes some beating.

Travels With Our Kitchen

Thai Stir Fry Vegetable with Thick Thai Noodles

This was cooked soon after we retired back to Edinburgh. I think it may have been the first time I had ever cooked Thai without assistance. I had always made a point of taking an interest, and helping where I could, when Angkana cooked for us in Hua Hin. This experience was a great help. Another incentive was the discovery that you could buy "Amoy" brand, gluten free, "Straight to the Wok" noodles. This meant that Sheila would be able to share the result. A final twist is we now use virgin coconut oil which is solid at Scottish kitchen temperature. It is expensive but you don't need a lot and it adds a special fragrance.

Serves 2

> For the "sauce"
> 2 tblsp fish sauce (eg "Squid Brand")
> Juice of ½ a lime
> 1 tblsp light soy sauce
> 1 tblsp chili sauce (or dry chilli flakes)
> 1 tsp soft brown sugar
>
> For the "stir fry"
> 2 cloves garlic finely chopped
> Large thumb ginger shredded into matchstick sized strips
> 4 - 6 spring onions
> 1 - 2 hot red chillies finely chopped
> 2 large or 4 small shiitake mushrooms
> ½ a red pepper sliced
> 250g prawns / sliced chicken / sliced pork (I used cooked pork)
> 2 - 4 small Pok Choy
> 1 packet Amoy Thai noodles

1) Combine the ingredients for the "sauce" in a small bowl and thoroughly mix together. Set to one side to amalgamate.

2) Now systematically prepare the ingredients for the stir fry. I like to have a row of bowls from 1st to be added being closest to the wok, with the last being at the end of the queue. First finely chop the garlic. Put in bowl #1. Then take your ginger and square off. Slice very thin lengthways slices. Then make a pile of a few slices and slice into thin matchsticks. Continue until completed. Add to the bowl with the garlic. Chop the spring onions cross wise into smallish slices. Finally cut the chilli(s) in half and deseed. Then make cuts in each chilli half, point to bottom, and then cut across the chili's making small squares. That's bowl #1 finished.

3) Slice the shitake mushrooms, and red peppers in finger width slices. Add to bowl #2.

4) In bowl #3 we place the diagonally sliced, cooked pork / chicken / prawns.

5) Bowl #4 is for the washed Pok Choy. Sliced the bottom stalks into 2 to 3 cm pieces and place to one side of the bowl. You will add these ahead of the leaves. If the leaves are large very roughly slice them. If the pok choy is baby sized you can cook them whole.

6) Bowl #5 is the "sauce" bowl.

7) Heat a wok over medium heat and a knob of virgin coconut oil, or a splash of vegetable oil. When hot add the contents of bowl #1 and keep stirring so that the garlic doesn't burn. With the flavours now aromatic add bowl #2 (shiitake mushrooms + red pepper). Continue to stir fry until they start to sweat down.

8) Increase the heat slightly and then add bowl #3 (the cooked pork in my case) to the wok and stir fry for a couple of minutes until the meat is heated.

9) Now add the contents of bowls #4 (pok choy) sliced stalks first if large. Once the pok choy leaves are added add the sauce from bowl #5. Stir fry for a minute or so and let the steam from the sauce wilt the pok choy.

10) Finally add the (Amoy gluten free in our case) "Straight to Wok" noodles and stir fry for 1 to 2 minutes.

Serve in warmed bowls.

Cote de Boeuf

This glorious piece of beef was chosen for us, and bought from, the excellent butcher at Craigies Farm shop. The art would seem to be in selection of the finest carcase and then "hanging" for at least 28 days. Our man at Craigies certainly knows his stuff so we have never been disappointed. This is an expensive piece of meat but for the two us it can provide us with at least 2 and maybe 3 meals meaning it's not too pricy per serving.

> **From the Butcher**
>
> *A single rib of beef (+/- 1 1/2 kg)*
>
> **To cook**
>
> *2 onions or shallots peeled and halved*
> *Salt*
>
> **For the Jue**
>
> *1 glass of red wine or red vermouth*
> *Vegetable cooking water*

1) Place a dry heavy bottomed, over proof, frying pan on a medium to high heat. When hot, using the rib as a handle, starting with the fatty side brown the rib joint on all sides. When it has started to take some colour lay flat in the pan, place the onions or shallot around the joint, and transfer to a pre heated oven at 190 C and cook for 10 minutes per 500 g, plus 10 minutes for medium rare. The core temperature should be +/- 55 C.

2) Remove the rib joint to a carving board, cover in aluminium foil, and leave to rest in a warm place for 15 to 20 minutes. The core temperature will have risen to 62 - 64 C.

3) Return the frying pan to the stove and deglaze the pan with the wine or vermouth. Bring to a boil and stir to clean the pan and sweat the onions. Add some vegetable cooking water and reduce the jue to the consistency you prefer. Pour the juices into a fat separator and then pour the separated jue to a sauce boat.

Traditionally this is served with chips and a salad.

Potato, Chorizo, and Shitake mushroom, frittata

The chorizo, shrink wrapped, needed to be used. I had some left over potatoes. Plenty of eggs and I had failed to find an inspiring (do able) black pudding recipe. Back to the frittata. I then added two other ideas / ingredients. The chives were still Ok after being transplanted to a bigger pot. And I had some Shitake mushrooms. The thought behind it all was a variation on the full British breakfast in one pot. The solution is set below.

Ingredients

6 eggs
¾ Chorizo sausage – sliced and cut in half (smallish bites)
6 or 8 left over cooked small potatoes
1/3 pack vacuum sealed Shitake mushrooms (I'm only being fancy here any sort would do)
Handful fresh chives – chopped into 1cm length
Pepper
No salt - I thought the Chorizo would be OK but you could add to taste

1) I gently fried the Chorizo (my experience is if you hit it with too much heat you set off the smoke alarm) slowly increasing the heat to get a little colour onto it

2) At the same time I sliced my potatoes into rings and fried in a little Goose fat

3) With this on the go I broke 6 eggs into a bowl & gave them a quick whip.

4) Get a deep'ish frying pan that could be put in the pre heated (yes put it on now) oven.

5) As the potatoes and chorizo were coloured I emptied them into this cold frying pan and neatly arranged them.

6) Then I quickly fried my mushrooms and added them to the cold pan.

7) I harvested a bunch of chives and chopped them into 1cm lengths over the cold pan. Then in with the egg mix and stir. Put on a medium heat. As the eggs begin to cook run a wooden specula around the edge to ensure they will leave the pan easily.

8) Once cooking has started put in the hot oven. Keep checking – when the centre is solid to the touch it's done.

Allow to cool for a few minutes and then serve with the option of Heinz Tomato ketchup.

Scottish Rope Grown Mussels

At the end of a visit to Belgium and Holland to see our good friends the van Rijmsdijks Eveline presented us with a typically Dutch, black enamel, lidded, mussel pot. We had seen them first when we lived in The Hague. We are always very keen to cook fresh rope grown Scottish mussels when they were in season and relatively small. Now with the appropriate equipment we could do the job properly. The cooked mussels are served in the pot and the lid is placed on the table to collect the shells.

Serves 2

1 bag of "rope" grown mussels
A splash of olive oil
A good knob of butter
1 or 2 leeks - white part finely sliced
Glass of Dry white wine or vermouth
A good handful of parsley - chopped

1) The first job, and in a way the most time consuming but vital, is to clean the mussels. Tip them into a bowl of cold water. Now one by one go through them. First check they are closed. If open, and they don't respond to a firm "knock" on the side of the sink discard. Pull off any beard and if present I chip off any small shells on the mussels. Finally give them a good scrub. When you have done them all you are ready to go.

2) Put your mussel pot / large casserole pot on a medium heat. Add a glug of oil and the knob of butter and melt. Add the sliced leeks and cook, stirring occasionally, until sweated down. Add the wine / vermouth and heat through to bubble off the alcohol.

3) Tip the cleaned mussels into the pan. Put a lid on the pan and bring to the boil to steam the mussels. Cook for a couple of minutes then give them a stir lifting the lower, and probably partially cooked, mussels to the top. Continue to steam until all the mussel shells are open.

4) Sprinkle the parsley over the mussels and give one last gentle stir to evenly distribute the parsley.

Bring to the table and ladle a helping of mussels into hot serving bowls. One last caution. Any mussels that do not open should be discarded.

Spiced Braised Venison with Chilli & Chocolate

Just the title of the dish makes you want to eat it. Our first Wee Restaurant cooking demo at Hopetown Farm Shop featured venison. The full story of Craig's demonstration is given below. Inspired we tried the recipe below. I think oft times venison can be a little dry. This we hoped would hit the spot. And indeed it did.

From the Butcher

2 tblsp vegetable oil
1/1/2kg diced stewing venison
3 large carrots - roughly chopped
1 large onion - roughly chopped
1 tblsp cumin seeds
1 tsp ground coriander
A large pinch of chilli powder
1 small cinnamon stick
1 hot red chilli - whole
500 ml red wine
300 ml beef stock
400 g can chopped tomatoes
A large sprig of thyme
2 Bay leaves
50g dark chocolate - more than 70% cocoa solids

1) Pre heat the oven to 180 C. Place a large flameproof casserole on medium heat and heat the oil, then brown the meat in batches. Add the vegetables to the dish and brown slightly. Then stir in the spices and the whole chilli and cook for 4 - 5 minutes. Pour in the wine, stock and the tomatoes. Finally add the thyme and bay and bring to a simmer.

2) Put a lid on the casserole and put in the middle of your pre heated oven. Cook for 1 ½ hours. Remove the lid and cook for a further 1 hour. If the meat is really tender remove from the oven and set to one side to slightly cool. Now gently stir in the melting chocolate.

Serve this rich and glossy venison stew in hot bowls with mashed potatoes, baby carrots, and the green veg of your choice.

Picnic Fish

The tradition started when we had the convertible Audi. It now continues, slightly less weather dependent, with the BMW's "sun roof". Given half a decent day we will pack the picnic hamper and set off, mostly, to the coast. On one such occasion we watched as this guy brought his inflatable out of the sea back to his car. Intrigued we went across for a chat. The upshot was the very generous gift, pictured below. The freshest of fresh mackerel.

On the drive home a detour was necessary. We stopped off at B & Q. One of the best ways to cook mackerel is to "blow torch" it. That was the cooking method we chose. First you have to fillet your mackerel leaving the skin on. Then you have to find any sort of steel plate the heavier the better. Finally you screw up your courage, light the blow torch, and admittedly using some care, blast the fish keeping the torch constantly on the move.

Ingredients -   Serves 2

3 or 4 very fresh whole mackerel - gutted and filleted
Rape seed oil

Equipment,

1 heavy duty blow torch
1 steel plate / metal baking tray
Heavy duty aluminium foil

1) To fillet the fish use sharp, flexible blade, knife. Lay the maceral flat on a board, head angled toward you. Make an incision just behind the fin at an angle toward the head and cut down to the back bone. Place your free hand flat on the body of the fish and carefully work the blade around. Holding the fish firmly now cut down the length of the fish keeping the blade gently pressed against the back bone. Turn the fish over and repeat on the other side. Trim the fillets of any thin belly parts and remove any discoloured or ragged bits of flesh.

2) Wrap the steel plate / baking tray in foil. Brush the foil / tray with oil. Neatly arrange the fillets skin side up on the foil.

3) Place the steel plate / tray in a suitable, non-flammable, place (top of the stove). Fire up the blow torch and keeping the flame constantly on the move begin to cook the fish. When the skin begins to bubble this is the sign to move the flame. Cook all the fillets evenly until the skin is slightly charred. Turnover and gently cook the flesh side until just taking colour.

Serve to warm plates and accompany with new potatoes, beetroot, and if you like gooseberry sauce.

The "Wee Restaurant" - Cookery Demonstrations

Over the years we, or more accurately Sheila, has attended several cookery courses and demonstrations. The first was in Brunei where a friend organised a series of cookery lesson that were given by a Brunei TV lady chef. These ran over a period of a month or so and included several well-known Far Eastern dishes. This tradition was extended via both formal demonstrations, and the joy of being invited into kitchens to witness many fine chef's (some professional, but mostly friends mothers or wives) cook their specialities.

On returning to Edinburgh we have kept the habit alive with help from Hopetown Farm Shop and local restaurant chefs. The farm shop started to run occasional cookery demonstration to promote both the chefs and their meat and veg products. In particular we have enjoyed evenings with two chefs of different styles. Craig and his wife Victoria of the "Wee Restaurant", and Mark Greenaway of the restaurant of his own name.

In the first demonstration we attended Craig cooked a cauliflower soup, and venison in three different ways. There were about twenty people in the audience. Each of us was presented with a tasting plate with all the trimmings. Between each course we were given a glass of wine chosen to complement each plate. A highly enjoyable, and very impressive, experience. We subsequently attended another evening with Craig in which he chose to cook chicken. As before doing it in three different ways. The confit chicken leg with spelt grain risotto & wild mushrooms was just outstanding. A French contact of Craig's chose the wines to complement each of these dishes.

When we attended Mark Greenaway's demonstration he invited all the guests to bring along a surprise ingredient which he subsequently used in the dishes he prepared. Sheila took juniper berries soaked in gin. The "Ready Steady Cook" theme was extended by Hopetown Farm shop also providing surprise ingredients. Quite a challenge. Mark rose to this challenge and as with the regular format we all got to try his efforts. His take on cauliflower and broccoli was the most interesting for us.

With our history of good home cooking; Sheila's large collection of cookery books all of which have been read if not used every day; a range of good friends with whom we cook and share recipes: two Thai daughter in laws and their families; access to a range of expert, and supportive, local suppliers; and learning opportunities as described above it is little wonder that cooking has infused our lives and continues to be a shared passion.

Index of Recipes

	Page
1.0 Introduction	8
2.0 Edinburgh - Student Days	16
Fried Egg Sandwiches	20
Potato and Leek Soup	21
Spaghetti Bolognaise	22
Bacon & Potato Pie	23
Grannies Lentil Soup	24
Smoked Haddock Kedgeree	25
Cottage Pie	26
Leg of Lamb	27
Queen of Puddings	28
3.0 London - First job With Shell	30
Vi's Pate	33
Potato & Watercress Soup	34
Fish Cakes	35
Taramasalata	36
Jamalat's Mousaka	37
Hare (Reserved for Cat)	38
Stifatho	39
Date Cake (Sheila's Mummies)	40
4.0 Aberdeen - Our Most Foreign Posting	42
The ZEN of Bread	45
Rose Hip Syrup	46
Macaroni & Cheese	47
Cullen Skink	48
Prawns in Tomato & Vermouth	49
Rowan Berry Jelly	50
Beach Barbeques	51
Fresh Johnshaven Scottish Lobster	52
5.0 Assen – North Holland	54
Apricot Chutney	56
Sardines & Spinach Pate	57
Carbonara	58
Cheese & Corn Soufflé	59
Guinea Fowl with Juniper Berries	60
Pork Fillet & Prunes	61

Roast Goose with Stuffing	62
German Red Cabbage	63
Geraldine's Chocolate Chiffon Cake	64

6.0 Brunei - First Overseas Assignment — 66

Tinned Seafood Pate	70
Barbequed Large Prawns	71
Banana, Bacon, & Prawn Kebabs	72
Rock Cornish Hen – Coronation Chicken	73
Beef in Guinness with Orange	74
Belly Pork, Apple, and Prune Casserole	75
Jungle Barbequed Chicken	76
Chilled Pawpaw Mouse with Hot Chocolate Sauce	77
Sylvie's Black Cherry Clafouti	78

7.0 London - Back to Reality — 80

Liver & Sage	83
Horseradish Sauce	84
Stuffed Shoulder of lamb	85
Grow Up Chocolate Marquise	86
Casseroled Pheasant	87
Mrs Dimbleby's Greek Island Chicken	88
Potato and Tomato with Garlic and Herbs	89
Bread & Butter Pudding	90
Grandma's Chocolate Cornflake Cakes	91

8.0 Damascus, Syria - Our Best Assignment — 92

Mayonnaise	96
Beetroot, Tomato, & Basil Salad	97
Bosra (Made up) Chutney	98
Koo Koo – Iranian Frittata	99
Chicken with Olives, Capers, and Prunes	100
Cauliflower Romagna Style	101
Butterflied Leg of Lamb	102
BBQ'd Red Peppers	103
Ayman's Mothers Green Bean Stew	104
Juniper & Gin Cabbage	105

9.0 Sarawak - Back to the Jungle — 108

Prawn Laksa	110
Saffron Rice	111
Saturday Morning Squid	112
Clam Chowder (Miri Style)	113

Travels With Our Kitchen

Old English Pork Casserole	114
Barbequed Spare Ribs	115
Stir Fried Ginger Beef	116
Salt & Pepper Squid	117

10.0 Den Haag - Dutch City Life — 120

Erwten Soup	122
Fish Pie	123
Bangers, Mash, & Onion Gravy	124
Asparagus Risotto	125
Rabbit & Prunes	126
Sheila's Fantastic Hamburgers	127
Sautéed Veal Kidneys in Brandy and Orange Juice	128

11.0 Cyprus - Life in the Holiday Home — 130

Elizabeth's Pate	133
Baked Fish With Fennel & Rosemary	134
Iman Bayildi	135
Cyprus Village Salad	137
Baked Sea Bass	139
Black Virgin Olive Oil	140
Prawn Saganaki	142

12.0 Oman - 3 Months Become 7 Years — 144

Basil Pesto	147
Salad Nicoise	148
Variation Jamies Chorizo & Tomato Salad	150
Masala Omelette	151
Barbequed Yabbies	152
Thai Chicken & Noodle Picnic Salad	153
Lobster Tails in Prawn Sauce	154
Curry Mix for Fish / Chicken / Veg	155
Fish of the Day Curry	156
Chilli Jam	157
Pomelo Thai Salad	158
Hamour - Two Tasty Alternatives	160
Thrice Cooked Chips	162
Roast (Oman) Chicken	163
Um Ali - Oman Bread & Butter Pudding	164

13.0 Thailand - Many Visits & Now Family — 168

Phad Thai – Cookery Lesson	172
Angkana's Pineapple Cucumber & Prawn	174

Barbequed Salted Fish	175
Thai Chicken Soup for the Soul	176
Squid Stuffed with Pork	177
Pork Burgers – For the Grandchildren	178
Massaman Beef Curry	179
Thai Mussels	180
Neua Yang Nam Tok (Waterfall Beef)	181
Poo Jaa (Thai Crab Cakes)	182

14.0 Edinburgh - Final Retirement   186

Heston Blumenthal's Pea & Ham Soup	189
Poached Seafood Ragout	191
Arbroath Smokies	192
Goose Egg Tortilla (Spanish Omelette)	193
Thai Squid Salad (Yam Pla-muk)	194
Baked Beetroot with Feta & Thyme	195
Fresh "Johnshaven" Brown Crab	196
Thai Stir fried Vegetables with Thick Thai Noodles	198
Cote de Boeuf	200
Potato, Chorizo, and Shitake mushroom Frittata	201
Scottish Rope Grown Mussels	202
Spiced Braised Venison with Chilli & Chocolate	203
Picnic Mackerel	204

Printed in Great Britain
by Amazon